Seventh-day Adventist

MINISTER'S HANDBOOK

Seventh-day Adventist
MINISTER'S HANDBOOK

Prepared and Published by
The Ministerial Association
The General Conference of Seventh-day Adventists
12501 Old Columbia Pike
Silver Spring, Maryland 20904, U.S.A.
1997

Printed in U.S.A.

Unless otherwise noted, texts in this book are from *The New King James Version.* Copyright © 1979, 1980, 1982, Thomas Nelson, Inc., Publishers.

Texts credited to KJV are from *The King James Version.*

Texts credited to NEB are from *The New English Bible.* © The Delegates of the Oxford University Press and the Syndics of the Cambridge University Press 1961, 1970. Reprinted by permission.

Texts credited to NIV are from the *Holy Bible, New International Version.* Copyright © 1973, 1978, 1984, International Bible Society. Used by permission of Zondervan Bible Publishers.

Bible texts credited to Phillips are from J. B. Phillips: *The New Testament in Modern English,* Revised Edition. © J. B. Phillips, 1958, 1960, 1972. Used by permission of Macmillan Publishing Co.

Bible texts credited to RSV are from the Revised Standard Version of the Bible, copyright © 1946, 1952, 1971, by the Division of Christian Education of the National Council of the Churches of Christ in the U.S.A. Used by permission.

Copyright © 1997 by the
Ministerial Association
General Conference of Seventh-day Adventists

ISBN 1-57847-005-6

TABLE OF CONTENTS

Acknowledgments 11
Preface 13

SECTION ONE
The Minister

Chapter 1 Calling 17
   A Personal Call From Christ 17
   A Personal Relationship With Christ 18
   A Personal Empowering by Christ 19

Chapter 2 Spiritual Formation 21
   Primacy of Spirituality 21
   Barriers to Spirituality 22
   Devotional Methods Helpful to Spirituality 24

Chapter 3 Interpersonal Relationships 27
   Impact on Ministry 27
   Loving People 27
   Intimate Friendships 28
   Community Relationships 30

Chapter 4 Time Management 31
   Tyranny of Time 31
   Timesaving Tips 31

Chapter 5 Personal Health 35
   Physical Health 35
   Psychological Health 36

Chapter 6 Personal Appearance 39
   Appearance Matters 39
   Appearance Should Attract to Christ 39
   Appearance Should Usually Go Unnoticed 40

Chapter 7 Personal Finance	43
Chapter 8 Family Life	47
Ministry Begins at Home	47
Prescription for a Happy Pastoral Family	49
Advantages of Clergy Families	51
Chapter 9 Pastoral Ethics	53
Ethics Code	53
Ethics and Fellow Ministers	54
Ethics and Job Placement	55
Ethics and Race	55
Ethics and Sex	56
Ethics and the Law	58
Chapter 10 Professional Growth	61
Why Grow?	61
Where to Grow	61
How to Grow	62
Chapter 11 Christian Example	65
Be What You Teach	65
Be Aware of Your Humanity	65
Be Willing to Admit Your Mistakes	66

SECTION TWO
The Minister and the World Church

Chapter 12 Relationship With Conference	69
Organization Is Needed	69
Pastors Help Conferences	70
Conferences Help Pastors	70
Cooperation the Key	71
Chapter 13 Church Policies	73
Church Manual	73
Membership Transfers	74
Chapter 14 Credentials	77
Purpose	77
To Whom Issued	78
Types	79
Internship	80

TABLE OF CONTENTS

Chapter 15 Ordination 83
   Ordination: a Statement 83
   Authorizing Ordination 86
   Examination for Ordination 89

Chapter 16 Ordination Service 93
   Ministers 93
   Local Elders and Deacons 100
   Induction Service 102

Chapter 17 Organizing New Churches 103
   New Churches Needed 103
   How to Start a New Church 103
   Preparation for Organizing a New Church 104
   Service Organizing a New Church 104

Chapter 18 Uniting Churches 107
   Before Uniting 107
   Service Uniting 108
   After Uniting 108

Chapter 19 Disbanding Churches 109
   Disbanding for Loss of Members 109
   Disbanding for Discipline or Apostasy 110

SECTION THREE
The Minister and the Local Church

Chapter 20 Church Leadership 113
   Leadership Versus Lordship 113
   Management Principles 114
   Setting Objectives 116
   Committees 116

Chapter 21 Members as Ministers 121
   Every Member a Minister 121
   Motivating Volunteers 123
   Choosing Lay Leaders 124
   Training Members 127

Chapter 22 Pastoring Large Districts 129
   Three Secrets to Success 129
   Quarterly District Meetings 131

Chapter 23 Church Growth 133
Finding New Members 133
Preparing New Members 135
Establishing New Members 139

Chapter 24 Worship Service 145
Purpose of Worship 145
Parts of Worship 147
Order of Worship 155

Chapter 25 Prayer Meeting 159
Importance of Prayer 159
Ways to Increase Attendance 159

Chapter 26 Visitation 161
Pastoral Visitation 161
Lay Visitation 164
Hospital Visitation 165

Chapter 27 Counseling 167
Counseling Limitations 167
Crisis Counseling 168
Lay Counseling 169

Chapter 28 Church Fellowship 171
Unity 171
Communicating With Members 171
Small Groups 175
Social Events 177
Additional Fellowship Options 178
Discipline 180

Chapter 29 Church Finance 185
Spiritual Giving 185
Handling Church Money 187

Chapter 30 Church Campaigns 189

Chapter 31 Church Facilities 191
Locating 191
Designing 192
Maintaining 194
Renting 194

Chapter 32 Christian Education ... 195
Importance of Christian Education ... 195
Practical Suggestions ... 195

SECTION FOUR
The Minister and Special Services

Chapter 33 Baptism ... 199
Importance of Baptism ... 199
Before Baptism ... 201
During Baptism ... 203
After Baptism ... 205

Chapter 34 Child Dedication ... 207
Biblically Appropriate ... 207
Planning the Service ... 208
Conducting the Service ... 209
Litanies ... 211
Additional Suggestions ... 213

Chapter 35 Church Dedication ... 215
Order of Service ... 215
Dedication Litany ... 218
Dedication Poems ... 219
Dedication Weekend ... 220
Dedication Booklet ... 220
Church Opening ... 221

Chapter 36 Communion ... 223
Importance ... 223
Problems ... 224
Sermon ... 225
Foot Washing ... 226
Lord's Supper ... 227
Additional Suggestions ... 228
Recipes ... 229

Chapter 37 Funeral ... 231
Before the Service ... 231
Typical Funeral Service ... 233
Typical Graveside Service ... 237
Additional Suggestions ... 239
Ministering to the Grieving ... 240

Chapter 38 Groundbreaking ... 243
Planning the Service ... 243
Order of Service ... 243
Stonelaying ... 244

Chapter 39 House Opening ... 245
Purpose ... 245
Who Officiates ... 245
Order of Service ... 245

Chapter 40 New Parish Induction ... 249
Difficulties of Transition ... 249
Smoothing the Transition ... 250
Pastoral Installation Service ... 252

Chapter 41 Prayer for Sick ... 255
When to Encourage Anointing ... 255
Who Officiates ... 255
Preparing for the Service ... 256
Order of Service ... 256

Chapter 42 Wedding ... 259
Legal Requirements ... 259
Denominational Guidelines ... 260
Congregational Guidelines ... 262
Premarital Counseling ... 264
Planning the Wedding ... 264
Order of Service ... 266
Bride Given Away ... 269
Sermonette ... 270
Vows ... 271
Reception ... 273
Additional Suggestions ... 273

Conclusion ... 275
Index ... 277

ACKNOWLEDGMENTS

The *Handbook for Ministers* was last revised in 1977. The basic handbook was written many years before that. Such dramatic changes in ministry have taken place since that time that it was felt that a new handbook was needed, rather than just a revision. This resource which was first published in 1992 as the *Minister's Manual* was further amended and renamed, *Minister's Handbook*, at the 1994 Annual Council. We gratefully acknowledge the help of all who contributed to any of the following four phases in preparing this handbook.

Researching. — Ministerial secretaries from the world divisions chose creative pastors from their fields who sent us ideas that might be included in the new handbook. *Ministry* magazine was researched. Floyd Bresee's files yielded ideas gleaned from more than 40 years of ministry. The former handbook was, of course, studied, along with the *Church Manual* and the *General Conference Working Policy*.

Writing. — Floyd Bresee wrote the original manuscript, with able help from secretaries Gwen Brown, Kathy Reid, and Debra Hill. John M. Fowler did the principal editing.

Reading. — The manuscript was sent to a worldwide reading committee of 100 pastors, ministerial secretaries, and administrators for suggested changes, many of which were incorporated in the handbook. Final approval was by the in-house Ministerial Association staff at the General Conference: W. Floyd Bresee, Carlos Aeschlimann, Ellen Bresee, Rex D. Edwards, John M. Fowler, J. David Newman, Sally Streib, Martin Weber, and Jim Zachary.

Publishing. — Rex D. Edwards headed the design, Ann Taylor the desktop layout, and Jim Zachary the printing and distribution.

Many others gave their counsel and time. To each, our heartfelt appreciation.

PREFACE

Every member of the church is called to ministry, but for some there is a call to full-time ministry as a vocation. It is for these that this handbook has been prepared.

Resources for Pastoral Excellence

Every Adventist pastor needs at least four resource books:
1. The *Church Manual* gives guidelines for the church's work.
2. The *Minister's Handbook* gives guidelines for the minister's work.
3. The *Elder's Handbook* helps the minister train local elders as associates in the church's and minister's work.
4. *Pastoral Ministry* is a compilation from the writings of Ellen G. White specifically for the pastor.

No minister should presume to function without all four. The Ministerial Association believes this so strongly that the four volumes have been published in the same size, to form a matched set.

Division ministerial secretaries voted not to repeat the loose-leaf form of the previous *Minister's Handbook*. Loose-leaf is more expensive, and some pastors complained that pages got lost.

Pastors who wish to have single pages for use in special services can have theirs duplicated.

Since this handbook assumes the pastor has a *Church Manual*, quotations from that manual will be less lengthy than in the previous handbook. However, because it is the most authoritative source, the *Church Manual* will be referred to often in some sections of this handbook. References will be made only by chapter number, inasmuch as pagination changes with each year's edition and with various language editions will cause page numbers to change periodically.

Pastors Plus

Much of this *Minister's Handbook* applies to all ministers. However, the principal focus is pastoral ministry, with the hope that specialized ministers will also benefit.

In some parts of the world the Seventh-day Adventist Church has women in pastoral ministry. However, women ministers sometimes feel forgotten and ignored and thus question whether or not they are truly welcome. In an effort to show they are remembered and important to the world ministry of the church, this handbook has gone to considerable length to omit gender reference wherever possible. We hope this gesture will be a reminder that they are important and that they are included.

Unity Without Uniformity

Adventist ministers are raised, trained, and serve in hundreds of differing races, cultures, and languages around the world. The church must show respect for cultures in which it functions. Thus, this handbook must be adaptable to local conditions. Yet there needs to be some coordination of pastoral plans and programs to create a united ministry throughout the world field.

It is to help foster such unity that this handbook was first prepared, and is now presented in revised form. Although no set order is established for the ceremonies of the church, it is desirable that unity be maintained in the general order of services and forms of worship. "Let all things be done decently and in order" (1 Cor. 14:40).

The world church is culturally diverse, and so the intent of the handbook is not to prescribe a rigid model, but rather to provide a general pattern for each given area. Additional options are suggested, from which the minister may choose those best fitting the local situation. Typically more options are included than could be utilized and pastors should select those which are most appropriate for the time limits and settings of the service. Where culture dictates, divisions may need to include further adaptation by adding footnotes or appendices.

Some poetry does not translate well into other languages. In such cases, divisions are free to omit or replace poems.

One small problem related to preparing a worldwide handbook was whether to quote from a contemporary Bible version or an older, more conservative one. Our compromise was to use the New King James Version. All Bible quotations are from that version unless otherwise specified.

Finally, the emphasis of this or any other handbook tends to be on techniques. We hasten to emphasize that our greatest need as ministers is not new techniques, but a renewed relationship with our Lord, leading to a revival in our own hearts. This handbook comes with the prayer that it will strengthen us spiritually as it assists us professionally.

James A. Cress, Secretary
Ministerial Association
General Conference of Seventh-day Adventists
October 1, 1997

SECTION ONE

The Minister

1. Calling
2. Spiritual Formation
3. Interpersonal Relationships
4. Time Management
5. Personal Health
6. Personal Appearance
7. Personal Finance
8. Family Life
9. Pastoral Ethics
10. Professional Growth
11. Christian Example

CHAPTER 1

Calling

A call to the gospel ministry is a uniquely personal call. It must come only from Christ. It includes three distinct spiritual qualifications.

A Personal Call From Christ

Ministry a privilege. — Preaching the gospel of Jesus Christ is the highest privilege and the most fascinating adventure ever given to human kind. "The greatest work, the noblest effort, in which men can engage is to point sinners to the Lamb of God. True ministers are colaborers with the Lord in the accomplishment of His purposes" (*Gospel Workers*, p. 18).

Henry Ward Beecher said it well: "Working for men! There is nothing so congenial. It is the only business on earth that I know of, excepting the mother's business that is clean all the way through; because it is using superior faculties, superior knowledge, not to take advantage of men, but to lift them up and cleanse them, to mould them, to fashion them, to give them life, that you may present them before God" (*Lectures on Preaching*, p. 48).

Ministry a divine appointment. — "God has a church, and she has a divinely appointed ministry" (*Testimonies to Ministers*, p. 52). You may choose a profession, but the ministry cannot be invaded that way, for the ministry is more than a profession; it is a calling. "And no man takes this honor to himself, but he who is called by God, just as Aaron was" (Heb. 5:4).

The true minister for God is not self-called. As with the apostle Paul, the initiative is not the individual's, but the Lord's. Paul did not choose; God chose. Paul's choice was whether or not to respond to God's choice. His testimony: "He counted me faithful, putting me into the ministry" (1 Tim. 1:12). (See also Isa. 6 and Jer. 1.)

A call to the gospel ministry is a call to be not a sociologist or a public performer, but an ambassador for Christ. A call to anything less is not a call to the ministry. This call demands a full-time, life-consuming devotion.

Question your call unless you feel that in any other work, no matter how large the salary, the job would seem too small. As Martin Luther counseled: "Lest thou art called, avoid preaching as thou wouldst hell." Christ has a work for you, a plan for your life. If you're in the wrong place, not only will you fill it poorly, but the right place is empty.

A Personal Relationship With Christ

Jesus "called to Him those He Himself wanted. And they came to Him" (Mark 3:13). Christ called—they came. The early apostles were successful in inviting others to come to Christ, because they themselves had already come. You cannot bring until you have been brought. To give others what you yourself do not have is an impossible and frustrating task.

And after the disciples came, they spent the next three years in an intimate, everyday relationship with Christ. Only then were they prepared to minister successfully.

Saul saw a vision of Christ on the Damascus road and it caused him to ask, "Lord, what do You want me to do?" (Acts 9:6). He was ready for ministry only after catching a vision of Christ. Young ministers sometimes seem to catch a vision of themselves: as sanctified divines, as powerful preachers, as leaders of adoring congregations. Stay away from the ministry unless you catch a vision of Christ. Your power in appealing to human hearts will be in proportion to your fellowship with Him.

Serve as He served. — An intimate relationship with Christ motivates us to live as He lived. To live as He lived means living to serve as He served. Jesus lived to bless others. He lived to love. Too many choose the ministry because they live to be loved.

We are all born selfish, and it's possible to get into the ministry for selfish reasons, but it's practically impossible to stay in. Successful ministry follows the motto of John the Baptist: "He must increase, but I must decrease" (John 3:30). When our selfishness decreases, our relationship with Christ will increase.

"Those who have the deepest experience in the things of God are the farthest removed from pride and self-exaltation. Because they have an exalted conception of the glory of God, they feel that the lowest place in His service is too honorable for them" (*Gospel Workers*, p. 142).

To enjoy serving is to enjoy the ministry. One lifelong pastor expressed it this way: "This business of helping other people become better people by bringing them closer to God is the most exciting, the most stimulating, the most challenging, the most rewarding work in the world, and quitting it would be like dying—only worse."

Ministers however, must not feel that gospel ministry somehow makes them more important than others or that it is the only vocation to which people are "called." The most important work for an individual is whatever work God asks that person to do. The grandest work in the world is the work of service, and God calls all—every member of every congregation—to some ministry of service.

Sacrifice as He sacrificed. — To live as Christ lived means to sacrifice as He sacrificed. Anyone near Jesus will be near the fire. The demands of the gospel ministry are many. The burdens are immense—often more than one person can bear. The life of ministry is a life of hard work and sacrifice.

Scripture counsels, "Therefore take heed to yourselves and to all the flock, among which the Holy Spirit has made you overseers, to shepherd the church of God which He purchased with His own blood" (Acts 20:28). When sheep are crossing the road, shepherds don't sit in the shade and say, "Look out, sheep, here comes a truck." They jump out in the road waving their arms. They hold up their hands offering themselves. They're the first to get run over. And ministers are called pastors—shepherds.

A Personal Empowering by Christ

Ministers need many gifts: moral earnestness, leadership, intelligence, common sense, relational skills, and teaching ability. If you lack these, you should probably question whether or not your call has really come from Christ. Those who are truly called by Christ will be empowered by Christ. Paul proclaimed, "And I thank Christ Jesus our Lord who has *enabled* me, because He counted me faithful, putting me into the ministry" (1 Tim. 1:12). Whomever Christ calls He enables. He does not call to failure. He has provided or will provide everything you need to succeed at whatever He has called you to do.

"Those who consecrate body, soul, and spirit to God will constantly receive a new endowment of physical, mental, and spiritual power. The inexhaustible supplies of heaven are at their command. Christ gives them the breath of His own Spirit, the life of His own life. The Holy Spirit puts forth His highest energies to work in heart and mind. The grace of God enlarges and multiplies their faculties, and every perfection of the divine nature comes to their assistance in the work of saving souls. Through cooperation with Christ, they are made complete in Him, and in their human weakness they are enabled to do the deeds of Omnipotence" (*Gospel Workers*, pp. 112, 113).

CHAPTER 2

Spiritual Formation

A call to ministry is first a call to spirituality. This is a great privilege rather than a heavy responsibility.

Spirituality is personal. It must have a private dimension before it can have a public influence. It is a response to God's initiative, not something we initiate on our own. It leads us to center ourselves in Him. Christ becomes the passion of our lives.

Primacy of Spirituality

On the wall of a seminary prayer room were these words, addressed to prospective preachers: "One thing you must learn to do. Whatever else you leave undone, you must not leave this undone. Your work will be stunted and only half developed unless you attend to it. You must force yourself to be alone and to pray."

Why is spirituality essential for pastors?

Essential to pastor's leadership. — One of the saddest texts in Scripture is, "They made me the keeper of the vineyards, but my own vineyard I have not kept" (S. of Sol. 1:6). If your church is to be revived, you must be revived. Unless something happens in you, not much will happen through you. Revival is unlikely to begin in your church until it has begun in you. As pastor, cry out, "Create in me a clean heart, O God, and renew a steadfast spirit within me" (Ps. 51:10).

Without the spiritual dimension, ministry will degenerate to implementation of psychological techniques, organizational methods, and motivational cheerleading. Real power in ministry springs from spirituality that comes from a personal encounter with Christ. As you unveil the beauties of a Saviour who has met your needs and meets the challenge of a society gone berserk over self-fulfillment and the sensational, your pastoral leadership credibility grows.

Essential to pastor's soul-winning success. — <u>Unless you set time aside for daily Bible study and prayer, your work will be powerless.</u> "The reason why our preachers accomplish so little is that they do not walk with God. He is a day's journey from most of them" (*Testimonies*, vol. 1, p. 434).

Knowing Jesus and holding Him up before your people is the first secret to soul-winning success. He promised, "And I, if I am lifted up from the earth, will draw all peoples to Myself " (John 12:32).

Essential to pastor's preaching. — Too much current preaching could better be done by a psychologist than a minister of the gospel. Such sermons rarely live beyond the church door, much less beyond their time. If the preaching of the gospel is to exercise a great power over your congregation, it must either enlist extraordinary preachers or endow ordinary preachers with extraordinary spiritual power.

Sermon preparation itself requires time for Bible study and prayer. <u>Never feed to others what has not already fed your own soul</u>. But this is not enough. Some devotional time must be dedicated to knowing Jesus for yourself, not just for sharing Him with your people.

Essential to pastor's courage. — Pastoral care, in the full sense of one's total ministry, is proclamation of the Word addressed to the human situation. But you, the minister, must receive pastoral care too. You too must hear the Word of God spoken to your personal situation.

Who pastors the pastor? Sometimes a ministerial secretary, a colleague, a local church leader, or a spouse. But sometimes what you need most of all is time to listen to and talk with God and let Him pastor the pastor.

Barriers to Spirituality

Here are five barriers to the pastor's spiritual growth:

1. *Lack of confidence.* — No one is likely to have entered the ministry without having had a strong spiritual experience—sometime. But you may have fallen into the success trap of which Ellen White warned: "As activity increases, and men become successful in doing any work for God, there is danger of trusting to human plans and methods. There is a tendency to pray less, and to have less faith. Like the disciples, we are in danger of losing sight of our dependence on God, and seeking to make a savior of our activity. We need to look constantly to Jesus, realizing that it is His power which does the work. While we are to labor earnestly for the salvation of the lost, we must also take time for meditation, for prayer, and for the study of the Word of God. Only the work accomplished with much prayer, and sanctified by the merit of Christ, will in the end prove to have been efficient for good" (*The Desire of Ages*, p. 362).

Or you may simply feel that God is beyond your grasp. You have lost confidence in your ability to be truly intimate with Christ. You have forgotten that God really wants to hear from you. But if you were fortunate enough to have had loving parents, remember how anxious they always were to hear from you? Your heavenly Father feels that way too.

Jesus promised, "Blessed are those who hunger and thirst for righteousness, for they shall be filled" (Matt. 5:6). There is nothing that stands between you and being filled except your own lack of hunger, your own absence of thirst. "And you will seek Me and *find Me*, when you search for Me with all your heart" (Jer. 29:13).

2. Lack of time. — Pastors never have enough time. More will be said about time management later, but finding time is basically an issue of priorities. If you feel private devotions are important, you'll find time. If you don't, you won't.

Jesus admonished, "But seek first the kingdom of God and His righteousness, and all these things shall be added to you" (Matt. 6:33). Seeking the kingdom is not unusual. Almost everybody does it—sometime. Seeking it first is very rare—perhaps even among preachers.

Set aside for your devotions your most creative time of day. Tired minds lead to dull devotionals.

3. Lack of privacy. — Private devotions should be at a time and place where phone and even family will not interfere. Only when we are completely alone with God do all the masks fall away and we become utterly honest, stripped to our real and ultimate aims and ambitions.

"All who are under the training of God need the quiet hour for communion with their own hearts, with nature, and with God. . . . We must individually hear Him speaking to the heart. When every other voice is hushed, and in quietness we wait before Him, the silence of the soul makes more distinct the voice of God" (*The Ministry of Healing*, p. 58).

One ideal is to plan a day of solitude each month. On that entire day, focus your whole attention on God and your relationship with Him.

4. Lack of planning. — If you promise to spend your spare time with God, the devil will see that you don't have any. Without a specific plan, you won't likely have much devotional life. With the pastor's hectic schedule, the plan must, of course, be flexible.

Daniel's secret of spiritual power was his prayer life. And one secret of his prayer life was his specific plan—three times a day (see Dan. 6:10). Even a royal edict could not interfere.

Make an appointment with God. How can you be sure that you

have one? First, when you make an appointment with someone, you usually write it down. Have you put in writing somewhere your appointments with God? Second, when you must break an appointment with someone, you usually reschedule it. Do you reschedule your broken appointments with God?

Make yourself accountable. A spiritual support group that meets once a week or once a month gives opportunity to share your spiritual journey as others share theirs with you. It also provides a group with whom you share your plan for spiritual growth. You hold yourself accountable to the group for following it.

5. Lack of discipline. — Spiritual growth does require self-discipline. Nothing of any importance is easy.

Devotional Methods Helpful to Spirituality

How should you spend your time in personal devotions? What methods work? Here are some basics:

Informed friendship focus. — Devotional life is not an end in itself. The focus must not be on the amount of time spent or the number of pages read, or on the feeling of a warm inner glow. Rather, it must be on friendship with God, the fascination of a person for a Person. This was the focus of Jesus' devotional life: "And this is eternal life, that they may *know You*, the only true God, and Jesus Christ whom You have sent" (John 17:3).

True spirituality is not self-centered, but God-centered. It says not only that you are forgiven, but that God is a forgiver; not just that you face judgment, but that He is the judge; not only that you can go to heaven, but that your Friend will be there when you arrive.

The focus on friendship with God must be an informed focus. The devotional life ought to include both learning and feeling. This informed friendship focus must not end when you return to life. Keep your mind open to God throughout the day. Be sensitive to His leading, tuned to His speaking. This is what it means to "pray without ceasing" (1 Thess. 5:17).

Reading. — Reading helps keep your friendship with God informed. It should primarily be in the Bible. Try journaling—reading your Bible, then writing your personal reaction to what you've read. Your reading ought to include some of the great Christian devotional classics.

Meditation. —Any line drawn between prayer and meditation is likely to be fuzzy. Prayer is talking; meditation is listening. Meditation invites God to tell you about yourself. Ask Him to help you see your true motives in ministry, in recent activities. How does He want to use you today? What should be the priorities among this day's tasks? What point of spiritual weakness does He most want to help you overcome just now?

Meditation also concentrates on thinking about God. "It would be well for us to spend a thoughtful hour each day in contemplation of the life of Christ. We should take it point by point, and let the imagination grasp each scene, especially the closing ones. As we thus dwell upon His great sacrifice for us, our confidence in Him will be more constant, our love will be quickened, and we shall be more deeply imbued with His spirit" (*The Desire of Ages*, p. 83).

Praise prayer. — Prayer should begin with praise. We spend too much time asking God to do things and too little thanking Him for what He's already done. We can learn much from the life of Jesus about the importance and effectiveness of prayer. He prayed early in the morning (Mark 1:35). He spent entire nights in prayer (Luke 6:12). He sometimes withdrew from His direct ministry to pray (Luke 5:16). His power for ministry came from His prayer life (Luke 3:21, 22). Prayer prepared Him for His darkest hour (Matt. 26:36-46).

Penitential prayer. — Never ask anything of God until you have confessed your sins and totally committed yourself to God. Prayer in the private devotional should not be modeled after public prayer, where it is necessary to pray in generalities. Devotional repentance should be highly personal and embarrassingly specific.

Intercessory prayer. — Paul challenged the young minister, Timothy, "Therefore I exhort first of all that supplications, prayers, intercessions, and giving of thanks be made for all men" (1 Tim. 2:1).

When there's an issue or a person you want especially to pray for, put it on a card and take these cards into your private devotional. If you are a person of your word, your promise to pray for someone or something every day may provide just the impetus you need to refuse missing your daily devotions.

Just God and I

Sometimes I shut the door on all the world
And go alone to that most secret place
Where there is only God—
Just God and I! Then
Together we go over subtle acts,

Mistakes, and small hypocrisies of mine.
I strip myself from shams, from shackles free,
And stand aghast at my duplicity.

We look, just God and I, into my heart,
And though I shrink, we gaze there to the depth;
And though I tremble, shamed by what we find,
I suffer, too, a kind of painful joy . . .
And while I often find it hard to bear
The burning of God's knowing eyes on me,
I feel me stronger grow, just from their gaze.
My nakedness, it seems to me, is clothed
In raiment new that is most wondrous fair.
When next I venture forth, I wear
Sincerity, the gift that God in secret gave to me.
—*Author Unknown.*

CHAPTER 3

Interpersonal Relationships

Every time you stand up to preach, your purpose is to lead your listeners into a new or deeper relationship with Jesus. You can attain this by logical argument and/or by emotional appeal. But like it or not, you do it or fail to do it mostly by the attitude of your listeners toward you as you speak. If your listeners don't like you, it is almost impossible for you to lead them to love Christ.

Impact on Ministry

If you can't get along with people, you can't get along in pastoral ministry. Your supreme interest must be people. If you like books, administration, or speaking more than you like people, you will never make a successful minister of Jesus Christ. People are your specialty.

A six-year study involving thousands of laypersons in 47 denominations surveyed members' expectations of ministers. The survey rated the personal characteristics of integrity and warmth higher than professional skills. The survey also found that the second most serious negative in congregational expectations of a pastor has to do with relationship: a minister who avoids intimacy and repels people with a critical, demeaning, and insensitive attitude.

Your attitudes more than your gifts determine your success in ministry. Ellen White declares, "Tact and good judgment increase the usefulness of the laborer a hundredfold" (*Gospel Workers*, p. 119).

Loving People

Pastors must love people. Ministers mean to be intimate disciples of Jesus, and Jesus said, "By this all will know that you are My disciples, if you have love for one another" (John 13:35).

Why do birds sing? Because the song is in them. Why do pastors pastor, and plan, and preach? Because of love within them for their people.

Jesus illustrated, "I am the good shepherd. The good shepherd gives His life for the sheep. But he who is a hireling and not the shepherd, one who does not own the sheep, sees the wolf coming and leaves the sheep and flees; and the wolf catches the sheep and scatters them. The hireling flees because he is a hireling and does not care about the sheep" (John 10:11-13).

Good shepherds give their lives for their sheep. Each has a place in the shepherd's heart. The young, the old, the leaders, the followers, are all dear to the true shepherd. Hirelings don't care about their sheep; to them shepherding is just a job.

Hireling pastors see people as stepping-stones to their own ambitions. They are willing to walk on them to get wherever they want to go. For such ministers, people are pawns in a game—to be manipulated and controlled more than understood or loved.

Moses, returning from Mount Sinai, demonstrated the ideal pastoral love for people. Following Israel's worship of the golden calf, he interceded for them: "His timidity was lost in his deep interest and love for those for whom he had, in the hands of God, been the means of doing so much. . . . His interest in Israel sprang from no selfish motive. The prosperity of God's chosen people was dearer to him than personal honor, dearer than the privilege of becoming the father of a mighty nation" (*Patriarchs and Prophets*, p. 319).

Loving unlovely people. — Loving people in general is both very popular and fairly easy. But loving certain people in particular is one of the toughest tasks of pastoral life. Pastors must be able to see people as they are, warts and all, and not lose sight of what they can become by God's grace.

To be Jesus' minister, you must minister as Jesus ministered: "But when He saw the multitudes, He was *moved with compassion* for them, because they were weary and scattered, like sheep having no shepherd" (Matt. 9:36). To be compassionate as Jesus was compassionate is to go beyond sympathizing to alleviating. It not only accepts people's imperfections, but longs to help them overcome.

Loving abusive people. — Even abusive people become lovable when you focus, not on what they do, but on the hurt that is causing them to do it. We are all sometimes abused, criticized, misunderstood, falsely accused. A test of Christian love is being able to forgive genuinely those who have abused you.

We must forgive even those who were wrong when we were right. "Bearing with one another, and forgiving one another, if anyone has a complaint against another, even as Christ forgave you, so you also must do" (Col. 3:13). We are to forgive others as Christ forgave us. And just how did Christ forgive you? Did He forgive you because He was wrong and you were right? Undeserved forgiveness is the most Christlike kind.

Intimate Friendships

Should pastors have intimate friends? Absolutely. Close, trustworthy, bare-your-soul friendships are not only permissible, but a sign of relational competence and emotional maturity.

Everybody needs close friends. — Jesus needed friends. He chose 12 disciples to be His special friends. He had a specially unique friendship with Peter, James, and John. John may have been His best, most intimate human friend (Matt. 17:1; 26:37; John 13:23; 19:26; 20:2).

Friendships help you develop a more realistic view of yourself and your personal limitations. An intimate friend not only supports you, but also exposes you. Nominal friends let you know what they like about you. Close friends also let you know what they don't like. And that may be why insecure pastors want only nominal friends.

Where does the pastor find intimate friendship? Hopefully, your spouse is your best friend. One definition of a close friend is someone to whom you open up, with whom you communicate freely. Although you love each other and live in the same house, your spouse cannot be all that an intimate friend must be unless you communicate your ideas, plans, fears, failures, and frustrations.

Friendship with your spouse should be the most nearly complete friendship. On the other hand, if your spouse is the only one in whom you completely confide, it places too heavy a burden on the spouse.

Your ministerial secretary should be a trustworthy friend. The Ministerial Association urges that the ministerial secretary's job description make that person available to ministers as a close friend. Research indicates that most ministers or their spouses will not intimately confide in anyone involved with ministerial placement or discipline.

You may prefer a fellow pastor as your confidant and friend. Other pastors share similar problems and frustrations and often understand more completely.

Close friends in the congregation can complicate. — There are at least three complications of having close friends in the congregation:

1. To maintain a wholesome spirit among all members within your congregation, you must guard against partiality toward any. You try hard to love the indifferent and unresponsive equally with those who are enthusiastic and cooperative.
2. Being too open about your personal life could threaten your image as pastor and leader.
3. The necessity of confidentiality restricts your freedom to share problems, especially within the congregation. All of these reasons have led many pastors and conference/mission administrators to discourage intimate friendships between your family and parish members.

On the contrary, the theology of spiritual gifts and individual priesthood teaches that every member of the congregation is a minister. It suggests that all should minister to one another in an interdependent community. If you, as pastor, minister to the church, but never practice mutual ministry by allowing the church to minister to you, you are not totally a part of the congregational community. The first source of help for any member of that community should be the community itself.

May the pastor have close friends within the congregation? Two suggestions:

1. It is at least partially possible, if you can maintain clear boundaries between friendship and ministry. In your official capacity, you must serve all members equally. You should attempt to have no favorites on the church board, the nominating committee or in any other church function.

During your personal time, however, some friendships may develop. These close friendships should not be hidden, but neither should they be too visible. The bottom line is that you must not cause anyone to feel excluded.

2. Close friendships with elders usually escape criticism. They are your colleagues—associates in ministry. Because you are also their pastor, there may be some things you dare not share. Theirs cannot be quite full-service friendships, yet they can be very satisfying and helpful in meeting your friendship needs.

Community Relationships

Adventists in general and Adventist pastors in particular tend to be rather isolated from the city communities and neighborhoods in which they live. We feel we are busy with our own mission and upholding our own standards. The community often interprets this as unfriendly aloofness and spiritual snobbery. You ought to be as involved in community activities as your time and conscience allow.

You should include clergy of other faiths in your ministry. If possible, be a part of the local ministerial association. You will not only be able to influence them, but also find in them valuable professional friendship.

We love to quote, "And the word of God spread, and the number of the disciples multiplied greatly in Jerusalem, and a great many of the priests were obedient to the faith" (Acts 6:7). We look forward to the time when this drawing of clergy from other faiths to Christianity under the early rain will be repeated in winning clergy to the three angels' messages under the latter rain.

We have no right to expect ministers of other faiths to join us if we have never ministered to them. Jesus, in His ministry, associated with other religious leaders—clergy of other faiths. For example, Nicodemus, in John 3. If there had been no John 3, there apparently would have been no Acts 6.

CHAPTER 4

Time Management

Tyranny of Time

No one seems to have enough time. Yet all of us have all that there is. How we manage it is the secret to why some accomplish so much more than others.

Jesus emphasized the urgency attached to time. "I must work the works of Him who sent Me while it is day; the night is coming when no one can work" (John 9:4).

Managing time has always been a problem for Christians in general and ministers in particular. Apparently this was true even in the first century, when Paul wrote, "Live life, then, with a due sense of responsibility, not as men who do not know the meaning of life but as those who do. Make the best use of your time, despite all the evils of these days" (Eph. 5:15, 16, Phillips).

Timesaving Tips

Here are eight suggestions:

1. Plan. — *Planning increases satisfaction.* The trouble with having no plan for the use of your time is that you have no way of knowing if you've used it well. "To him that knoweth not the port to which he is bound, no wind can be favorable." If you don't know where you're going on a given day, week, or year, how can you enjoy the satisfaction of having gotten there? Planning increases satisfaction.

Planning increases efficiency. First, set long-term goals and objectives based on what you want most to accomplish. Then develop a time schedule to accomplish them. Without such a plan, you will drift from task to task, finishing few and not really tackling the most important.

Every year set aside a few hours to sit down with your spouse and schedule the typical week: hours in the office, in church meetings, visiting, at home. The general weekly schedule for a pastor of three churches might go like this:

Sunday:	Family.
Weekday Mornings:	Study and office work.
Monday:	Afternoon and evening—Bible studies, meetings, visitation at Church A, your largest.
Tuesday:	Afternoon and evening—same at Church B.
Wednesday:	Afternoon and evening—same at Church C.
Thursday:	Afternoon and evening—same back at Church A.
Friday:	General Sabbath preparation.
Sabbath:	Church services and family time.

Planning must be flexible. Don't plan too tightly. Pastoral ministry has too many exceptions and emergencies. Expect the unexpected. A plan so precise and detailed that it cannot realistically be followed will soon be abandoned.

Planning must be communicated. Members will never respect your time as completely as you wish, but you have no right to complain about their interfering with your time schedule if you haven't told them what it is. Discuss your schedule with the church board and get their advice, approval, and support. Then announce it to your congregation. You must always add that you're available anytime for emergencies, but that you are endeavoring to make the best use of your time so you can contribute most to the congregation.

Communicate your schedule in writing. Post it on your office door. Include it in the bulletin. Out of fairness to your members, be available in the scheduled time. Out of fairness to you, your members must understand you cannot be available for just any thing at any time.

Communicate personally. This is most difficult and delicate. How can you handle drop-ins or telephoners with no real need other than wanting to talk? If someone asks, "Are you busy?" don't be too kind to give an honest answer. A balanced reply is "Yes, I'm terribly busy just now. How can I help you?" If that person still wants to chat, give your full attention for a few minutes. Then, if it's a drop-in, stand, thank the person for coming, shake hands, and perhaps say a little prayer. Never be unkind. But never let a few so control your time that you become ineffective in helping the many.

2. Prioritize. — Efficiency experts speak of the 80/20 rule. According to this, we tend to spend 80 percent of our time doing what gets 20 percent of the results. Pastors spend far too much time doing things that don't really matter. Too many make a career of hunting ants rather than elephants, because they get a quicker kill and thus a higher body count. The most successful are not those who work hard, but those who work hard at hard work.

TIME MANAGEMENT

At the beginning of each week, make a list of what needs doing that week. Each morning, decide which items on the list should be done that day. "When you rise in the morning, take into consideration, as far as possible, the work you must accomplish during the day. If necessary, have a small book in which to jot down the things that need to be done, and set yourself a time in which to do your work" (*Evangelism*, p. 652).

Now prioritize. The 80/20 rule says that 80 percent of your day's value will come from 20 percent of the list. Resist the tendency to do the easy tasks first and leave the hard tasks undone. ABC your list. Do the most important A items first and the least important C items last. Your goal is not to finish everything on the list, but those things that are most important.

3. Create at your prime time. — Certain hours of the day energy level tends to be highest. For many, this is first thing in the morning. For others, it takes most of the morning to wake up, but they are bright and energetic into the night. No one else has the right to tell you when to do your creative, hard-thinking work. Do it whenever your energy level is highest.

4. Use a secretary. — A good secretary can double your effectiveness by handling much of the church's paperwork, taking phone calls, making appointments for you, etc. Unfortunately, very few churches are willing or able to finance the salary. Perhaps a part-time secretary is possible. A volunteer, such as a retired secretary, may be available. Your spouse might be interested in working with you in exchange for your having more time for the family. A shut-in might use the telephone to make appointments for your visitation, helping you see up to twice as many people in the same amount of visitation time.

5. Group your calls. — Group your visits. Try never to be in the same part of your district twice in the same week. Group your phone calls. Let your congregation know when you will be available to receive or return phone calls so you or your family are not interrupted so many times throughout the day. Use the phone for much of your visiting. A phone call is worth half a visit, and you can usually make five to ten phone calls in the time it takes to make one visit. If someone is sick in a satellite church, you can't go every day; but if phones are available, you could call.

6. Do it now. — Settle trifles quickly. Be democratic, but don't call committees to make minor decisions that could just as well be made by one or two. Make it your ideal to handle a piece of paper only once.

Leave your mail until you have time to give it proper attention. Then, if a letter needs answering, do it immediately and be done with it. If something can be delegated, pass it along right away.

Efficiency and effectiveness are powerful twins. Efficiency says, "Do the job right." Don't be so pushed by time that you do the job poorly and end up wasting time by having to do it again. Effectiveness says, "Do the right job right." Don't waste your ministry concentrating on minor jobs because they're easier. Tackle the most important job, even if it's the toughest. Do it first and be done with it.

7. Use time twice. — Most ministers spend much of their time traveling. All spouses and parents spend time waiting here and there for family members. Use such times to read, listen to tapes, answer your mail, catch up on the radio news, etc.

8. Delegate. — Eliminate things you shouldn't be doing. To be effective, ministers must be reflective. You must take time to think, to study, to pray, to plan. Ellen White counsels, "It is a great mistake to keep a minister who is gifted with power to preach the gospel constantly at work in business matters. He who holds forth the Word of life is not to allow too many burdens to be placed upon him." (*Evangelism*, pp. 91, 92).

The apostles learned this the hard way. When they tried to do the work of the church by themselves the work didn't get done. And so they delegated that part to which they were not directly called, saying, "But we will give ourselves continually to prayer and to the ministry of the word" (Acts 6:4). Results? "And the word of God spread, and the number of the disciples multiplied greatly" (verse 7).

CHAPTER 5

Personal Health

"A merry heart does good, like medicine, but a broken spirit dries the bones" (Prov. 17:22). People in touch with God are less likely to get sick— and better able to cope when they do. Since your business is to further religion, and since religion and health are so interrelated, you ought to both teach and practice personal health.

Physical Health

Get a physical checkup on a regular basis as prescribed by your conference/mission. Most problems can now be treated successfully if detected early. Unwillingness to undergo a regular physical exam is not a sign of superior strength, but of short-sighted judgment.

Three basic ingredients of good physical health are:

1. Diet. — *Eat the right foods.* Eat foods high in fiber and low in sugar, salt, and animal fats. "Many of our ministers are digging their graves with their teeth" (*Testimonies*, vol. 4, p. 408). "Ministers, above all others, should economize the strength of brain and nerve. They should avoid all food or drink that has a tendency to irritate or excite the nerves. . . . God cannot let His Holy Spirit rest upon those who, while they know how they should eat for health, persist in a course that will enfeeble mind and body" (*Counsels on Diet and Foods*, pp. 55, 56).

Eat the right foods in the right amounts. You may be able to hide many things about your personal life. Being overweight is not one of them. When your appearance disagrees with your doctrine, it's embarrassing to teach and preach temperance and self-discipline. Besides, it's harder to get your work done while carrying those extra pounds everywhere you go.

2. Exercise. — How can a pastor who is badly out of shape presume credibility when dispensing advice for either this life or the next? "The whole system needs the invigorating influence of exercise in the open air. A few hours of manual labor each day would tend to renew the bodily vigor and rest and relax the mind. In this way the general health would be promoted, and a greater amount of pastoral labor could be performed" (*Testimonies*, vol. 4, pp. 264, 265).

3. Rest. — Too many Adventist ministers preach against addiction while they themselves are being addicted—to work! If you are proud of overwork, you may well have both an ego problem and a theological problem. Get your sleep each night. Take your day off each week. Take your vacation each year. Jesus would. Although He had only three and a half years to get His work done, He made sure His disciples got their rest. On several occasions He took them aside for the purpose of resting.

Jesus also practiced a unique type and source of rest we never quite comprehend, yet should continually strive for. On one single Sabbath He preached at the synagogue, healed a man with an unclean spirit, cured Peter's mother-in-law, and taught His disciples; after sundown, He healed many sick in the city (see Mark 1). Does that sound a little like some of your Sabbaths?

How did Jesus rest up after such a day? He apparently slept for a while, but then He turned to His very special method of rejuvenation: "Now in the morning, having risen a long while before daylight, He went out and departed to a solitary place; and there He prayed" (Mark 1:35). Private prayer was one of Jesus' favorite ways to rest and recharge Himself when He needed special energy most.

Psychological Health

Ministry is stressful work. Stress, in itself, is not bad. When you are completely relaxed, you fall asleep. You work more efficiently under some stress. It's overstress, unrelieved stress, that should be avoided. One recent study showed that 75 percent of clergy experienced periods of major stress. Other research has indicated that women pastors experienced significantly greater personal strain than men pastors.

Burnout. — Overstress causes burnout. Burnout is defined as a cluster of physical, emotional, and mental exhaustion reactions. It is the result of repeated emotional arousal resulting from constant involvement with people.

Pastoring is stressful because it is a people-centered occupation, and people cause stress. Also, you have more to do than you can get done. You are expected to be skillful in more areas than you are good at.

Moreover, you stand between the expectations of your congregation and your conference/mission, and unfortunately, these expectations are often different. This has the "hourglass effect," making you feel in the middle of an hourglass, where the grinding sand comes at you from both directions.

Pastoring is stressful because, generally, pastors tend to have less recreation than most people.

Burnout prevention. — On the positive side, research indicates that pastors tend to have better personal resources for coping with stress than the general population. A vigorous faith experience is one of the best hedges against burnout.

Jesus teaches a lesson that too many pastors seem not to have learned. According to Him, satisfaction comes not from what we do, but from what we already are—greatly loved children of God. Christians should feel forgiven, saved, loved. Thus Christianity tends to make us optimistic rather than pessimistic. Pessimists' negative attitudes often blind them to solutions. The optimist is happier, healthier, and a better problem-solver.

Even then, you will need some special help from other people at times. This may come from your spouse, a fellow pastor, a friend, or a support group. Some conferences/missions have a plan to pay anonymously at least part of the fee for counseling with a professional counselor. Don't be too embarrassed or proud to accept counsel. Plan your life around the expectation that "we all need help sometimes."

CHAPTER 6

Personal Appearance

"God expects His ministers, in their manners and in their dress, to give a fitting representation of the principles of truth and the sacredness of their office" (*Gospel Workers*, p. 174).

Appearance Matters

When you meet someone for the first time, even before you utter a word, that person makes a judgment about you based on your appearance. The way you look not only impacts on the people you meet, but affects how they treat you.

"But appearance doesn't matter much to me," you might argue. Does influencing people matter to you? Is helping people important to you? If so, then appearance must matter, for what people see sometimes speaks so loudly that they cannot hear what you say. "A minister who is negligent in his apparel often wounds those of good taste and refined sensibilities" (*Testimonies*, vol. 2, p. 613).

Clothing ranks you and your profession. If your dress is second-class compared with other professionals in your community, the community will assume yours is a second-class profession.

Appearance Should Attract to Christ

Paul counsels, "Therefore, whether you eat or drink, or whatever you do, do all to the glory of God" (1 Cor. 10:31). Dress to impress—for Christ. "The God of heaven . . . is honored or dishonored by the apparel of those who officiate in His honor" (*Gospel Workers*, p. 173).

Dress will open or close doors for Christ. If people expect persons in a particular profession to dress in a certain manner, they are more likely to believe them and trust them if they appear in the expected garb. Research also indicates that unusual dress cuts into credibility. People don't quite know whether to trust and believe a person dressed differently than they expect.

Don't go for cheap clothes; they are sometimes the most expensive. Good-quality clothing lasts longer. Also, it holds its shape better and thus looks neater.

Three appearance factors most likely to attract people to Christ:

1. Good taste. — The first rule of dress is common sense. Shun fads. Typically, the respected ministerial garb is conservative as defined by the local culture.

Good taste means clothing should be not only appropriate but appropriate to the occasion. Conservative dress does best in the pulpit, and certainly at a wedding or funeral, but don't dress so conservatively around young people that they think you belong only to the past.

Men should be teachable enough to listen to their wives' counsel about dress. Women tend to be more interested in appearance, and more intelligent about good taste.

2. Neatness. — You can hardly teach neatness or preach self-discipline while dressed like an unmade bed. "The loss of some souls at last will be traced to the untidiness of the minister" (*Testimonies*, vol. 2, p. 613). Neatness need not be expensive. It includes such things as well-pressed clothes and shined shoes.

3. Cleanliness. — The pastor's clothes should be kept clean—and so should the pastor. Preaching and other parts of our work tend to excite our nerves. When nervous, we perspire. When perspiration grows stale, it gives off an embarrassingly indelicate odor.

Appearance Should Usually Go Unnoticed

Your dress should be adapted to the culture in which you work. When static comes over your radio, you may fidget and tune the radio for a while, trying to get rid of the noise, but if it continues, you'll simply turn the radio off. An undesirable physical appearance, dress, and gestures on the part of the preacher causes static. It interferes with what you want people to hear. And when there's too much static, people simply turn the preacher off.

Research indicates that 7 percent of what speakers communicate comes from their words, 38 percent from their manner of speech, and 55 percent from the expressions on their faces and from their bodily movements. You may not like it, but your body language can speak so loudly your people hardly hear your sermons.

You can't portray the joy of following Christ if you preach with a frown on your face. The pale-faced preacher is a horrible representative of the robust Jesus.

PERSONAL APPEARANCE

It's best if your appearance goes mostly unnoticed. Is it appropriate to wear a gold watch, gold-rimmed glasses? How about a sparkly tie clasp, cuff links, or trendy hairstyle or beard? The objective should be: dress so people hardly notice. If your appearance is cheap and shoddy, people notice. If your appearance is either too gaudy or too elegant, people notice. If you dress like 20 years ago or like 20 years in the future, people notice. Don't make static with your clothes. Dress so your appearance doesn't interfere with your message.

CHAPTER 7

Personal Finance

"Moreover it is required in stewards that one be found faithful" (1 Cor. 4:2). Here are 10 good rules for being a faithful steward of personal finance.

1. *Enjoy frugality*. — Christian workers have virtually always been underpaid. So if you are to live on a minister's salary, learn to enjoy frugality and simplicity. Adopt Solomon's prayer of contentment as yours: "Give me neither poverty nor riches" (Prov. 30:8). On the other hand, if you see yourself principally as a professional entitled to live on the economic level of other professionals in your church, you're probably doomed to disappointment. A Christian minister is a divinely called servant-leader of the congregation as a whole. As such, you're expected to live on the economic level of your membership as a whole. The tithing system is designed to make this generally possible.

Church members resent denying themselves and giving of their funds to leaders who live economically above the donor's financial level. They do not wish to give money to leaders to possess things the giver cannot afford. If you're financially discontented, do not be too certain that more money would solve your problem. Almost everyone, regardless of how high or low the income, thinks the same way. The solution to financial problems is not just getting more money, but learning how to manage what you have. It begins with knowing the difference between your wants and needs. It involves finding ways to make do. Stretching a budget can challenge one's creative genius and can be fulfilling.

One minister's wife summed up her obligation to live frugally: "My husband's salary isn't what it should be, but I will not let this rob my contentment. I guard my attitude toward things and finances carefully, spend wisely, and consider the blessings I enjoy from being a pastor's wife as unlimited riches. My attitude toward my husband's salary can make my lot in life a blessing or a curse, and I want a blessing attitude."

2. *Be absolutely honest*. — Because they mean to be honest, ministers can take their honesty too much for granted. Your temptation may be to cheat just a little on your taxes, misrepresent something you're selling, or shift church funds from one account to another. Discipline yourself to be absolutely honest.

Never take personal financial advantage of the church funds you handle. They are not yours, but the people's—and God's! Church money must be handled with a greater sense of responsibility and accountability than your own funds.

Conference, union, and General Conference leaders with travel budgets and other funds available to them must not use these to gain personal privileges not available to pastors.

3. Pay bills promptly. — Not only your own reputation, but that of your church, depends on prompt payment of bills. When moving to another field, faithfully repay any indebtedness to your mission/conference.

4. Shop wisely—but not selfishly. — Never be a discount specialist, always pleading with merchants for a special clergy discount. It degrades your calling and can be selfish. The merchant must make a living too.

5. Shun debt. — Ellen White counseled church leaders, "Let them guard themselves as with a fence of barbed wire against the inclination to go into debt" (*Testimonies*, vol. 5, pp. 235, 236). Borrow as little as possible, at the lowest rate you can find, for the shortest period of time you can afford. Live on a budget, even if it is a loosely structured one. A budget teaches you self-discipline in financial matters.

Beware of the credit card (where available). It is a blessing only if you are able to pay the bill before interest is added. On a minister's salary you can't afford the exorbitant interest charged by credit cards.

Have adequate insurance. Ellen White warned against speculative life insurance schemes where you invest large sums of money with the hope that you or your heirs will become wealthy. But sensible insurance is necessary to protect your personal finances.

6. Avoid sidelines. — Church administrators and members are responsible to provide ministers a living wage. Ministers are responsible for living within that wage so they can devote their full energy to their ministry. "The minister who is wholly consecrated to God refuses to engage in business that would hinder him from giving himself fully to his sacred calling" (*The Acts of the Apostles*, p. 366).

7. Never borrow from members. — Borrowing from members tends to lead to one of two problems: (1) an eventual misunderstanding and strained relationship with the lender, or (2) favoritism toward the one to whom you're indebted.

8. Don't seek gifts from members. — Playing on the sympathies of your members to your financial advantage is unfair to the members and belittling of your calling.

9. Be an exemplary giver. — No minister who does not return a faithful tithe should be employed. Give offerings generously. Don't ask people to sacrifice for the church more than you do.

10. Save a little. — Plan for the unexpected: emergency repairs, replacement of appliances, sudden medical expenses. You also need to rely on savings to pay cash for large items, educating the children, and preparing for retirement.

Sometimes you may not be able to save very much, but the habit of saving is more important than the amount saved. Give to God first, then give to yourself—put something in savings. The trick is to live just a little beneath your means. One rather painless way to begin saving is to wait until you receive a pay raise. If you have been getting along with the former salary, put the additional money in savings.

How to handle personal finance? Do your best, then trust God to do the rest. "And my God shall supply all your need according to His riches in glory by Christ Jesus" (Phil. 4:19).

CHAPTER 8

Family Life

Ministry Begins at Home

Traditionally, the pastor's family experiences special stresses. — Pastors experience stress. Generally pastors are overloaded. Some even feel guilty if they take time off for their families. They work all day as "saints" even though they actually aren't. They must smile and be loving no matter how they're treated. Only when they get home do they dare to explode or vent their feelings and frustrations—on their families.

No other area so emphatically reminds pastors of their humanity and sinfulness as their relationships at home. No matter how successful they may be in helping others solve relational problems, if they cannot solve their own they will feel a failure.

Pastors' spouses experience stress. Ministerial stress affects spouses as well. Frequent moves may lead to an experience of loneliness and isolation. Spouses may feel guilty for resenting their mates' putting church work first. They may face other stress factors such as not having enough time for the family, financial problems, feelings of personal inadequacy, criticism by church members, and concern about conference approval.

Pastors' children experience stress. Sometimes children are confused by the difference they perceive between what the preacher preaches and how the preacher lives. A limited sampling of pastors' children of high school and college age indicates that most felt strong pressure to conform to church members' expectations. Eighty-eight percent said adults treated them differently because they were PKs (preachers' kids). Fifty-six percent answered that their house rules were different from their friends'.

On the positive side, 88 percent expected that their adult belief system and moral attitudes will be much the same as their parents'. Eighty percent said that, on the whole, they enjoyed being PKs.

Historically, the pastor's family has been neglected. — If the apostles had families, they seemed to pay little attention to them. Paul

47

was probably married at one time, but emphasized the benefits of ministers being single. The Roman Catholic Church insists on clergy celibacy. Adventists trace their roots to Methodism, whose founder, John Wesley, did not marry until age 48. Even then, he cut his honeymoon short with the explanation that a Methodist preacher should not preach one sermon less or travel one day less married than if he were single.

This historical background may seem to excuse the modern minister's neglect of family. The counter argument, however, is much stronger. Jesus was family-oriented in His relationship to His mother. The apostles could not have normal family relationships, because they were confined to a unique, itinerant ministry.

As the New Testament model for the pastor, we might consider the bishop of 1 Timothy 3, usually thought of as a local elder. Here the apostle strongly encourages the concept of pastoral family (verse 2). In fact, failure at home is suggested as indication of failure in ministry: "For if a man does not know how to rule his own house, how will he take care of the church of God?" (verse 5).

"The minister's duties lie around him, nigh and afar off; but his first duty is to his children. . . . The world is not so much in need of great minds, as of good men, who are a blessing in their homes" (*Gospel Workers*, p. 204).

Theologically, the pastor's family is the pastor's first ministry. — Christian theology should make a minister a model spouse. Why?

1. *Christianity is love-centered living.* "He who does not love does not know God, for God is love" (1 John 4:8).
2. *Love is a developed capacity.* Nobody is born loving, not even when we're "born again." We are born with a need for love and with a potential for love, but love is learned behavior. And so God created the home.
3. *The home is a place to test love.* It's where we most emphatically and consistently learn our love imperfections.
4. *The secure home is a place to learn love.* Surrounded by love, children learn love. Surrounded by loved ones with whom they dare to be vulnerable, adults learn to love more fully.

Thus, if love is at the heart of Christianity, and if home is where love is tested and developed, the home must be at the center of Christianity. If Christian love won't work at home, it won't work anywhere.

Important as the Sabbath is, there's much more home than Sabbath in the Ten Commandments. Five of the commandments refer directly or indirectly to the home:

- Second—Children tend to follow the example of their parents.
- Fourth—Sabbath rest involves parent, son, and daughter.
- Fifth—Children at any age have a responsibility to their parents.
- Seventh—Adultery is still sin.
- Tenth—Admire your own spouse, not your neighbor's.

Since there's more home than Sabbath in the Ten Commandments, only home reformers should call themselves commandment keepers.

At the first wedding ceremony God said, "Therefore a man shall leave his father and mother and be joined to his wife, and they shall become one flesh" (Gen. 2:24). Husband and wife are to be closer to each other than to anything or anyone else in the world. Pastor, that relationship is to take precedence over your church members, your studies, your hobbies, conference goals, over everything except God Himself.

Prescription for a Happy Pastoral Family

1. Devote quality time regularly. — *Give time.* A survey of Adventist ministers' wives indicated they felt their husbands' time priorities were as follows: (1) church work, (2) time with God, (3) his health, (4) wife, and (5) children. Seventy-two percent worried about not having enough family time.

The greatest gift you can give your family is yourself. "Nothing can excuse the minister for neglecting the inner circle for the larger circle outside. The spiritual welfare of his family comes first" (*Gospel Workers*, p. 204).

Give dependable time. Pastoral families complain less about ministers failing to give enough time than about failing to give dependable time. When you promise family time and then frequently cancel it because of church emergencies, the family feels second-class and in competition with the church. Never cancel. Seldom postpone, and if you do, make sure to keep the family appointment at the first possible opportunity.

Give quality time. Set aside time when you're not worn out. Spend time with the children. Give them your undivided attention, rather than just being in the same room while you are doing your own thing. Spouses need time away from the children, where just the two of you can be alone together.

Give chore time. Instead of doing your chores alone, include your spouse or child. You not only spend time together without it taking any extra time, but you both enjoy the satisfaction of having accomplished something together.

When Martin Luther was hanging out diapers the neighbors laughed. Luther exclaimed, "Let them laugh. God and the angels smile in heaven."

2. Communicate deeply. — Communicate with your child. The word "communicate" comes from the same root as "common." How much we have in common with our children will depend on how well we communicate with them. Verbal communication must include both talking and listening. We talk to (or past) our children too much and listen too little. Body language also communicates. Children never outgrow their need to be touched and hugged.

Communicate with your spouse. Your spouse needs your ear, not just your heart. Paul counseled, "Husbands, give your wives much love; never treat them harshly" (Col. 3:19, Phillips). Listen lovingly. Listen nonjudgmentally.

Talk. You get the thrills of success in ministry. Share them with your spouse. Spouses hear too many church problems and too few church triumphs.

Communicate at a deeper, feeling level. There is little relational communication taking place when we talk about buying groceries or paying bills. We know persons intimately only to the extent that we know their deepest feelings. People dare to open themselves and talk about such things only when they are certain they won't be shamed, put down, or made to look foolish.

Pastors should talk about their spouses' niche in the church. Where do they see themselves fitting in? Do they feel comfortable in their role?

Talk about romance and lovemaking. To be fully satisfying, physical intimacy must be preceded by mental and spiritual intimacy. If you are close enough to practice sexual intimacy, you ought to be close enough to talk about it.

3. Affirm frequently. — Make it a habit to look for something good and beautiful in your spouse and children each day—and tell them. Write one-minute memos to your children. A one-minute memo is one that takes only a minute to write and less to read. Use them to share congratulations, thank-yous, or inspirational thoughts, or just to let your family know you're thinking about them.

Be with your spouse in public. Your spouse will love it, and members will notice that you don't need any more romance than you're already getting. If you both feel comfortable doing it, stop by your spouse's pew as you exit down the aisle on Sabbath morning, then greet your congregation together at the door. Say only kind, appreciative things about your mate in the pulpit. In your sermons, never hold your children up as examples or illustrate your sermons with their failures. Affirm your family.

4. Pray daily. — Give the family altar first priority in your day.

FAMILY LIFE

Make family worship a happy experience. Be the priest, but not always the professor. That is, you must be the spiritual leader of your home, but you mustn't assume that only you know all the answers. Christianity is meant to be an intensely personal experience. Nobody has all the answers for anybody else. Families need to talk about beliefs and standards, not just impose them as family traditions or church rules.

On occasion, affirm a chosen member of the family in family worship by inviting each family member to suggest a Christian character trait you've observed in that person. Before prayer, ask, "What may I pray for, for you today?" As you pray, use a culturally accepted touch to express family togetherness.

Advantages of Clergy Families

Yes, there are unique stresses in the pastoral family. But there are also special advantages. Research indicates only 10 to 15 percent of preachers' children have trouble with their role. PKs surveyed felt they have wider exposure to people and ideas, and usually a more secure family, spiritually committed to making Christian love work.

Other advantages listed by clergy couples:

- A strong sense of purpose and mission in life.
- Opportunity to work as a team on tasks of eternal significance.
- A people-oriented vocation that really has the answers.
- Satisfaction of helping people in the very best way they can be helped—finding God's love.
- Being surrounded by the love of Christian friends.

Maintaining a happy, exemplary pastor's family has enough problems to make it challenging, but it's well worth the effort. If something goes wrong, don't settle for the burial of family relationships gone dead. Be Christian. Seek a resurrection. It will bless your family and multiply the effectiveness of your ministry. "One well-ordered, well-disciplined family tells more in behalf of Christianity than all the sermons that can be preached" (*The Adventist Home*, p. 32).

CHAPTER 9

Pastoral Ethics

Ethics Code

The General Conference Ministerial Association, with counsel from pastors and church administrators around the world, has prepared and recommends to every Adventist minister the following code of ethics:

Seventh-day Adventist Minister's Code of Ethics

I recognize that a call to the gospel ministry of the Seventh-day Adventist Church is not for the purpose of bestowing special privilege or position, but rather for living a life of devotion and service to God, His church, and the world. I affirm that my personal life and professional activities shall be rooted in the Word of God and subject to the Lordship of Christ. I am totally committed to the fundamental beliefs of the Seventh-day Adventist Church.

I am dedicated to the maintenance of high standards of professional conduct and competence in my ministry. I purpose to build relationships based on the principles expressed in the life and teachings of Christ.

I shall, by the grace of God, apply these standards in my life so as to include the following:
1. Maintain a meaningful devotional life for myself and my family.
2. Give full time and attention to the ministry as my only vocation.
3. Commit myself to continuing professional growth.
4. Initiate and maintain supportive professional relationships with fellow ministers.
5. Practice strictest professional confidentiality.
6. Support my employing organization and the world church.
7. Manage church and personal finances with integrity.
8. Perceive and treat my family as a primary part of my ministry.
9. Practice healthful living.
10. Relate with propriety to those of the opposite sex.

11. Respect the personhood of every individual, without bias or prejudice.
12. Love those to whom I minister and commit myself to their spiritual growth.

Ethics and Fellow Ministers

Your fellow pastors. — We ministers love our Lord, we love our work, we love our people. But we ought to love each other more than we do. We must decrease the spirit of competition among us and increase the spirit of cooperation and support. We need to make our pastors' meeting not only a get-together for instruction, but an occasion for warm fellowship. We need to be sharing our problems with a fellow minister. We need to be sensitive and available to the hurts of other pastors.

Your intern supervisor. — Intern, support your supervising pastors and their ministry. Your education may be superior, your personality may be more charismatic, and your gifts may be greater, but never underestimate the value of the wisdom your supervisor has gained through experience. Supervising pastors always have persons in the congregation who disagree with them. The pastor may have had to deal very frankly with some. Don't let these gain a disloyal ear when they lift you up and put your supervisor down.

The General Conference Ministerial Association has prepared *A Manual for Ministerial Interns and Intern Supervisors* to assist in the internship training process. It is available through the GC Ministerial Supply Center.

Your predecessor. — When you move to a new district, don't be too quick to discard your predecessor's program. Yours isn't better just because it's yours. Show both wisdom and respect by keeping what's working.

Your successor. — Leave good church records, such as street maps marked to show membership, missionary territories, etc., a church directory including officers and committees, evangelistic interests, and ingathering records.

Share helpful personal information about shopping, doctor and dentist, hospital, bookstore, etc. The rule: "Therefore, whatever you want men to do to you, do also to them" (Matt. 7:12).

Your disciplined peers. — Disfellowshipped ministers should not be "disfriendshipped" by other ministers. Don't take a holier-than-thou attitude toward those dismissed from the ministry. They usually feel they've failed, and failure is deeply painful. Their homes are often in jeopardy. They are suddenly alienated from their former circle of friends and very lonely. They need a pastor. They need a friend.

Your non-SDA fellow ministers. — You have a lot more in common with these ministers than you may realize. Get acquainted. If feasible, join the Ministerial Alliance or Ministers' Fraternity.

Ethics and Job Placement

Don't seek promotion. — Never let restless feet make you more solicitous for promotion than for principle. In God's work, promotion is His business, not yours, "For promotion cometh neither from the east, nor from the west, nor from the south. But God is the judge: he putteth down one, and setteth up another" (Ps. 75:6, 7, KJV).

Shun self-pity. — If you feel pushed aside or passed over, be patient. Your turn may come later. Instead of feeling sorry for yourself, use the experience for self-examination to see if the fault lies with you. "If any are qualified for a higher position, the Lord will lay the burden, not alone on them, but on those who have tested them, who know their worth, and who can understandingly urge them forward" (*The Ministry of Healing*, p. 477).

Seek a high standard, not a high position. — Aim high, but aim at a high standard, not a high position. Keep your performance standards high, and the position will, under God's guidance, take care of itself. The best way to get out of a low position is to be consistently effective in it. Work hard where you are, keep improving, and leave promotion to God.

Ethics and Race

The Seventh-day Adventist Church is just moving from believing in a world church to truly being a world church. Over 89 percent of its membership now live outside the North American Division, where the movement began. Those who fear this church has lost its mission should feel reassured by this hard evidence that the three angels' messages really are going "to every nation, tribe, tongue, and people" (Rev. 14:6). Even within North America, the growth of membership among ethnic minorities is outstanding. The race of the majority of early Adventists is becoming a minority. And it takes a lot of Christian love for a majority to become a minority gracefully.

Racism is sinful. Christian love pulls down barriers that separate people. "There is neither Jew nor Greek, there is neither slave nor free, there is neither male nor female; for you are all one in Christ Jesus" (Gal. 3:28). If Jesus is your brother and my brother, then you and I are brothers; and color or caste or tribe or language or nationality is irrelevant.

Ethics and Sex*

Paul's admonition to young Timothy should be ours: "Be an example to the believers in word, in conduct, in love, in spirit, in faith, in purity" (1 Tim. 4:12).

The call to ministry is a sacred trust, involving among other things a respect for the personhood of people as envisioned in the seventh commandment. Any breach of trust in this area brings reproach to ministry, to the church, and to God. Since it is unreasonable to ask members to trust pastors who have engaged in sexual misconduct (adultery, pedophilia, homosexuality, fornication, etc.), and since the church is at legal risk when employing or transferring, as pastors, those with a history of sexual misconduct, such ministers are expected to return their credentials to the conference/mission. While violation of the seventh commandment makes pastors ineligible for employment in pastoral ministry, they need and can experience God's forgiving grace and love. The church should seek to restore and nurture their spiritual and family relationships.

Since some ministers are women, we have attempted to eliminate gender in this handbook as much as possible. However, since male ministers seem more often guilty of unethical sexual conduct, we will address this section primarily to men.

Professionals specializing in counseling pastors with sexual problems have drawn a portrait of the typical minister most subject to a moral fall. He tends to be a middle-aged male who is disillusioned with his calling, is neglecting his own marriage, is a lone ranger isolated from his clerical colleagues, and has met a woman who needs him.

It's happening too often. A study of Protestant clergy reported that 13 percent have had extramarital affairs involving a church member. The incidence was almost double what has been reported for other helping professionals, suggesting that ministers are particularly vulnerable in this area. Let's look at a few reasons for this moral problem among pastors.

The problem. — Some behaviorists have labeled five characteristics

---

*To help increase awareness among ministers in these areas the General Conference Ministerial Association has prepared a video, "Sexual Ethics for Church Professionals."

in addition to physical attractiveness that make a person appear romantically attractive to the opposite sex. These five characteristics were not meant to apply specially to pastors, but notice how closely they do:

1. *Self-confidence.* Not all ministers feel self-confident, of course, but they generally appear confident. And confidence attracts.
2. *Power.* People are attracted not only to power but to powerful persons. The pastor is usually perceived as a powerful person within the church. This power is magnified because he speaks with authority—the authority derived from God and Scripture.
3. *Public recognition.* Pastors enjoy some degree of celebrity status within their constituencies; and fame is an aphrodisiac. Ministers tend to have a special longing and need to be loved. If they are not receiving the love and recognition from their congregation that they need, they may be overwhelmed by someone who does give them recognition.
4. *Showing interest and concern.* Pastors are expected to be attentive, interested, responsive listeners. It is only a short step from intimate communication to intimate behavior. Successful counseling requires a counselor who truly cares and a counselee whose needs are being met. Romance can seem almost a natural next step.

Pastors work mostly with female church volunteers. Any two people of opposite sex who are of similar age, who enjoy working together, and are alone a lot have a likelihood of arousing some sexual feelings.

5. *Gentleness.* Gentleness is a romantic quality. It is also a stock in trade for ministers.

All five of these characteristics, that contribute to romantic attractiveness, are typical of ministers. Our office and calling give us additional attractive characteristics that we would not ordinarily have. Without our being aware of it, or any woman's planning it, we can become romantic and fantasy objects.

Solutions. — Here are some solutions.

1. *Be in love with your wife—and let it show.* Work to make your home work. The grass doesn't always look greener on the other side of the fence if you've watered the lawn at home. Be often seen expressing affection to your wife as culturally appropriate.
2. *Be aware of your vulnerability.* Too many of the pastors who said "It could never happen to me" are now ex-pastors. It can and will happen to you if you think you can toy with little flirtations and sexual fantasies and remain unscathed. Respect the compelling nature of the sex drive. If indulged, erotic and romantic longings inevitably win over rational thought.

3. *Be perceptive.* Be perceptive of your own feelings. Candidly face up to the beginning of an attraction such as mutual looks, a desire to be in her company. See red flags if you become preoccupied with a counselee's presence, clothes, or erotic signals.

Be perceptive of women's feelings. When a pastor has an affair, it is not necessarily with a scheming seductress. More likely, it's with an individual who is hurting, whose self-esteem is low, and who thus feels drawn to one who listens and counsels. If you aren't perceptive to women's romantic feelings, trust your wife—she very likely is. If you feel significant attraction, tell your wife. Verbalizing your feelings helps you sort them out, and when your wife knows, no affair is likely to develop.

4. *Be accountable.* Pastors take risks secular counselors are afraid to take. Professional counselors typically are required to report periodically to someone else about each client. Regularly tell someone what's going on in your counseling relationships.

Seldom counsel with women when alone. In many countries, pastors are the only professionals still making house calls. Someone else should be present when you counsel a woman in her home. Don't counsel in your office when no one else is in the building. Put a window in or beside your office door. Counseling demands auditory privacy, but not visibility privacy!

5. *Be cautious of sexual counseling.* Men find it difficult to talk with women about their sexual problems without themselves being sexually aroused. Women would be wiser to share such things with another woman.

6. *Be ready to run.* Kindly but persistently separate yourself from a tempting situation. The counselee should not be left feeling rejected and without help, but you should arrange for her to see another counselor.

Solomon surely knew from experience a great deal about being tempted by a woman. He insisted, "Remove your way far from her, and do not go near the door of her house, lest you give your honor to others, and your years to the cruel one" (Prov. 5:8, 9). It's a fool's bargain to trade your family and your future for one sensuous moment.

7. *Be spiritually strong.* Keep your spiritual resistance high. Remind yourself that "thou shalt not commit adultery" means you. Feel about it as Joseph did: "How then can I do this great wickedness, and *sin against God?*" (Gen. 39:9). See adultery as a sin, not only against yourself and your family, but against your God!

Ethics and the Law

Suits against the church. — Separation between church and state tends not to protect the church from lawsuit when there has been sexual abuse by a pastor or other church leader. Victims, congregations, and church administrators have historically tried to protect the church by hiding sexual misconduct. Law and society, however, are becoming increasingly active in protecting the unempowered from the empowered.

The law now tends to hold a pastor accountable for sexual intimacy with a counselee, no matter how willing the counselee might have been. The pastor's position of power and presumed emotional maturity often causes the law to hold him and his employing organization responsible.

Some therapists insist that counselors who have sex with their counselees should be prosecuted for rape, no matter how willing the counselee was. Rape is when one person overpowers another. This is true, they would argue, whether the overpowering is physical or psychological.

Churches and conferences are also being sued for misconduct of local church leaders, especially their sexual abuse of children. Such abuse can happen at Pathfinder retreats, Sabbath school division socials, the church school, etc. When it does, parents may be angry enough to sue, and courts and juries tend to sympathize.

Generally, law holds churches responsible for only those injuries that result from their negligence. Typically, lawsuits against churches are based on either negligent hiring or negligent supervision.

Negligent hiring. — When a volunteer or a paid worker is abusive, the church may be held responsible if it has placed that person without reasonable attempt to uncover and deal with any previous abuse. Two examples that would apply in many countries:

1. If a conference or mission moves a pastor to another church, knowing that the pastor has been guilty of moral misconduct in the previous church, and if the new church has not been notified and the pastor given counseling help, the conference may be held accountable by law for future misconduct.

2. If a youth leader has been guilty of child abuse in the past and the present church did nothing to learn of this, the local church and conference may be held accountable by law for future misconduct.

Negligent supervision. — Negligent supervision means that a church did not exercise sufficient care in supervising a worker. If such is proved, the local church and conference may be legally accountable for immoral acts.

CHAPTER 10

Professional Growth

Why Grow?

When is a child grown? When he/she reaches five feet in height? six? It all depends on what size God designed the child to be. When is a minister fully grown? When you are assigned a large church? When you're given a desk at the conference/mission office? The most noble reason for professional growth is not for position or importance. It is not to become the size of anybody else. It is to become all God designed you to be.

Where to Grow

Evaluation is essential. — Evaluation is how you learn where you need to grow. Practice does not necessarily make perfect. It may only make permanent. If you do anything wrong often enough, it becomes the only way that feels right. Pastoral skills are best learned by practice, followed by evaluation, followed by a plan for improving.

Evaluation is frightening. — Overcome your fear of your own limitations. Refusing evaluation is hiding not only from your weaknesses, but from your strengths. Evaluation encourages you by pointing out your two-talent and five-talent areas so you can build your ministry around what you do best. But it also encourages you to see your one-talent areas from which you may have been hiding. It helps you lay plans to do your best with what you do have.

Evaluation is available. — You will find helpful evaluation tools in *Evaluation Instruments for Pastors, Churches, and Church Administrators.* Prepared by the General Conference Ministerial Association, the handbook is available through the GC Ministerial Supply Center or through your division or union ministerial association.

How to Grow

Perpetual student. — To a large degree, ministers function as teachers. Like teachers, they must keep learning all their lives. Ministerial training should assist the student to become a self-learner. It should create a lifelong thirst for study and growth.

The 1986 Annual Council voted the following: "To urge the controlling bodies of Seventh-day Adventist organizations to make it possible for Seventh-day Adventist ministers to take at least 20 clock hours of continuing education for ministry each year, or an average of 20 clock hours for each year of licensure. (For example, if the minister's license/credential is voted for three years, he should, during that time, accumulate 60 clock hours of credit.) Courses taken by a minister for academic credit in connection with a formal education program approved by the employing organization may be accepted in lieu of continuing education units. If at the time a minister's license/credential is renewed, the annual average of his CEU is less than the standard 20 clock hours indicated, a representative from the employing organization [should] personally counsel with and encourage him to become involved in the Continuing Education Program for Ministry."

Continuing education may come in the form of an approved degree program, or intensives offered by Seventh-day Adventist or, occasionally, non-Seventh-day Adventist educational institutions. Such intensives may be held on campus or off. Properly planned workers' meetings may include continuing education. The GC Ministerial Association has prepared video courses for this purpose. Self-study courses, including textbook, study guide, and sometimes audio or video tapes are available through the General Conference Ministerial Supply Center or your union or division ministerial association.

Be an avid reader. Use the local library, borrow from a fellow pastor, frequent bookstores, including those offering secondhand books. Set yourself a weekly reading goal. Include some secular reading in that goal. Ministers whose messages are accused of irrelevance have usually not been reading about and becoming sensitive to the society to which they bring God's Word.

Perpetual spiritual renewal. — To the minister, professional growth is always toward God. We must overcome the temptation of thinking that, because we are doing spiritual things, we must be spiritual. Paul warned, "Lest, when I have preached to others, I myself should become disqualified" (1 Cor. 9:27). His commitment should become our own: "For I determined not to know anything among you except Jesus Christ and Him crucified" (1 Cor. 2:2).

In speaking of John the Baptist, Scripture declares, "There was a

PROFESSIONAL GROWTH

man sent from God, whose name was John" (John 1:6). Those sent from God are invariably the most professionally prepared to lead others to God.

In ministry, perhaps more than in any other profession, "the secret of success is the union of divine power with human effort. Those who achieve the greatest results are those who rely most implicitly upon the Almighty Arm. . . . The men of prayer are the men of power" (*Patriarchs and Prophets*, p. 509).

CHAPTER 11

Christian Example

"In all things *showing yourself to be a pattern of good works*; in doctrine showing integrity, reverence, incorruptibility, sound speech that cannot be condemned, that one who is an opponent may be ashamed, having nothing evil to say of you" (Titus 2:38).

Be What You Teach

What Jesus taught He was. That's what made His teaching so effective. As preachers, we must be what we ask others to be, believe what we expect them to believe, and love Christ the way we want them to love.

The ministry, perhaps more than any other profession, presumes that your vocation and your personal life are inseparable. In choosing a surgeon or a mechanic, you probably want competence more than you want character. Not so with ministers. What we are as persons takes precedence over what we do as pastors.

We Christian ministers live in a community not only for the purpose of preaching Christ, but to show, at least to a small extent, what Christ was like. We are Christianity with skin on. We are not perfect people, but we ought, like Christ, to be persons of principle.

God needs pastors who are both good and able. But in the long run a congregation will likely be helped more by the good than by the able.

Be Aware of Your Humanity

Ministers must overcome their pride. — Beware of the assumption that your holy calling makes you holy. Your congregation tends to assume you are the local "holy person." Tragically, this can cause you to assume it too. While our goal is to be Christlike, the more like Christ we become, the less aware we will be of it. Anything else is pride masquerading as piety.

Ministers must accept their humanity. — Christ had to become human before He could become our "minister." "Therefore, in all things He had to be made like His brethren, that He might be a merciful and faithful High Priest. . . . For in that He Himself has suffered, being tempted, He is able to aid those who are tempted" (Heb. 2:17, 18).

Jesus became "like His brethren" so He could mercifully and faithfully serve them. His pastors should accept their humanity so they can more effectively serve their people. Jesus suffered, "being tempted." This enables Him to aid those who are tempted. His pastors should face and, through Christ, conquer their own temptations to qualify them to help their people face and conquer theirs.

Ministers must know their limitations. — According to professionals involved in counseling ministers, the most common problems ministers face are low self-esteem, self-doubt, and feelings of inferiority. This may be because of people's overidealistic view of ministers and their ministry. Congregations expect them to be more than they are. Ministers try to live up to those expectations by pretending to be more than they are. This pretension is inevitably discouraging. It is hypocritical. It devastates self-esteem.

Know your spiritual limitations. If you are to lead your people to heaven, you must be on the road there, but you don't have to pretend you have already arrived! You are, after all, human, not God. It's all right to admit it.

Know your physical limitations. Don't be misled by people who think you're 10 feet tall and able to walk on water. You cannot work a 20-hour day and keep sweet. You cannot do everything everybody wants done. Besides, you're not supposed to.

Ministers must share their ministry. — You don't need to be in control of everything in your church. Omnipotence is a characteristic God has not given you. The purpose of the pastor-teacher gift is to equip "the saints for the work of ministry" (Eph. 4:12). Admit your humanity by sharing your ministry with your members. You are colleagues in ministry. Only your roles are different. Minister with them, not just to them.

Be Willing to Admit Your Mistakes

With God, the only "unpardonable sin" is the unconfessed sin. With congregations, the most unpardonable ministerial mistake is probably the one everybody knows about, but you can't admit. God freely forgives sins we confess. Congregations usually forgive mistakes we admit.

Be a Christian example to your flock, but remember that a first step in Christianity is admitting you were wrong.

SECTION TWO

The Minister and the World Church

12. Relationship With Conference
13. Church Policies
14. Credentials
15. Ordination
16. Ordination Service
17. Organizing New Churches
18. Uniting Churches
19. Disbanding Churches

CHAPTER 12

Relationship With Conference

Organization Is Needed

Organization is needed for theological reasons. — God has always organized. Wherever God is, there is organization. Heaven is organized. "Order is the law of heaven, and it should be the law of God's people on the earth" (*Testimonies to Ministers*, p. 26). Our universe is organized. Whether you focus a microscope on a single cell or a telescope on the stars, you see precise, predictable organization. "System and order are manifest in all the works of God throughout the universe" (*Ibid*).

God has always organized His church. He gave ancient Israel an impressive system of organization. Jesus founded a literal church organization and ordained its leaders. The Holy Spirit led the New Testament church in choosing leaders and organizing itself.

The church is like Noah's ark. The ark was no doubt an imperfect boat, for it was made by people, but it did the job of helping God save His people, because it was made after God's plan. The church is an imperfect organization, for it is made up of people, but it will do the job of helping God save His people, because it is a part of God's plan.

To be Christian is to love His church, for Christ "loved the church and gave Himself for it" (Eph. 5:25). "I testify to my brethren and sisters that the church of Christ, enfeebled and defective as it may be, is the only object on earth on which He bestows His supreme regard" (*Testimonies to Ministers*, p. 15).

Organization is needed for practical reasons. — A nation, a business, or even the human body would fail without organization. A church with the task of taking the three angels' messages to the world would surely fail without organization. Any group going anywhere has to get organized. And so, despite their fears of organized religion, early Adventists organized this church. Ellen White summarizes, "As our numbers increased, it was evident that without some form of

---

For details on church organization and the minister's relationship to it, see *Church Manual*, chapters 2-4, 9, and 16.

organization there would be great confusion, and the work would not be carried forward successfully. To provide for the support of the ministry, for carrying the work in new fields, for protecting both the churches and the ministry from unworthy members, for holding church property, for the publication of the truth through the press, and for many other objects, organization was indispensable" (*Ibid.*).

Pastors Help Conferences

The position of the conference/mission president is similar to that of Paul, who writes of his "deep concern for all the churches" (2 Cor. 11:28). The conference president is overseer of all the churches, under guidance from higher church organizations, but is largely dependent on pastors in carrying out the plans and policies of the conference. Nothing in the conference moves much without pastoral participation.

The responsibility of pastors and elders is in the local congregation, where they are to "take care of the church of God" (1 Tim. 3:5). They shepherd the flock. "Therefore take heed to yourselves and to all the flock, among which the Holy Spirit has made you overseers, to shepherd the church of God which He purchased with His own blood" (Acts 20:28).

Conferences depend almost totally on pastors for church growth and nurture. Conference money comes from churches. The income of the conference depends on the ministry of its pastors.

Conferences Help Pastors

Administrators help. — Through actions of the conference executive committee, administrators provide significant financial security to their ministers. Unlike many clergy, Adventist pastors don't have to raise their own wages. Salaries may not always seem generous, but they are almost always dependable.

Conference/mission administrators help pastors by providing significant job security. No quarrelsome faction in your church can fire you. If you run into difficulty, hopefully conference leaders will counsel and help you through. If a move seems appropriate, they almost always arrange a new appointment.

Departments help. — Pastors must be generalists. Departmental directors should be specialists, who make their expertise available to pastors and work with them in training their members. They do not have direct authority over the pastors. They are resource providers and advisers, not bosses.

Departments ought to make pastors aware of programs and materials available. With this information in mind, pastors should lead their churches in developing their own objectives and plans, and then ask departments for advice and assistance.

The conference/mission ministerial association should be of special interest to ministers and provide significant services for them, such as; a personal visit, a listening ear, an internship that meets your educational needs, training in pastoral evangelism, a *Ministry* magazine subscription that keeps you abreast of ministerial issues, soul-winning tools to aid you in your ministry, continuing education opportunities, assistance in training your elders, and a training and support system for your spouse.

Cooperation the Key

Organization limits freedom. — You are free to make your own individual choice in accepting church employment. However, when you do become an employee and leader in the church, you accept a responsibility to the church that may curtail your personal freedoms. You obligate yourself to:

1. *Trust your leaders.* They may have weaknesses, but not any more than you have. They will make mistakes, and so do you. Talk out differences. There's little pleasure and less Christianity in working together without trusting each other. "Let us cherish a spirit of confidence in the wisdom of our brethren" (*Testimonies to Ministers*, p. 500).

2. *Support your leaders.* Even when you differ, give your support in every way not contrary to your own conscience.

3. *Consult your leaders.* Counsel with your conference/mission leadership before you enter into any activity that makes inroads upon time normally meant for your regular work. Get their advice before you buy or build a home, or enroll in a study program. Consultation assures future safety.

4. *Hold your leaders accountable.* Ours is a representative form of church government. At election time the democratic process gives you both a right and an obligation to hold leaders accountable.

Think freely, but speak loyally. — Pastors have freedom to study for themselves in order to "prove all things." The church never claims to have found all the truth. Study. Discuss with your peers. Consult other theologians within the church. Nevertheless, a line must be drawn between freedom and responsibility. You do not have the right to discuss your personal studies in a way that will undermine the faith of any member.

One right surrendered while in the employ of a denomination is the freedom to preach, print, or propagate views that contradict the official or accepted position of the church. Although the Holy Spirit does lead individuals, He also instructs the whole people of God so that new understandings result in harmony among the believers. Seek and accept counsel. "Never should a laborer regard as a virtue the persistent maintenance of his position of independence, contrary to the decision of the general body" (*Testimonies*, vol. 9, p. 260).

While God made us all free and independent, it is as that freedom is cooperatively given to the church that God's work goes with power. The gift of our individual wills, for the good of the whole, is basic to organization. It is of God. If you have "new light" that other responsible leaders cannot affirm, then you should seriously question and eventually reject your independent stance. God will not reveal truth to you only.

CHAPTER 13

Church Policies

The *General Conference Working Policy* and your division's and union's adaptation of it provide specific guidelines for your conference/mission. Conference/mission administrators must have these two policy books and accept a special responsibility to apply their policies in the local field. Policy is updated at the General Conference by Annual Council, and the division by the year-end meeting.

The *Church Manual* provides specific guidelines for local churches. Pastors must accept responsibility to apply its policies in their churches. They are no more free to ignore it than administrators are free to ignore the policies that apply most directly to conferences/missions.

The *Church Manual* is the most significant policy book of the denomination. It was approved by General Conference session and can be updated only at succeeding General Conference sessions, which occur only every five years.

The *Minister's Handbook* provides additional pastoral guidelines. It is prepared by the General Conference Ministerial Association in consultation with pastors and other leaders from the world field. It is updated as needed. It is imperative that every pastor have these two volumes.

Church Manual

Authority. — Since the *Church Manual* is endorsed by the world church in session, it carries all the authority of the church. "When, in a General Conference, the judgment of the brethren assembled from all parts of the field is exercised, private independence and private judgment must not be stubbornly maintained, but surrendered." (*Testimonies*, vol. 9, p. 260).

Close adherence to the *Church Manual* is not only your responsibility as pastor, but it is also to your advantage. If you support it even where you might wish to see it changed, you can rely on its authority to support you when others press for unacceptable change. On the other hand, if you belittle these policies of the world church, your members will learn to belittle policies you establish in the local church.

Flexibility. — The *Church Manual* does, on the other hand, have flexibility built into it. It permits adaptation to varying cultures and is sensitive to social changes. You should feel free to experiment with church changes that do not go contrary to either the letter or intent of manual policies.

Ideally changes should come up from the local church rather than down from administrative entities. Thus, when you feel a change should be made in the *Church Manual*, you have both the right and the responsibility to suggest such changes by passing them to the General Conference through your local conference/mission.

Membership Transfers

Consult your *Church Manual* for details of membership transfers. We will consider here only what impacts the pastor.

Significance of church membership. — Church membership is a divinely initiated privilege. Guarding the local church's membership list as well as the persons it represents is a sacred responsibility. Both the local and the world church need to evaluate themselves continually, and this is done largely on the basis of local church records. Unless pastor and church clerk keep local records updated and accurate, the world church cannot accurately assess either its successes or its failures. Also, it is a discourtesy to another church that is either recommending or receiving a member, if your church doesn't act promptly on letters of membership transfer.

Transferring by letter. — The *Church Manual* recommends that if a member moves and is absent from the local congregation for more than six months, the membership should be transferred. For the sake of the member, it is good to encourage this. However, people should not feel pushed. A letter of transfer should never be initiated against the member's wishes or knowledge.

The church board must not overstep its authority in dealing with membership status. The board can advise, but only the church body can act.

It is both improper and unwise to elect a person to church office before the membership transfer is completed. What if the former church cannot recommend membership in good and regular standing? It's better to be cautious than to be embarrassed.

Transferring disciplined members. — In no case should a church vote a letter of transfer to a member who is under discipline. This would be an extreme discourtesy to the church receiving the new member.

Be cautious about accepting by profession of faith, or even by baptism, persons formerly members of another congregation. The safe and courteous thing to do is to contact a pastor or elder from the former church and learn why the membership was dropped.

CHAPTER 14

Credentials

Purpose

"The churches in their collective capacity through the conferences confer upon certain men the authority to represent and speak for the church as ministers and gospel workers. This authority is represented by the granting of credentials, which are written commissions, properly dated and signed by the officers of the conference" (*Church Manual*, chapter 9).

Unions carry special responsibility to oversee issuing of credentials. "The union and local conferences share the responsibility for safeguarding the integrity of the ministry and are required by denominational action and practice to assure that credentials issued within their respective territories shall indeed certify that the holders are in good and unquestioned standing, properly subject to invitation to any other field of service" (GC *Policy* L 60 05).

Credentials protect congregations from those who might mislead the church. "In order that enemies of the work may not gain access to our pulpits, it is most strongly urged that no one be allowed to speak to any congregation unless he presents valid and up-to-date denominational credentials. It is recognized, however, that there are times when it is proper for our congregations to be addressed by government officials or by civic leaders; but all unauthorized persons should be excluded from the pulpit" (*Church Manual*, chapter 9). This, of course, is not meant to prohibit established members of the congregation from speaking.

Disciplined ministers. — Ministers may be disciplined because of a moral fall, apostasy (falling away to the world, giving continuing support to an activity subversive to the denomination, persistently refusing to recognize church authority), or continued and unrepentant dissidence regarding the fundamental beliefs of the Adventist Church (see GC *Policy* L 60 15).

Discipline may affect ministers in four ways: (1) withdrawal of credential/license in case of a moral fall or apostasy, or dissidence; (2)

annulment of ordination in case of a moral fall or apostasy; (3) their church membership; and (4) loss of employment in gospel ministry, the teaching ministry, or denominational leadership (see GC *Policy* L 60 20).

Cutting ministers off from the ministry should, however, be done very carefully and prayerfully. When you lose a limb, it is painful and you miss it terribly. Losing a fellow minister should be just as painful. Provision has now been made for reaching out to disciplined ministers. "Where practical the organization involved shall provide a professional program of counseling and career guidance for the minister and family to assist them in transition" (GC *Policy* L 60 22).

Expired credentials. — "Credentials are granted for the duration of the conference term, either annually, triennially, or quinquennially. The credentials are renewed by a vote of the conference in session. If for any reason it is deemed inadvisable to renew credentials to any minister, he ceases to function as a worker in the conference. The possession of out-of-date or expired credentials does not authorize him to function in any of the offices of a minister. In such a case he has no more authority or standing than any other lay member in the church" (*Church Manual*, chapter 9).

To Whom Issued

Employees. — "Credentials/licenses shall be issued only to full-time denominational employees and to those under the supervision of conferences/missions or denominationally owned institutions. They shall expire when denominational employment is terminated. In special cases a credential/license may be issued to a nondenominationally-employed individual while serving the church under the supervision of a denominational organization" (GC *Policy* D 10 70). Credentials may also be granted to chaplains and to ministers attending school (see GC *Policy* D 10 71-73).

"Any organization with authority to issue credentials and licenses has the power to withdraw the papers it has granted" (GC *Policy* D 10 75).

Retirees. — "Honorary credentials, corresponding to the credentials they held while in active service, may be granted to retirement beneficiaries who are members of the Seventh-day Adventist Church" (GC *Policy* D 05 35). In most cases, "employees receiving benefits from the Retirement Plan and retired military chaplains receiving military retirement pay, if entitled to credentials or other papers, are to receive the same from the union conference in which they reside" (GC *Policy* D 10 60).

Retired ministers usually hold their membership in a church near their place of residence. Their relationship to the church is the same as that of any other church member, except that they may still be called upon to baptize, perform weddings, ordain local leaders, etc., especially when the pastor is not authorized to do so. They may be elected to any office in the local church.

Types

Ministerial credential. — The ministerial credential is granted only to ordained ministers.

Ministerial license. — The ministerial license is given to nonordained pastors, evangelists, and Bible teachers who are on the path toward ordination.

"The responsibility and authority of the licensed minister may in certain circumstances be extended to include the performance of specific functions of the ordained minister in the churches to which he is assigned. The authority for extending this responsibility belongs to the division committee which shall clearly outline for its territory the ministerial functions which may be delegated to licensed ministers" (GC Policy L 25 05).

For example, the North American Division has the following provision: "A licensed minister is authorized by the conference to perform substantially all the functions of the ordained minister for the members in the churches or companies to which he is assigned and elected as a church elder, and for the communities he serves" (NAD Policy L 20 10). Licensed ministers, however, are excluded from presiding over organizing churches, uniting churches, and ordaining local elders and deacons (see NAD Policy L 20 10).

"The conference/mission executive committee shall authorize, in harmony with the division policy, which functions of the ordained minister the licensed minister may perform" (GC Policy L 25 15).

Minimum requirements to be met by licensed ministers before being given extended ministerial functions include: completion of the ministerial training program, holding a current ministerial license, appointment to a ministerial or pastoral responsibility, election as a local elder in each church to which they are assigned, and ordination as a local elder (see GC Policy L 25 10).

Commissioned minister credential. — The GC Working Policy does not specifically designate a commissioned minister credential. However, divisions are free to bestow such a credential if they choose. The North American Division, for example, does grant the commissioned minister license and credential as follows: "To associates in pastoral care; Bible instructors; General Conference, division, union, and local conference treasurers and departmental directors including associate and assistant directors; institutional chaplains; presidents and vice presidents of major institutions; auditors (General Conference director, associates, area and district directors); and field directors of the Christian Record Services" (*NAD Policy* D 05 10).

When the commissioned minister credential is granted, an appropriate commissioning service may be conducted.

Commissioned minister license. — This license is given to employees in the above commissioned minister categories who have fewer than five years' experience. It is not the normal practice to ordain an individual holding this license (see *NAD Policy* D 05 10). Ordinarily an associate in pastoral care is granted a commissioned minister credential after four years of denominational service (see *NAD Policy* L 21 25).

Bible worker. — The Bible instructor is of such significance in the organization of the denomination that a job description is included in chapter 9 of the *Church Manual*. Although this *Minister's Manual* was not specifically written for Bible workers, much of it applies to them.

Bible instructors normally carry a missionary license for up to five years, then receive a missionary credential. Where the commissioned minister license and credential are awarded, Bible workers should be included in that category.

Internship

Interns receive a "license" rather than a "credential," not only because they are new in the ministry, but also to designate that their ministerial training is not complete until after their internship. Granting a ministerial license is not a commitment on the part of a conference that ordination is ultimately assured. It merely provides the opportunity for licentiates to prove their calling.

Purposes. — Ministerial internship "designates a period of service spent in practical ministerial training, to be entered upon after the completion of the prescribed ministerial training course, this training period to be served under supervision in a local conference/mission, at a limited wage, for the purpose of proving the divine call to the ministry" (*GC Policy* L 10 10).

Privileges. — While internship limits the beginning minister in some ways, it does provide significant privileges. Here are two:

1. Experience in all phases of ministry: "Local conferences/missions shall place ministerial interns in the conference/mission where there is prospect for well-rounded development in all the phases of the ministry—evangelistic, pastoral, teaching (i.e., personal and group instruction), and various departmental activities" (GC Policy L 15 40).

2. Supervision: "When a conference gives a young man a ministerial license it should be recognized as a pledge on the part of the conference leadership to foster that employee's growth" (GC Policy L 35 35).

A special financial plan makes it possible for the conference to fulfill this pledge: "The plan is designed to assist the local conferences/missions in such ministerial training by a sharing of the salary and expenses by the division, union, and local conference/mission as provided by division committee action" (GC Policy L 15 25). This training period is to be served under supervision and "conferences/missions shall assume obligation for direct supervision in training ministerial interns" (GC Policy L 15 40).

Conferences/missions should not use the internship subsidy to fill pastoral openings with interns. While such a temptation is understandable, the practice is not only contrary to church policy but crippling to the development of a professional ministerial force. Conference/mission administrators should ensure that interns get adequate, supervised, and varied experience under trained experienced ministers. The General Conference Ministerial Association has developed a *Manual for Ministerial Interns and Intern Supervisors*. The manual aims first to train intern supervisors, then to assist them in training interns.

Every intern should spend significant time with at least one and preferably several supervisors during internship. Supervisors should be considered qualified to supervise only after taking special training such as the intern manual provides.

CHAPTER 15

Ordination

"The licensed minister is ordinarily ordained to the gospel ministry after he has satisfactorily fulfilled a period of pastoral/evangelistic service during which time he has given evidence of his call to the ministry. The spiritual rite of ordination constitutes the official recognition by the Seventh-day Adventist Church of his divine call to the ministry as a life commitment, and is his endorsement to serve as a minister of the gospel in any part of the world" (GC *Policy* L 25 30).

The length of service prior to ordination cannot be prescribed, because there are too many variables. Ordinarily, however, a licensed minister is ordained after about four years of field experience.

Ordination: a Statement*

"The Christian church is that body of people who have been reconciled to God and their fellow beings by Jesus Christ (Eph. 2:16; Rom. 12:5). United to God by baptism (Matt. 28:19), Christians are incorporated into His work of redemption as 'a royal priesthood' to 'declare the wonderful deeds of him who called [them] out of darkness into his marvelous light' (1 Peter 2:9) [citations are from the Revised Standard Version]. This means, among other things, that Christians are to be ministers of reconciliation, forwarding God's mission in the world (2 Cor. 5:18, 20). Ministry, therefore, is the function of every Christian as well as the corporate church and is carried on by means of the gifts that the Holy Spirit imparts (Rom. 12:4-8; 1 Cor. 12:4-7; Eph. 4:8-16; 1 Peter 4:10).

"***Ordination for particular service.*** While all Christians render spiritual service, the New Testament portrays an organized church, administered and nurtured by persons who are specially called by God, set apart by the laying on of hands to a particular service. Apart from

---

* This section reproduces the statement on ministerial ordination prepared by the General Conference Ministerial Association and the GC Biblical Research Institute. The statement received broad input from the world field and went through numerous revisions. It purposely omits the gender issue in ministerial ordination, seeking rather to lay down basic principles by which all ministerial ordination issues can be measured.

the appointment and ordination of the twelve apostles for their unique, unrepeatable role (Mark 3:13, 14; *The Desire of Ages*, p. 296), the Scriptures distinguish three categories of ordained officers: (1) the gospel minister, whose role may be seen as preaching/teaching, administering the ordinances, and pastoral care of souls and churches (1 Tim. 4:14; 2 Tim. 4:1-5); (2) the elder (sometimes in Scripture called *bishop*), who exercises oversight of a local congregation, performing necessary pastoral functions as well (Acts 14:23; 20:17; Titus 1:5, 9; 1 Tim. 3:2, 5); and (3) the deacon, to whose care the poor and the benevolent work of the congregation are entrusted (Phil. 1:1; Acts 6:1-6; 1 Tim. 3:8-13).

"Ordained elders and deacons minister to the well-being of local congregations, attending to their outreach. But, possibly reflecting the unique role of the apostles, greater responsibility rests upon ordained gospel ministers. Supported by the elders and deacons, they, in any locale, serve the church in word and ordinance, continuously recalling it to its scriptural foundations (2 Tim. 4:1-5).

"The Gospel ministry: a special call. While elders and deacons are appointed on the basis of spiritual experience and ability (Titus 1:5; Acts 6:3), the gospel ministry, Seventh-day Adventists believe, is a special calling from God. Regardless of the means by which the Lord initiates it, His call becomes an all-absorbing passion, a relentless drive that leads its possessor to exclaim: 'Necessity is laid upon me. Woe to me if I do not preach the gospel!' (1 Cor. 9:16). The conviction becomes a 'fire in the bones' that will not be denied expression (Jer. 20:9). Historically, Seventh-day Adventists have insisted on an ordination procedure for those thus called.

"Significance of ordination. Just as prophets, priests, and kings were anointed by oil for special roles, so the rite of ordination by the laying on of hands recognizes that God calls some, who are already His, for special purposes (cf. Mark 3:13, 14). Ordination to the gospel ministry acknowledges special needs in the church body: (1) the need for leadership that provides to the membership both example and challenge to move forward in God's program (1 Cor. 11:1; 1 Tim. 4:12); (2) the need for sentinels 'on the walls of Zion,' burdened with the responsibility to inform and alert the people of God (Eze. 3:17-19; 2 Cor. 11:2, 3); (3) the need for the Word and the authoritative preaching of the will of God to church members and in evangelistic outreach to the unsaved that rises from serious study of the Scriptures (Acts 6:2-4; 2 Tim. 4:2-4).

"Ordination, an act of commission, acknowledges God's call, sets the individual apart, and appoints that person to serve the church in a special capacity. Ordination endorses the individuals thus set apart as authorized representatives of the church. By this act, the church delegates its authority to its ministers to proclaim the gospel publicly, to administer its ordinances, to organize new congregations, and, within the parameters established by God's word, to give direction to the believers (Matt. 16:19; Heb. 13:17). In short, ordination invests ministers with full ecclesiastical authority to act in behalf of the church anywhere in the world field where they may be employed by the church (*The Acts of the Apostles*, p. 161). Seventh-day Adventists do not believe that ordination is sacramental in the sense of conferring some indelible character or special powers or the ability to formulate right doctrine. It adds 'no new grace or virtual qualification' (*Ibid.*, p. 162).

"The biblical background of the rite indicates that it 'was an acknowledged form of designation to an appointed office and a recognition of one's authority in that office' (*Ibid.*). By this means the church sets its seal upon the work of God performed through its ministers and their lay associates. In ordination, the church publicly invokes God's blessing upon the persons He has chosen and devoted to this special work of ministry.

"***Qualifications for ordination.*** The Lord qualifies those whom He calls to special service (Ex. 31:1-5; 1 Tim. 4:14; 2 Tim. 1:6). By ordination the church recognizes the work of Christ—the Head of the Church—in the making of a minister. Since ministers carry out their ministry within an earthly organization, that organization must determine whether the individual's inner conviction is only a general call to serve Christ as all members should, or is, indeed, a genuine call to the gospel ministry. God's call and His equipping constitute the first step to the ministry; the recognition and confirmation of that call by those authorized to evaluate its validity comprise the second (cf. 1 Tim. 5:22).

"Candidates for the gospel ministry should evince:

"1. *Spiritual experience.* They must have a deep, experiential knowledge of and devotion to the person of the Lord Jesus Christ that reveals itself in an exemplary lifestyle and reputation, in sound judgment, in representative home life, and in positive character traits (1 Tim. 3:1-7; Titus 1:6-11).

"2. *Knowledge of the Scriptures.* Christian pastors are primarily called to the ministry of the Word. Therefore ordinands should have a mind furnished with the truth, utterly subject to the Word of God, and prepared to penetrate and make plain its right meaning. They will have given evidence that they have mastered and are able to apply the discipline of theology in their preaching, teaching, and counseling (Titus 1:9; 2 Tim. 2:15, 24-26; 2 Cor. 4:1, 2; cf. *Gospel Workers*, p. 105).

"3. *Competence for the tasks of ministry.* Ordinands must manifest that God has equipped them with the gifts necessary to the ministry— the gifts of intellect and utterance that enable them to proclaim, defend, and teach the faith (Eph. 4:12; 1 Tim. 3:1; Titus 1:9; 2 Tim. 2:2) and the gift of leadership that enables them to guide, motivate, and train the congregations entrusted to their care (1 Peter 5:1-4).

"4. *A fruitful ministry.* It is unthinkable that Christ would call and equip His servants without blessing their efforts. Ordinands will reveal their call to the ministry both by soul-winning success and by their ability to nurture those under their care (1 Cor. 9:2).

"Responsibility of ordination. Though ordination conveys no special powers upon the recipient, it does impose solemn responsibilities and for that reason should not be accepted lightly. Ordained ministers are not their own, but God's. Their time, talents, and lives are dedicated to Him without reservation, for they are His mouthpiece and representatives of His church. Ministers proclaim the word of the Lord to judgment-bound people whose eternal destiny is in the balances. The care and salvation of souls is a weighty commission entrusted to them both 'in season and out of season' (2 Tim. 4:2). It is God's intention that there be no release from this vocation while life and strength last—until the Lord, 'the righteous judge,' shall award 'the crown of righteousness' to all His faithful servants on 'that Day' of His appearing (verse 8)."

Authorizing Ordination

Jesus chose certain ones for ordination. "And He went up on the mountain and called to Him those He Himself wanted. And they came to Him. Then He appointed twelve, that they might *be with Him* and that He might send them out *to preach*" (Mark 3:13, 14). Thus, the example of Jesus authorizes His church to ordain those experiencing an intimacy with Christ, who are prepared to preach Christ.

Barnabas and Saul labored in the ministry for some time, and the seal of success was on their work as soul-winning evangelists. Then the Spirit authorized their ordination. "As they ministered to the Lord and fasted, the Holy Spirit said, 'Now separate to Me Barnabas and Saul for the work to which I have called them.' Then, having fasted and prayed, and laid hands on them, they sent them away" (Acts 13:2, 3).

Ellen White comments: "God had abundantly blessed the labors of Paul and Barnabas during the year they remained with the believers in Antioch. But neither of them had as yet been formally ordained to the gospel ministry. . . . Before being sent forth as missionaries to the heathen world, these apostles were solemnly dedicated to God by fasting and prayer and the laying on of hands. Thus they were authorized by the church, not only to teach the truth, but to perform the rite of baptism and to organize churches, being invested with full ecclesiastical authority. . . . Both Paul and Barnabas had already received their commission from God Himself, and the ceremony of the laying on of hands added no new grace or virtual qualification" (*The Acts of the Apostles*, pp. 160-162). Thus, the church today should authorize the ordination of only those whom God has already both *chosen* and *proven*.

Ordination not a reward. — "Ordination must never become simply a reward for faithful service or be considered an opportunity to add title and prestige to an employee. Neither is it an honor to be sought by the individual or his family or friends on his behalf " (GC *Policy* L 35 50).

Ordaining nonpastors. — "Workers who are ordained to the gospel ministry are set apart to serve the world church, *primarily as pastors and preachers of the Word*, and are subject to the direction of the church in regard to the type of ministry and their place of service. It should therefore be understood by those accepting ordination and who are engaged in specialized ministries such as administration, teaching, and departmental leadership, that they *may be reassigned by the church to pastoral, preaching and evangelistic duties*" (GC *Policy* L 40).

Calls to serve the church in other than pastoral ministry may be just as divine in origin, but should be recognized in some way other than ordination to the gospel ministry.

Who authorizes ordination. — "Ordination to the ministry is the setting apart of the employee to a sacred calling, not for one local field alone but for the world church and therefore needs to be done with wide counsel" (GC *Policy* L 45 05). The proper procedure is as follows:

1. *Preliminary examination by the local conference/mission administration.*
2. *Recommendation by the conference/mission committee.*
3. *Approval by the union.*
4. *Final examination.*

"The time and place for the ordination ceremony, including the examination of the candidate, with his wife, shall be arranged by the approving organization in counsel with the union" (GC *Policy* L 45 10). This final examination is usually given by a group including guest ministers from outside the local conference and union, thus emphasizing that ordination is by and for the world church.

"The examination of candidates for ordination is conducted by ordained ministers. Ordained representatives of conferences/unions/divisions/General Conference, who are present, may be invited to assist in the examination. Where it is deemed advisable by the conference/mission executive committee, one or more laypersons may be selected to participate" (GC *Policy* L 50).

In-depth examination is essential. "Before any ordination is carried out, there shall be careful, unhurried, and prayerful examination of the candidates as to their fitness for the work of the ministry. The results of their labor as licentiates should be reviewed, and the examination should cover the great fundamental facts of the gospel" (GC *Policy* L 50). "There has been too little done in examining ministers; and for this very reason churches have had the labors of unconverted, inefficient men, who have lulled the members to sleep, instead of awakening them to greater zeal and earnestness in the cause of God" (*Gospel Workers*, p. 437).

The best place for an in-depth examination of ordinands is under step 1 above, preliminary examination by the local administration. This is where time is most adequate and information is most available. The ministerial secretary should have gathered detailed information about the ordinand's life and ministry. Candidates can be examined individually by conference/mission leaders, including the ministerial secretary.

Examination by visiting ministers from higher organizations just before the ordination takes place comes very late in the ordination process. Ordinands have already been informed of their ordination. Plans have been laid. Family and friends have been invited. It's almost too late to deny ordination. This is not so much a time for making ordination decisions as it is for giving affirmation, counsel, and encouragement.

Marriage before ordination is recommended but not required. If a candidate for ordination is married, homelife and the commitment of the spouse should be weighed. Some research indicates that more ministers leave the ministry because of unhappy spouses than for any other reason.

Neither hasten nor delay ordination. "Undue haste has sometimes been apparent in recommending candidates for ordination. On the other hand, there has also been undue delay, extending as long as 20 years and more. Both these attitudes are wrong. Although no employee should be hurried into ordination, it is just as important that when a man is ready to be thus set apart, the service should not be unduly delayed" (GC *Policy* L 35 25).

Communicating with possible ordinands. — Ministerial ordination is not a thing to be sought after. On the other hand, the church plainly teaches that it is the rite by which the church expresses approval of the licentiate's ministry. Licensed ministers and their families should not be blamed for being deeply concerned about whether or not their work is approved. Conference/mission leaders ought to communicate with them openly. Remove the mystery surrounding ordination. It is a solemn step, not a secret one.

Reordaining clergy converts. — "When a minister from another denomination accepts the Adventist message and desires to become an Adventist minister, he shall, before he becomes involved in a formal study program, be expected to give evidence of his stability in the message and of his aptitude as a candidate for the Adventist ministry by being active in a local church" (GC *Policy* L 30).

After six months to a year working under the local pastor, such ministers may be sent to an Adventist college or seminary for at least one year. Then they could be considered ready to accept a call to the Adventist ministry.

"Ordained or unordained ministers from other denominations who accept the Advent message and continue in the ministry may be issued ministerial licenses after they have completed their period of study and orientation and have entered upon regular employment in any conference, mission, or institution. Ordained ministers received thus into denominational work shall be ordained to the ministry of the Seventh-day Adventist Church prior to issuing ministerial credentials to them" (*Ibid.* L 30).

Examination for Ordination

Self-examination. — The most thorough preordination examination of ordinands should not come from any committee or group, but from themselves. Ellen White wrote to a minister, "You do not closely search your own heart. You have studied many works to make your discourses thorough, able, and pleasing; but you have neglected the greatest and most necessary study, *the study of yourself*" (*Testimonies*, vol. 1, p. 433; italics supplied).

Formal examination. — Below are three sources listing areas that might be included in an ordination examination. Questioners should feel free to choose any one of the three as the basis for their questions.

1. GC *Policy* L 50. Thirteen areas are suggested:
   a. A call to the ministry as a lifework.
   b. Belief in and knowledge of the Scriptures.
   c. Acquaintance with and full acceptance of the vital truths we believe we are called to proclaim to the world.
   d. Experience in various kinds of ministerial responsibility.
   e. Entire consecration of body, soul, and spirit.
   f. Spiritual stability.
   g. Social maturity.
   h. Aptness as a teacher of truth.
   i. Ability to lead souls from sin into holiness.

j. Fruitage in souls won to Christ.
k. A cooperative attitude and confidence in the organization and functioning of the church.
l. A life of consistent exemplary Christian conduct.
m. An exemplary family.

2. *Intern Manual.* This manual includes 50 ministerial functions, divided into seven categories. The conference/mission is responsible for having given each intern some training in each of the 50. Thus, questions from this list test both the conference and the candidate.

Any examination testing an individual's preparedness to enter either a calling or a profession ought to be based on that profession's job description. These 50 functions cover the areas in which every pastor needs expertise and thus, although they are not written in job description form, do provide the church's most official outline of what a Seventh-day Adventist pastor is expected to be and to do:

a. Personal growth: (1) personal devotions; (2) Adventist doctrine, Adventism as a unique, worldwide movement; (3) attitudes, ministerial call, commitment to ministry; (4) church policies, organizational structure; (5) continuing education; (6) development of a personal support group; (7) filing system; (8) leadership ability; (9) ministerial ethics; (10) personal appearance; (11) personal finance; (12) personal health; (13) team ministry with spouse; (14) time management, family time.
b. Personal relationships: (15) relationships outside the church—home, community, race; (16) relationships within the church—Christ, congregation, conference.
c. Evangelism and church growth: (17) church growth awareness systems; (18) church growth outreach systems; (19) church growth planning and strategy; (20) getting decisions; (21) personal evangelism; (22) public evangelism; (23) small group evangelism; (24) specialized outreaches, prison, etc.
d. Lay training: (25) recruiting and training volunteers, officers, spiritual gifts.
e. Preaching and worship: (26) baptism; (27) child dedication; (28) Communion; (29) funeral; (30) planning and leading worship; (31) prayer meeting; (32) preaching; (33) wedding.
f. Pastoral care and nurture: (34) assimilating new members; (35) church discipline; (36) counseling; (37) former members, inactive members; (38) spiritual formation through communication with members; (39) visitation of members.

g. Organization and administration: (40) Christian education; (41) church building, maintenance; (42) church social life; (43) committees; (44) conference departments; (45) finance; (46) pastoring multi-church district; (47) problem solving, conflict resolution; (48) promotion, campaigns; (49) Sabbath school; (50) youth leadership.

3. *Seventh-day Adventist Minister's Code of Ethics.* This code (see p. 51) provides an excellent basis for examining an ordinand's commitment to ministry. Some suggest that such a statement be signed by ordination candidates.

CHAPTER 16

Ordination Service

Ministers

Audience involvement. — Adventists teach that ordination is the church-at-large setting aside its ministerial leaders. However, in practice, the ordination service tends to involve ministers almost exclusively. Audiences have so little participation that individuals sometimes feel like uninvolved spectators, witnessing an exercise of ministers for ministers.

Fellowship between ministers is important and might be enjoyed in a special reception ordained ministers give for the ordinand and his spouse. Ordination, however, is not something ministers do for each other, but something the whole church does for its ministry. If ordination is principally for service in local churches, the churches that ordinands serve ought to be involved.

Four suggestions for increasing audience involvement:

1. Invite members of all churches the ordinand has served to stand, along with his family, as he is introduced and escorted to the platform.

2. Include some responses in the ceremony for the audience to read.

3. At some point in the service, bring to the platform the elders of the churches the ordinand is currently serving. Perhaps they could congratulate their pastor just after the ministers.

4. Hold the ordination service in a local church where the ordinand is currently pastoring. This will surely make the ordination more significant to the church, and may be appreciated more by the pastor.

Spouse involvement. — Five suggestions for increasing spouse involvement in the ordination service:

1. Escort the wife to the platform along with her husband.

2. Invite the wife to kneel beside her husband for the ordination prayer.

3. Have the wife remain beside her husband for the charge and welcome.

4. Let a minister's wife give a special welcome to the ordinand's wife.

5. Give the wife flowers at the same time the husband is given the ordination certificate. (If the custom is for the husband to receive a gift, give the wife a gift also.) This might come from the local

Shepherdess chapter and be given by its president.

Order of service. — If practical, all ordained ministers should be seated on the platform as the ministerial ordination service begins. The order of service might be as follows:

Hymn
Prayer
Presentation of candidate(s) and spouse(s)
>Have the candidates and spouses seated on the front row of the audience until this time. As each couple's name is called, the couple stands and goes to seats on the platform. It is well for them to be escorted by the seasoned ministerial couple of their choice. As the couple stands, their family and members of churches they've served might also stand and remain standing until the couple is seated on the platform. Meanwhile, the ministerial secretary, or whoever is presenting the candidate, tells about his background and ministry. The wife's unique gifts and chosen role in ministry should be mentioned.

Special music
>It is nice if a group of ministers' wives can give this.

Sermonette
>This should be brief. Candidates and their spouses ought to be seated where the speaker can address them directly. It should conclude with a challenge to the ordinands.

Candidate's response
>This may need to be eliminated if many are being ordained at once. It should not be a sermonette, but a brief, personal testimony.

Ordination prayer (see below)
Charge (see below)
Welcome (see below)
Ministers' chorus (if practical) or other special music.
>The ministers are already on the platform. This song can be their welcome and challenge to the ordinands.

Benediction
>At this juncture the ministers often take considerable time congratulating and welcoming the new ministers and their spouses, but the audience is not involved and becomes restless. The audience could be dismissed just before the receiving line. Individuals are then free to sit and watch, get into the receiving line, or leave.

Receiving line in this order:
>Officers giving ordination certificates, gifts, flowers, etc.
>Ministers.

ORDINATION SERVICE

Elders from churches presently served by ordinands.
Family and special guests of ordinands. These could be seated in a reserved area.
Audience.

Ordination prayer. — The congregation is usually seated with bowed heads for the ordination prayer. The ministers and the candidate kneel, the latter in the center of the group. The spouse may kneel too by the side of her husband, but she does not receive the laying on of hands. Those who have a special part in the service, and as many others as may conveniently do so, kneel close to the candidate so as to join in the laying on of hands.

The ordination prayer thanks God for the family who raised the candidate, for the wife and children who stand by his side, for the local congregations that support him. The prayer recognizes God's call of the minister to his sacred work and the need of divine strength to fulfill that call. It asks that, as the hands of the ministers are laid upon the candidate in recognition by the church of the divine call, the Lord may bestow in yet larger measure the Holy Spirit's power.

As the laying on of hands is mentioned in the prayer, each ordained minister places a hand upon a candidate's head, or on those laying hands on candidates, so that all are joined. They continue thus to the close of the prayer.

Charge. — Rising from prayer, all the ministers stand while the charge is given:

> Brother _____, God has called you to the work of the ministry, and the church, having recognized that call, has set you aside by the laying on of hands. You are now invested with full ecclesiastical authority. No higher honor can come to any person. But such honor also involves great responsibility.
>
> *I charge you to minister as a servant.*
> As a servant, *make the Master your lifelong study.* Know what you teach, but first know whom you teach. By spending time with Jesus, you will become like Jesus. For it is by beholding that we become changed. "A disciple is not above his teacher, nor a servant above his master. It is enough for a disciple that he be like his teacher, and a servant like his master" (Matt. 10:24, 25).
> As a servant, *live like your Master lived:*
> Like Jesus, live *simply.* "Let this mind be in you which was also in Christ Jesus, who, being in the form of God, did not

consider it robbery to be equal with God, but made Himself of no reputation, taking the form of a servant" (Phil. 2:5-7). "You therefore must endure hardship as a good soldier of Jesus Christ. No one engaged in warfare entangles himself with the affairs of this life, that he may please him who enlisted him as a soldier" (2 Tim. 2:3, 4).

Like Jesus, *be what you expect others to become.* "Be an example to the believers in word, in conduct, in love, in spirit, in faith, in purity" (1 Tim. 4:12).

I charge you to minister as a shepherd.

Jesus said, "I am the good shepherd. The good shepherd gives His life for the sheep. . . . The hireling flees because he is a hireling and does not care about the sheep" (John 10:11, 13).

Be a shepherd, not a hireling. Work for the sake of the sheep, not for the sake of mere money. Love Christ supremely, and He will help you love His stubborn, wayward sheep as He loved them. "Be gentle to all, able to teach, patient" (2 Tim. 2:24).

And remember, your own family is the first flock you are charged to shepherd.

I charge you to minister as a watchman.

As a watchman, *warn.* "So you, son of man: I have made you a watchman for the house of Israel; therefore you shall hear a word from My mouth and warn them for Me. When I say to the wicked, ' O wicked man, you shall surely die!' and you do not speak to warn the wicked from his way, that wicked man shall die in his iniquity; but his blood I will require at your hand. . . . Say to them: 'As I live,' says the Lord God, ' I have no pleasure in the death of the wicked, but that the wicked turn from his way and live. Turn, turn from your evil ways! For why should you die, O house of Israel' " (Eze. 33:7, 8, 11).

As a watchman, *win.* Jesus said, "You did not choose Me, but I chose you and appointed you that you should go and bear fruit, and that your fruit should remain" (John 15:16).

"I charge you therefore before God and the Lord Jesus Christ, who will judge the living and the dead at His appearing and His kingdom: Preach the word! Be ready in season and out of season. Convince, rebuke, exhort, with all longsuffering and teaching. . . . But you be watchful in all things, endure afflictions, do the work of an evangelist, fulfill your ministry" (2 Tim. 4:1, 5).

I charge you to minister as a teacher.

Teach *pastorally*, by training your members to be leaders. "And the things that you have heard . . . , commit these to faithful men who will be able to teach others also" (2 Tim. 2:2).

Teach *intelligently*, by being a lifelong reader of books and student of the Word. "Study to shew thyself approved unto God, a workman that needeth not to be ashamed, rightly dividing the word of truth" (verse 15, KJV).

Teach *doctrinally*. "If you instruct the brethren in these things, you will be a good minister of Jesus Christ, nourished in the words of faith and of the good doctrine which you have carefully followed. . . . Take heed to yourself and to the doctrine. Continue in them, for in doing this you will save both yourself and those who hear you" (1 Tim. 4:6, 16).

Teach *plainly* and *practically*, so even the children listen and understand. "Take heed therefore unto yourselves, and to *all* the flock, over the which the Holy Ghost hath made you overseers, to feed the church of God, which he hath purchased with his own blood" (Acts 20:28, KJV).

The poet summarizes:

> We bid thee welcome in the name
> Of Jesus our exalted head:
> Come as a *servant*: so He came;
> And we receive thee in His stead.
>
> Come as a *shepherd*: guard and keep
> His fold from hell and earth and sin;
> Nourish the lambs, and feed the sheep;
> The wounded heal, the lost bring in.
>
> Come as a *watchman*: take thy stand
> Upon the tower amidst the sky;
> And when the sword comes on the land,
> Call us to fight, or warn to fly.
>
> Come as a *teacher*, sent from God,
> Charged His whole counsel to declare:
> Lift o'er our ranks the prophet's rod,
> While we uphold thy hands with prayer.
> —James Montgomery

And when your work is ended, may you say with Paul, "I have fought the good fight, I have finished the race, I have kept the faith. Finally, there is laid up for me the crown of righteousness, which the Lord, the righteous Judge, will give to me on that Day, and not to me only but also to all who have loved His appearing" (2 Tim. 4:7, 8).

Welcome. — The platform party remains standing as a designated minister gives the welcome:

> My dear Elder (or Pastor), it is my happy privilege to extend to you a hearty welcome into the ranks of the gospel ministry.
>
> *I welcome you on behalf of your conference and the world church.* Be loyal to its leadership. Make use of its services to assist in your work. Never lose sight of our mission of "having the everlasting gospel to preach to those who dwell on the earth—to every nation, tribe, tongue, and people" (Rev. 14:6).
>
> *I welcome you on behalf of your fellow ministers.* Every problem or frustration you will ever face has already been faced and successfully worked through by other ministers. Choose one as your pastor. Let your fellow ministers minister to you.
>
> *I welcome you on behalf of the congregations you will serve.* They are entitled to expect much of us. It is an inspiration and a comfort to remember that their prayers ascend in our behalf, as in turn we look to them as coworkers in soul winning.
>
> As a soldier of Christ, you will not be without bruises and scars. None of us can escape them. But when at last we stand victorious on the sea of glass with those for whom we have labored, the nail-scarred hand of our Commander will rest lovingly upon those scars. To us, our scars will seem so small compared with His, as we hear Him declare, "Well done, good and faithful servant; you were faithful over a few things, I will make you ruler over many things. Enter into the joy of your Lord" (Matt. 25:21).

Welcome to wife. — The platform party continues standing as a designated minister's wife welcomes the ordinand's wife. The candidate's wife should be standing by her husband.

> Welcome, _____, to the family of women whose husbands are ordained to the gospel ministry of the Seventh-day Adventist Church.
>
> Welcome to a team ministry with your husband. In Eden it took both Adam and Eve to represent the image of God

adequately. In the pastorate it takes both the strength of a husband and the sensitivity of a wife to represent Christ to the church fully.

Your husband's ministry needs you as a team partner. To whatever extent you are able, work with him to develop a team ministry fulfilling to you both. Your unity will be an example to youth, an attraction to unbelievers, and a source of help to those seeking counsel.

Welcome to life in the pastoral family. You must not be expected to do everything the church, and maybe even your husband, expect of you. There will be some things you do not feel able to do. Nobody should be expected to do everything, but every church member can do something. I encourage you to find your own place of ministry and fill it. Do not try to be all things to all people. But do consecrate yourself to being all that God wants you to be.

Welcome to the problems of a minister's wife:
- Loneliness and isolation resulting from too many moves, too few roots, and uncertainty whether or not it's OK to have close church friends.
- Feelings of inadequacy, fearing you will not always smile when you should, say the right words, or have all the gifts members expect.
- Longing for privacy while living in a fishbowl, continually expected to be a role model for others when you're sometimes not certain who you are yourself.
- Wiping away the tears as you pray for the people who do not respond to the ministry offered them.
- Tight budgets and tight schedules.
- Tensions when you want to shout defensively because your husband is under attack—and all you dare do is bite your lip.

Welcome to the pleasures of a minister's wife:
- Living with a man who, though imperfect, intends to be a dedicated Christian.
- Being as much a part of your husband's work as you choose to be.
- Offering the gospel to people, the only thing in the world that can really answer all their needs.
- Feelings of accomplishment in a cause that counts.
- Being needed.
- Understanding that living to serve, though sometimes

frustrating, brings life's greatest satisfaction.
- Knowing your members love you and many pray for you daily.
- Finding that Jesus never fails, and that you can trust Him.
- Knowing that God planned for this day before you were born. He has not brought you here to fail, but will make available everything you need to do everything He wants you to do.

Please remember that your fellow ministers' wives are praying for you. We offer ourselves to be your special support. Welcome.

Additional suggestions. — Five additional suggestions that might be considered in planning the ordination service:

1. Conference leaders could take the candidate and his spouse out for an evening of fellowship and encouragement. Or, the wife of a conference leader might invite the ordinand's wife out or to her home.
2. Bring the ministerial staff together for a Communion service and special recognition of the couple. A gift would be appropriate in remembrance of the occasion.
3. Use the Code of Ethics on page 51 of this manual. It could be incorporated into the sermon, be read as the ordinand's commitment to ministry, or be printed on the back of the ordination certificate or elsewhere to be signed as the ordinand's commitment.
4. As part of the service, husbands could speak to wives and wives to husbands as they share their commitment to ministry.
5. In some places it is traditional to give ordinands a Bible at the time of their ordination. If so, give a gift to the spouse as well; perhaps a hymnal matching the Bible, or some other gift appropriate in the local culture.
6. Use a beautiful and representative certificate of ordination such as the one available through the GC Ministerial Association.

Local Elders and Deacons

The conference/mission does not need to approve candidates for ordination as elder or deacon. They are elected by the local church. However, only an ordained minister may perform the service of ordaining an elder or deacon. This is to help assure that individuals are not ordained without careful consideration under seasoned leadership in the local church.

In some countries ordination of elders or deacons is rather rare. This may be because of local tradition and culture of other churches that assume the candidate is making a lifelong commitment much like a pastor or priest. The Adventist Church teaches that deacons and elders should be persons of experience and chosen wisely. But once they have been chosen and trusted by the local congregation, their ordination should not be unduly delayed. It is well for these officers to receive training, but it should not be assumed that their ordination depends on it.

Elders. — A proper form of elder ordination embraces the following features:

1. An ordained minister is in charge. Ordained ministers and elders in the congregation may be invited to assist.
2. At the proper time, usually during the Sabbath morning service, invite the candidate to the rostrum. Read a Scripture passage such as 1 Timothy 3:1-7. You may speak briefly on the work of an elder (see *Church Manual*, chapter 6). Reference to the spouse is appropriate.
3. Candidate and minister kneel. The minister prays that God will approve the recognition the church is giving that the Holy Spirit has called the candidate to this office. The hand of ordination is laid on the candidate's head during the prayer. Assisting ministers and elders may join in this.
4. After prayer, the minister and those assisting clasp the candidate's hand and share a word of blessing. A certificate of ordination may be given. The one newly ordained then returns to the congregation or is seated on the platform to take part in the remainder of the service.

Having once been ordained as a church elder, it is not necessary to be ordained again upon reelection, or upon election as elder of some other church, provided the person has maintained good and regular standing in the church. One who has been ordained as elder may later function as a deacon without further ordination.

Deacons. — The ordination service for a deacon is quite identical with that of an elder. The suggested Scripture passage is 1 Timothy 3:8-13. Further comments on the work of a deacon may be found in the *Church Manual*.

Ordination as a deacon does not qualify one for serving as elder. Once ordained as deacon, a person need not be ordained again upon reelection to the same office.

Additional suggestions. — Options such as the following might be considered in planning the ordination of either elders or deacons:

1. Wives of those being ordained could be invited to sit on the front row of the church. At a designated time they could receive a flower or similar memento. This both gives recognition to the wives, and identifies them for the members.
2. Following the ordination, the head elder could lead out in

welcoming new elders; the head deacon in welcoming new deacons.

3. Candidates for ordination might kneel around the minister, with those already ordained kneeling behind them. After the ordination, these ordained individuals extend the right hand of fellowship to the one who knelt in front of them.

An adaptation would be for each candidate to choose (or the church to assign) from the congregation one person already ordained to the office. These persons would be the sponsors, each charged with helping to train the new ordinand. They could even escort the candidates to the platform, later kneel behind them, and then give the hand of fellowship.

Induction Service

In some parts of the world two types of church leaders are set aside for special spiritual service in an induction rather than an ordination service:

Commissioned ministers. — (See page 71 for those included in this category.)

Ministerial ordination is a public sign of the church's acceptance by the church of the ordinand's ministry. The church has not agreed to ordain women ministers, but it has accepted women in pastoral ministry. There needs to be a public sign of acceptance by the church of their ministry. This is also true of others in the commissioned minister classification. An induction service provides this public sign.

The North American Division encourages such a service: "It is recommended that an appropriate commissioning service be conducted when an employee is granted a commissioned minister credential" (*NAD Policy* D 05 10).

Suggested order of commissioning service:

Hymn	**Candidate response**
Prayer	**The commitment**
Purpose of commissioning	(A litany spoken by leader, candidate, and congregation.)
Presentation of candidate(s)	**Dedicatory prayer**
Special music	**Presentation of credentials**
Sermonette	**Benediction**

Deaconesses. — The *Church Manual* suggests, "The church may arrange for a suitable service of induction for the deaconess by an ordained minister holding current credentials" (*Church Manual*, chapter 6).

Such a service could be very similar to that ordaining elders and deacons.

CHAPTER 17

Organizing New Churches

New Churches Needed

Don't be afraid to start new churches. Mother churches that purposely reach out to foster new congregations seldom suffer. Sometimes they are revived. The biblical principle "Give, and it will be given to you" (Luke 6:38) applies.

When a church reaches a size at which its officers can best perform their task of shepherding, nurturing, and training members, it is well to foster a new congregation. Under ordinary circumstances, churches that have grown to 200 or 300 members are probably large enough to consider spawning a new congregation.

As a church grows beyond the level of maximum efficiency, the dangers inherent in its administration increase. Largeness may impede fellowship.

Giving birth to a new church will have the double effect of involving more members in the work of the church and establishing a congregation in a new area that must also be reached with our message. The best way to produce more fruit is to plant more trees.

New churches win new members. In most parts of the world it is difficult to attract unchurched people to a church more than a half hour away from their residence.

New churches win former members. Church growth studies show that new churches revive inactive members more easily than do old churches.

How to Start a New Church

1. Plan. — Find out where the need for a church is greatest. Put the new church where the population is, not where some strong member lives, or where land is donated. Study demographics. Where is the population growing? Where is the significant population with needs a new church would be uniquely qualified to meet?

For details on organizing new churches, see *Church Manual*, chapter 14.

2. Probe. — Do some probing before you do too much investing. Learn what interest can be created in the proposed area. Begin home Bible study groups that could develop into home churches. Start a branch Sabbath school. Hold evangelistic meetings in the area.

3. Form a company. — One workable suggestion is to form a company made up of volunteers from the mother church who offer themselves to attend and support the embryo organization for a specified time—perhaps two or three years. Chapter 5 of the *Church Manual* gives details for organizing a company.

Preparation for Organizing a New Church

When it becomes evident that the new church can thrive, ask your conference/mission leaders to approve its formal organization. The organization must be presided over by an ordained minister. The president should be invited.

See that letters of transfer from previous churches have been granted for members wishing to join the new congregation. Arrange for necessary record books and materials to be available for the new treasurer, clerk, and other officers to be chosen.

Provide Communion equipment. Although Communion at the time of the organization may make the program too long, the service should at least be held shortly thereafter, perhaps at the first regular worship service.

Service Organizing a New Church

An order of service that would include the recommendations of the *Church Manual* might be as follows:

Opening song
Prayer
Brief review of fundamental doctrines
    (This has greater significance when the church is to be made up mostly of new Adventists rather than members transferring from another congregation.)
Forming of nucleus
Accepting of membership by vote of nucleus
Forming of nominating committee
Congregational singing and special music
    (While the nominating committee meets.)
Voting of new officers

Ordination of new elders and deacons
Challenge to the new church and its members
Church's response
Prayer of dedication

Under some circumstances several meetings might be held to organize a new church. For example:

Communion	Friday evening: held at the new church with the parent church invited.
Commissioning	Sabbath morning: a service at the parent church acknowledges departing members.
Commencement	Sabbath afternoon: the new church is established.
Congregating	Sabbath evening: plan a fellowship meal and social event.

CHAPTER 18

Uniting Churches

The term uniting churches needs to be defined. When church B (presumably small) decides to unite with church A (presumably larger), and simply moves its members to church A and closes its former facility, that is hardly the definition of the term uniting churches as used here. Under the above circumstances, only some of the steps below would be necessary. All of these steps apply only when both churches cease to exist as previously organized.

The following steps for uniting churches are based on chapter 14 of the *Church Manual*:

Before Uniting

1. Consultation with conference/mission. — As pastor, you are in the best position to know when two or more churches should unite, and thus you may be the one to initiate the proceedings. However, your tenure as pastor is limited, and the uniting of churches is presumably a very long-term decision. Also, the two churches may presently be under different pastors, creating a potentially sensitive issue between you and your fellow-minister. In addition, you may be tempted to want churches united because this would seem to make your work easier and more manageable.

For all these reasons, uniting of churches should involve much counsel from the conference/mission at the very start. The uniting must be voted by the conference executive committee. The conference president or president's representative should preside over the more significant meetings involved with the uniting.

2. Each church discusses informally. — It may be wise to start preliminary discussions with smaller groups, such as elders, or the Church board. However, only during a duly called business meeting can one church body decide to unite with another.

For details on uniting churches, see *Church Manual*, chapter 14.

3. *Each church votes to unite.*

4. *Churches work together to prepare a unification agreement.* — A meticulously prepared document will prevent misunderstandings later. The agreement should include the reason for uniting, disposal of property, financial arrangements, new church name, etc.

5. *Approval by conference executive committee.*

Service Uniting

1. *Adoption of unification agreement by a joint meeting of the churches.* — If possible, any differences over the agreement should have been worked out beforehand. It is imperative that this meeting be in an atmosphere of warm Christian love.

2. *Choosing a nominating committee.* — With the adoption of the agreement, all leaders of the churches involved are released from their offices. It is imperative, of course, that at least principal officers are chosen within a few days. The new church cannot function without leaders.

3. *A time for fellowship.* — A Communion service may provide the spirit of unity needed to get the church started right. A fellowship meal following the service might also be helpful.

After Uniting

1. *Transfer local records.* — Records, books, and bank accounts from both churches become a part of the new church.

2. *Update conference records.* — The new church applies to the conference for acceptance into the sisterhood of churches, replacing the former church bodies.

CHAPTER 19

Disbanding Churches

Reasons for disbanding a church are: (1) loss of members, (2) discipline, and (3) apostasy or rebellion. Fortunately, church disbandings are rare in the Adventist Church. You may never preside over a disbanding. If it appears that you must, first make sure you have done all you can to help any needed church survive.

Disbanding for Loss of Members

We have no precise criteria for deciding when a church has gotten too small to continue. The *Church Manual* criteria may be the best available: "So many of the members may move away that the number remaining is not sufficient to support the organization." Even then, ask such questions as:

Is the church needed? — Does the church serve a significant population that needs to be evangelized? Could present members be well served by a nearby church?

What is the depth of congregational loyalty? — A pastor may become exasperated over being expected to serve a tiny congregation where little seems to be happening. You become frustrated because the smaller the group, the fewer the leaders. And the fewer the leaders, the more the church wants pastoral leadership. On the other hand, if the members are content and deeply loyal to their church, disbanding becomes very difficult and probably unwise.

Could you hold a revival? — Maybe evangelism is the answer. If you cannot do it yourself, a little church is a good place for lay evangelism.

Could members from nearby churches transfer? — Members whose

For details on disbanding churches, see *Church Manual*, chapter 14.

leadership potential is not being tapped in another congregation might be willing to transfer their membership and provide leadership. They could become lay assistants and free you from ministering to the little group so often.

Disbanding for Discipline or Apostasy

Things to try before disbanding an apostate church:

In-depth study. — Churches moving toward apostasy usually have some theological disagreement with the world church. Almost invariably, among them are individuals whose dissidence is extreme and whose influence has confused others. You may not be able to help the former, but you surely must offer help to the latter. If necessary, bring in a guest specialist in the subjects involved. Pray that a revival of loyalty to and enthusiasm for Christ, the church, and its teachings will result.

Visitation. — People need to be loved and listened to individually. Getting the confused members alone, away from the extreme dissidents, will help you understand much better what they are really feeling.

Removal of dissident elements. — Dismissal of such persons from membership may be difficult, but it's sometimes necessary to cut off some fingers in order to save the rest of the body. Discipline may be needed. Just remember that love-less discipline is never needed.

SECTION THREE

The Minister and the Local Church

20. Church Leadership
21. Members as Ministers
22. Pastoring Large Districts
23. Church Growth
24. Worship Service
25. Prayer Meeting
26. Visitation
27. Counseling
28. Church Fellowship
29. Church Finance
30. Church Campaigns
31. Church Facilities
32. Christian Education

CHAPTER 20

Church Leadership

Leadership Versus Lordship

Leaders must lead. — Pastors may be many things, but one thing they must be: spiritual leaders. On assignment to a local church they assume principal leadership of the congregation. Ordination to the ministry and assignment by the conference/mission authorize them to function in all church rites and ceremonies. They should care for such services unless they choose to delegate the responsibility to other authorized church leaders.

"All branches of the work belong to the ministers" (*Testimonies,* vol. 5, p. 375). This does not mean that they must attend to the entire church work, but that all work does come under their supervision. They are responsible for overseeing and fostering every department and program (see *Church Manual,* chapter 9).

Pastors, however, must not set up an independent body of counselors to guide and control the church. They are to work in cooperation with the local elders and other duly elected officers of the body.

Leaders as servants. — Research indicates that growing churches usually have strong pastoral leadership. Strong does not mean dominating or manipulative leadership. We must not confuse leadership with lordship. Peter prescribed, "Be shepherds of God's flock that is under your care, serving as overseers . . . not lording it over those entrusted to you" (1 Peter 5:2, 3, NIV).

The Jesus model shows that, whereas worldly rulers are *over* those they lead, Christian leaders are to be *among* those they lead. "You know that the rulers of the Gentiles lord it over them, and those who are great exercise authority over them. Yet it shall not be so among you; but whoever desires to become great among you, let him be your servant. And whoever desires to be first among you, let him be your slave—just as the Son of Man did not come to be served, but to serve" (Matt. 20:25-28).

Christian leadership is servant leadership. The Gospels speak of this at least seven times. In one instance, Jesus insisted, "Neither be ye called masters: for one is your Master, even Christ. But he that is greatest among you shall be your servant" (Matt. 23:10, 11, KJV). When tempted to use their leadership role to exercise power over their people, ministers need to remind themselves of how contrary this is to the teachings of Christ.

Servanthood, of course, is not servitude. Servitude is demeaning because it is a status forced on you by others, depriving you of the freedom of choice. Ministry must not become servitude. Servanthood, on the other hand, is a voluntary action. It is choosing to be of service to others.

For example, servitude causes a congregation or conference to force an evaluation process upon its ministers and their ministry; but servanthood causes ministers to want and seek evaluation of their work so they can serve more effectively. Too few are able to make this application of servanthood without feeling personally threatened. Pastors may be tempted to think they are accountable only to the Lord. Servant leadership suggests they are also accountable to those they serve.

(The General Conference Ministerial Association has instruments available for pastors who wish to be evaluated by themselves, their congregations, or their conferences.)

Management Principles

Personality and leadership style are so intimately related that we seldom adopt a leadership style different from our personality. To the best of your ability, however, you need to adapt your leadership style to the church or churches you lead. When your present leadership seems much less effective than your leadership in a previous congregation, you need to ask yourself if it is because your present church requires a different leadership style. Servant leadership demands the flexibility to adapt your leadership style to meet the needs of different congregations.

We could hardly imagine a stronger leader than Paul. Yet he understood this principle of servant leadership: "For though I am free from all men, I have made myself a servant to all, that I might win the more; and to the Jews I became as a Jew, that I might win Jews; . . . to the weak I became as weak, that I might win the weak. I have become all things to all men, that I might by all means save some. Now this I do for the gospel's sake, that I may be partaker of it with you" (1 Cor. 9:19-23). Servant leadership demands adaptation and flexibility.

A church board made up of educated, professional people used to weighing big issues and making important decisions may not allow the pastor a dominant role in decision-making. A board made up of people who work for others and are accustomed to obeying orders may accept a very different style of pastoral leadership.

Leadership style comes in four types: telling, selling, consulting, and participating. The telling or selling style may work fairly well with the second group above. The consulting and participating style is much preferred and will work with both groups.

Leadership style must be flexible. Management mechanics are important. But your leadership style is not nearly as important as your leadership spirit. How you lead attitudinally is far more important than how you lead mechanically.

Here are four management principles well adapted to pastoral leadership:

1. *Visualize*. — Visualize what is and what ought to be. As pastor of a church or church district, you need to ask a lot of questions. Where has the church been? Where is it now in terms of mission, programs, facilities, and finances? Where does the church want to be a year from now? five years from now?

2. *Organize*. — How can the church get from where it is to where it wants to be? What programs are needed? What personnel are available? There's little value in making plans unless the church has the personnel with the skills and interest to carry them out. How can these programs be most effectively organized? How will the leaders be trained?

(Churches with a computer available can purchase from the General Conference Ministerial Association software that will assist the organizing process by keeping record of members' interests, experience, and abilities.)

3. *Deputize*. — Delegate the work. Much of what pastors do can be done as well or better by church members. One reason pastors don't delegate more responsibility is that it requires delegation of authority as well, and this they are reluctant to do. Servant leadership does not feel threatened when authority is shared.

A second reason pastors don't delegate responsibility is that they dread dealing with the failures of others. It is often easier to do a job ourselves than to get someone else to do it. The argument is: "If you want it done right, do it yourself." This kind of reasoning, however, has a fatal theological flaw. The argument would be valid if our primary business were getting church work done. But it isn't. Our first business is the growth of the church member, and members who work for the Lord get closest to the Lord. Members who work for the church stay in the church.

4. *Supervise*. — Give assistance at crucial times. If somebody is failing, find a way to help that person succeed. Reward performance. "Let us have real warm affection for one another as between brothers, and a willingness to let the other man have the credit" (Rom. 12:10, Phillips).

Setting Objectives

Objectives clarify what the church wants to do and how it plans to go about doing it. The process need not be complicated or frightening. At least once a year, and preferably once a quarter, the church should look at its objectives—the goals it has set for itself.

The most important time to review old objectives and form new ones is just before new officers are chosen. Leaders chosen and committees formed should not depend just on what was done the previous year, but on what you plan to accomplish in the coming year. Planning for the future can make all the difference between a dying and a growing church.

Objectives must grow out of some kind of dialogue within the congregation. Pastors, or even board members, should not set objectives without consulting the congregation at large. Goals which people have had a say in setting become "owned" goals.

Essential elements of an objective can be expressed as an acronym, SAM: specific, attainable, measurable.

1. Is the objective specific? — Suppose one of your objectives is to help your youth grow spiritually. But that's not specific enough. How about this: to hold a Friday vespers for youth each week.

2. Is the objective attainable? — You might wish that every member would win a soul during the year. Unfortunately, it's not likely that everyone will, and so such a high goal sets the church up for failure. Set goals that are high but attainable.

3. Is the objective measurable? — Baptisms are easily measurable. Perhaps that's one reason we place so much emphasis on baptism. But helping those new members grow spiritually is harder to measure, and perhaps that's one reason we don't emphasize this as we should. Yet spiritual growth is measurable. Sabbath school participation, church attendance, stewardship, witness, and caring relationships to some degree help in measuring growth. Strive for measurable objectives; otherwise there's no accurate way of knowing when or whether you achieve them.

(The General Conference Ministerial Association has instruments available for your use in helping your church set objectives.)

Committees

Committees are Christian. — The church believes strongly in the committee system (see *Church Manual* under committees, boards, and councils). This is so not just because of our tradition, but because of our theology. The Bible says a church is like a human body. Each part is important. The body operates on the basis of group participation.

Christians are to love and trust each other. If we do, it will be proven by our respect for each other's judgment and point of view. We take the Bible seriously when it says, "Where there is no counsel, the people fall; but in the multitude of counselors there is safety" (Prov. 11:14). All of us together are bound to be wiser than any one of us alone.

Ellen White agrees: "In counseling for the advancement of the work, no one man is to be a controlling power, a voice for the whole. Proposed methods and plans are to be carefully considered so that all the brethren may weigh their relative merits and decide which should be followed" (*Testimonies*, vol. 7, p. 259).

Committees are costly. — Committees take up a lot of time. Here are some timesaving suggestions:

Don't chair too many committees. Committees may run the church, but that doesn't mean that you as pastor must run every committee. You, or an elder you designate, should presumably be an ex officio member of every committee. Sometimes you need to attend to show your interest in and support of the group. When especially significant items are considered, committee chairpersons appreciate pastoral support. On the other hand, a pastor's perpetual presence can be at times intimidating.

As pastor, you have a right to chair the church board, and probably should (see *Church Manual*, chapters 6, 7). Sometimes, depending on your availability, personality, leadership style, and local available leadership you may wish to delegate this to a church elder.

Eliminate the trivial. Make decisions at the lowest level possible. For example, don't take to a business meeting items that can be settled by the church board. Don't take to the board items that can be settled by the Sabbath school council. And don't take to the Sabbath school council items that can be settled by the Sabbath school superintendent. This not only saves time, but improves committee attendance when committee members know that only significant items will be considered.

On the other hand, don't handle at lower levels the most significant items that affect the whole congregation. The business meeting, not the church board, is the highest authority in the congregation.

Combine a simple supper with your business meeting to increase attendance, and make it a time of fellowship for the entire church.

Double up. Hold committee meetings before or after other services such as prayer meeting. Have several committees going on at once, perhaps starting at different times. This way you may be able to spend some time with each committee.

Evaluate annually. Review the work of each committee every year. Is a particular committee necessary? Are the right personnel on it? A good rule of thumb is that one third of a committee's membership should be new each year.

Is the committee size-efficient? Research indicates that committees should not be larger than 6 to 12 members. When committees become large, members feel less obligated to attend and are less likely to speak up if they do attend. In such situations the more aggressive members tend to take control.

Does each committee have properly defined terms of reference—its areas of concern, its authority to act or recommend for approval by another body?

Chairing committees. — Ten rules for successfully chairing a committee:

1. *Prepare agenda.* An agenda is a list of items for the committee to consider and upon which to act. Each committee member should receive a copy of the agenda. If practical, this should be done well before the meeting date so that members can come prepared. Under some circumstances it is wise to screen the agenda through a smaller group, such as the elders' council. When there is consensus among the elders, there will usually be agreement by the church board.

What if a committee member interrupts the agenda with an additional item? In informal settings this is no serious problem. Sometimes, however, the issue introduced could be an explosive one. No one person should be allowed to control the group, neither the one interrupting nor even the chairperson. If the group votes to consider the issue, it might be added at the bottom of the agenda. A safer way is to use a screening committee as suggested above. Then the chairperson can, without seeming dictatorial, explain that items are to be passed through the screening committee before being placed on the agenda.

2. *Begin and end on time.* Speaking of long committee meetings, Ellen White counsels: "In the hope of reaching a decision, they continue their meetings far into the night. . . . If the brain were given proper periods of rest, the thoughts would be clear and sharp, and the business would be expedited" (*Testimonies*, vol. 7, p. 256).

Listing agenda items can help keep a committee on time. Not everyone ever arrives on time, and so list first items that do not require everyone's presence, such as a treasurer's report or routine business. And then begin the meeting on time. Starting meetings late produces a vicious circle; next time people will come even later.

Next on your agenda, put the heavy, lengthy items. After the committee talks for an hour and members realize they've gone through only a fourth of the agenda, they'll become more businesslike. Next, place the more brief, shorter items. Finally, include items that must be considered sometime, but could be postponed if you run out of time.

3. *Provide information.* Committees working in the right spirit with the right information will invariably make the right decision. Inadequate information often leads to wrong decisions. The chairperson need not be the source of all information, but should ensure that the committee gets the information it needs to act intelligently.

4. *Create a team spirit.* Research shows that committees become ineffective when there is a hostile spirit within the group. Members must want to work together, want to agree. The chairperson has much to do with creating this kind of team spirit.

Don't overcontrol. Unless the committee is oversized, members shouldn't have to address the chair when they wish to speak. Dialogue should flow freely and directly from person to person. If two persons disagree vehemently, turn to others and hear their comments while the antagonists cool down.

Understand and at least informally observe the rules of parliamentary procedure. This gains respect for your leadership, establishes an organized sense of fairness, and protects the democratic process.

And nothing helps create a team spirit more effectively than a wholesome sense of humor. If you can smile together, you can usually work together.

5. *Control participation.* Ensure a broad spectrum of participation, and encourage everyone to join in the discussion. Gently bypass those who have already shared their point of view and tend to dominate. Ask, specifically, the more timid to share their thinking. When these nonparticipating members speak once and find their contribution is heard and respected, they will usually speak again and continue to participate.

6. *Respect others' ideas.* Pastors and other denominational chairpersons tend to be too autocratic. You know more about the subject than your committee members, because you have probably been more involved. But this does not mean your judgment is superior to that of the group. Some chairpersons may manipulate a committee to get their own way. But people resent such an approach; it's neither wise nor Christian.

Settle the process theologically in your own mind. Do you really believe in the wisdom of the church body as a whole? If so, you will respect the will of the committee, not only out of necessity, but out of your ecclesiological understanding.

As chairperson, remain as unbiased and neutral as possible. If there is an issue in which you cannot do this, give the chair to someone else during discussion of that item. One advantage in asking someone else to chair the church board is that you can then argue openly and fairly in favor of a given plan that is especially important to you.

Frank discussion of delicate issues should never leave the committee room. If it does, discussion will be less frank and open next time. Practice and preach confidentiality.

On the other hand, understand the tendency of human nature to betray confidence. Practice the principle of Matthew 18—limiting the discussion of controversial issues to the smallest group possible. You may sometimes need to ask the permission of your board or business meeting to delegate the discussion of highly confidential details to a designated small group. The elders' council may be one such group.

7. *Stick to the problem.* A committee *solves problems* by a *cooperative pooling* of *information* and *judgment.* We have addressed each section of this committee definition except the first—a committee solves problems.

But when the problem proves difficult to solve, the group or some of its members will begin talking about something that has no relevance to the main issue. The chairperson must kindly but relentlessly keep the committee on the problem at hand.

8. *Summarize periodically.* Rather than spending a lot of time on your own arguments, as chairperson concentrate more on rephrasing and summarizing the arguments given by others and work on areas of consensus. Voting, though absolutely essential, need not be a source of concern, for thorough and fair discussion by a good committee usually leads to a unanimous or near-unanimous decision.

Large problems can be solved in small steps. When faced with a difficult problem, the chair should watch for consensus developing on a portion of the problem and encourage a decision on that before continuing the discussion. For example, if the group is having difficulty deciding whether or not to put red tiles on the roof, the chairperson can listen for consensus on a part of the problem—does the church need a new roof?

9. *See that decisions are recorded.* This may seem unimportant in smaller, informal groups. But forget that you can remember, and remember that you can forget. Minutes of a meeting should be read and approved at the next meeting. Recorded minutes can keep the pastor out of a lot of trouble.

10. *Support the decision.* See that assignments are made for its implementation. Few things aggravate a committee more than finding out that the pastor or other church leaders ignored the committee decision and did things their own way anyway. When you're voted down, either accept the committee's wish or bring together additional information and ask the group to reconsider. Everyone together is more likely to be right than anyone alone—including the pastor.

CHAPTER 21

Members as Ministers

Every Member a Minister

The biblical word *laos*, from which we get our word "laity," has nothing to do with amateur or secondary status within the church. Rather, it includes the entire people of God—including pastors. We really misuse the term when we use it to describe assistants in or supporters of the ministry. We use it correctly when we mean associates in ministry. "Not upon the ordained minister only rests the responsibility of going forth to fulfill this commission. Everyone who has received Christ is called to work for the salvation of his fellow men" (*The Acts of Apostles*, p. 110).

Christ's plan. — At His ascension Jesus gave to His church an overwhelming task: "Go into all the world and preach the gospel to every creature" (Mark 16:15). To His tiny group of followers the work seemed an impossible assignment until they understood His plan for its fulfillment.

Here's the plan. "But each of us has been given his gift, his due portion of Christ's bounty. Therefore Scripture says: 'He ascended into the heights with captives in his train; he gave gifts to men.'. . . And these were his gifts: some to be apostles, some prophets, some evangelists, some pastors and teachers, to equip God's people for work in his service, to the building up of the body of Christ" (Eph. 4:7-12, NEB).

The gospel commission is overwhelming, but the provision for its fulfillment is overabundant. When Jesus went away, the Holy Spirit was given to His followers, bringing to each a gift or gifts for ministering, "distributing to each one individually as He wills" (1 Cor. 12:11). Everyone receiving the Holy Spirit receives a ministering gift designated by the Spirit to be used in a ministry for Christ. To say we have no spiritual gift is to say we have no Holy Spirit.

This spiritual gift is presumably related to some talent we already have. And the Holy Spirit urges us to find a ministry whereby the gift can be used to serve others and attract them to Christ. Under this plan there is no hierarchy. Everyone is a minister performing some ministry for which he or she has been specially gifted.

Christ's plan neglected. — This plan deeply disturbs the devil. He must find a way to stall the church. The name of his plan is separation. A line is drawn between clergy and laity. Clergy study the Bible, do the teaching, perform the work of the church. Laity are no longer obligated to minister; they are ministered to. Their only obligations are to pray, to pay, and to obey.

It's a popular plan. The clergy like it, for it gives them prestige and authority. The laity like it, for they no longer feel obliged to minister. But the fire of the church goes out. When a church is taken over by the clergy, it grows cold.

We tend to think of the church primarily as an organization or institution, rather than as a fellowship or community of faith, which is the predominant meaning of "church" in the New Testament. We assume that the role of church members is to help the professional ministers do their work, when in fact it is the function of the ministers to help the people do their work.

Only Christ's plan will succeed. — *Everybody should be doing something.* "If pastors would give more attention to getting and keeping their flock actively engaged at work, they would accomplish more good, have more time for study and religious visiting, and also avoid many causes of friction" (*Gospel Workers*, p. 198).

Pastors must understand the "pyramid principle." Keep pouring sand on a table, and gradually it will pyramid higher and higher. But eventually the pyramid can go no higher, the sand will begin spilling over the table edges, and you cannot add more sand unless you enlarge the table.

The table represents the leadership base of the church. The sand represents the work done by the church. It is unrealistic to presume the church program can keep increasing and the pastor, with a little help from a tiny group of church leaders, can somehow work hard enough to keep up. More people must be working if more work is to be done.

Everybody should not be doing the same thing. Christ's plan is that everyone in the church should have the Holy Spirit. Everyone receiving the Spirit receives a gift for ministry. But not everyone receives the same gift.

We're each responsible only for the gifts God gives us, "so there also may be a completion out of what you have. For if there is first a willing mind, it is accepted according to what one has, and not according to what he does not have" (2 Cor. 8:11, 12).

The church program is in error if it presumes everybody should perform the same ministry. Do not make your members feel guilty for failing to exercise your gift. When members do not enjoy serving and sharing, it is often because they have tried to use a gift they don't have. And so they have failed.

The pastor laments that the people don't want to witness anymore. It isn't because they don't want to witness. They don't want to fail. Help them find a ministry for which they're gifted, and they'll succeed. And when they succeed, they'll want to witness again.

Christ's plan will finish the work. "The work of God in this earth can never be finished until the men and women comprising our church membership rally to the work, and unite their efforts with those of ministers and church officers" (*Christian Service*, p. 68). The true test of evangelism is not so much how many come into the church to worship, but how many go out from the church to serve.

Motivating Volunteers

Managing voluntary leaders in the church is very different from managing paid employees, who have to do a job whether they want to or not. As servant leaders you do not presume authority over church workers. They work only because they want to. Maximum pastoral success is possible only as you become a specialist in motivating volunteers. Here are six suggestions that will help you succeed:

1. Preach inspirationally. — Hopefully, people do church work for altruistic, spiritual reasons. No motivation is more profound than spiritual motivation. And hardly anything engenders more effective spiritual motivation than Christ-centered, Bible-based preaching. Spend more time working on your sermons, and that will inspire your members to spend more time working for the church.

2. Involve members in the planning. — The planning process may be more helpful than the plans that result. It clarifies the mission and, if done wisely, gets people involved. When the planning process gets members enthusiastic about a given program, they'll want to help lead it.

3. Prepare job descriptions. — It's unfair to expect members to help with a job when they don't know what the job is. Clear-cut job descriptions are essential. And they're not difficult. Those presently holding the job can write the first draft.

4. Catch leaders doing something right—and tell them. — A manager increases or decreases initiative by the frequent or infrequent use of praise, criticism, feedback, information, etc. A study of volunteer church leaders showed that one third felt the job they did was not really important or that no one really cared what kind of job they did.

Church leaders may not always be looking for a compliment, but they are looking, especially to their pastor, for any clues that might indicate whether they are doing well or poorly. They like to see signs that you value their work.

When volunteers do something well, tell them immediately. But be specific. General statements of appreciation smack of flattery and are often interpreted as hypocritical and manipulative.

Train your elders to do the same. You cannot observe everyone's good work and express appreciation. Provide some kind of support system for every leader so someone is available to give encouragement and counsel when the going gets rough.

5. Protect leaders from burnout. — A study of church volunteers revealed that at least one in four was clearly experiencing burnout. Most of these are extremely busy people, involved in their work, community affairs, and family, besides doing church work. The same study indicated the average volunteer church leader was spending only seven evenings at home per month. Overworking church leaders not only overstresses them, but often leads to their eventually dropping out of church work altogether.

6. Believe in people. — You may have moments when you wish you had hired all your church workers so you could fire about half of them. Working with volunteers over whom you have very little direct control can be exasperating. Overwhelmed with the inconsistencies and blunders of humanity, you may succumb to the desire to manage everything yourself.

Rather, remember that every person reflects at least some of the image of the Creator. The good is there somewhere, and it's your job to help find and enlarge it. People tend to live up to whatever it is they think you expect of them. Losing faith in people leads to pastoral failure. Remember that Christ's plan is for the members of the church to do the work of the church. Ellen White insists, "The burden of church work should be distributed among its individual members" (*Review and Herald*, July 9, 1895).

Choosing Lay Leaders

Admit your limitations. — The range of work is too broad, the needed skills are too many. No one Christian, including the pastor, has all the attributes of Christ. However, the congregation as a whole does.

A prism breaks light down into its component parts and thus reflects all its colors. Spiritual gifts are the colors of Christ broken down into their component parts. No person alone represents the body of Christ, but each represents a part of His body. Only the congregational body as a whole represents fully Christ's body. Thus, you as a pastor should be not only free but internally compelled to admit your limitations and your need of help from the rest of the body.

When you, whether out of pride, guilt, or duty, spend your time doing things for which you're not gifted, everyone suffers. You suffer because you don't enjoy your work, and the church suffers because it never gets the maximum benefit of what you do best. Too many pastors spend most of their time doing things at which they are second-best.

Ellen White confirms: "I have been instructed in regard to the importance of our ministers' keeping free from responsibilities that should be largely borne by businessmen. . . . Your work is not the management of financial matters. . . . If you carry lines of work for which you are not adapted, your efforts in presenting the word will prove unsuccessful. . . . Those who are employed to write and to speak the word should attend fewer committee meetings" (*Testimonies*, vol. 7, pp. 246, 247).

Depend on your elders. — The idea that pastors dare not be open with or confide in anyone within the congregation is probably overly hierarchical, and theologically questionable. Pastors, like everyone else, need a support group. Ideally, this support should come from the church community with whom they serve, especially local church elders (see *Church Manual*, chapter 6).

The *Church Manual* states: "The minister should not gather to himself all lines of responsibility, but should share these with the local elder. . . . The pastoral work of the church should be shared by both. The elder should, in counsel with the minister, carry much of the pastoral responsibility" (chapter 6).

One model for the pastor/elder relationship is that of the specialist/general practitioner relationship in medicine. The elder (general practitioner) can take care of the day-to-day business of the church—chairing committees, organizing visitation, and planning worship services. An elder may be assigned to be either adviser or leader of each of the main departments and programs of the church. The pastor (specialist) is then freed to do preaching, evangelism, counseling, and nurturing.

Instead of complaining about pastors' weaknesses, elders should encourage pastors to work in the areas of their strength. Meanwhile, leaders whose strengths may fill in for pastors' weaknesses can be chosen to serve in those areas. This, of course, is possible only if pastor and church are willing to delegate both responsibility and authority to these leaders.

Match program and gifts. — In planning the church program, don't just consider what the church wants to accomplish. Focus also on what gifts are available in the congregation. Recognize abilities, and match those gifts with the program.

New converts should be put to work. However, don't hurry them into difficult and controversial assignments, no matter how gifted they may be.

Nominate wisely. — Your work with the nominating committee is one of the most important things you do. Before the committee meets, finalize the plans for the upcoming year and the job descriptions of offices that need to be filled. This provides the list from which the nominating committee operates.

Do not allow your church board to have too much control in choosing the nominating committee. They must not appoint the committee. Although they can be a part of the process, this is the time when control of the church is given to the church at large and not just the "in" group (see *Church Manual*, chapter 10.)

Shortly before it meets, the nominating committee should survey the congregation. A sheet, listing offices to be filled, may be passed out to all church members. Members could write which offices they feel gifted for, have had experience with, or are interested in.

Offices that are ongoing may, under some circumstances, be filled for a two-year term. This will facilitate better long-term plans. It will also simplify the work of the nominating committee.

Install formally. — A formal installation service for lay leaders at the beginning of the officer year enhances the seriousness of the office. It also provides an opportunity for dedication. You may have a service like the following during a regular worship hour:

Leader:	To the worship of God and the work of the Church—
Officers:	We dedicate ourselves.
Leader:	To the fulfilling of our assigned duties under the guidance of God, and for the edification and leadership of young and old—
Officers:	We consecrate our services.
Leader:	To the setting of a right example of Christian living in our homes, at our work, and before all with whom we come in contact—
Officers:	We commit our lives.

Leader (addressing congregation):	You have heard your leaders promise to fulfill faithfully the duties of the offices to which you have elected them. Will you pledge to your officers your support, assistance, and prayers as they work with you in doing Christ's work in the Church?
Congregation:	We will.
All:	Heavenly Father, we have given our pledge before our friends and Thee to do our work as leaders and followers. Grant, O God, that what we say with our lips we may believe in our hearts and practice in our lives. Give us wisdom to lead this Thy church. And may we so love and serve our Saviour together here that we may soon live together in the hereafter. Amen.

Training Members

"Every church should be a training school for Christian workers. Its members should be taught how to give Bible readings, how to conduct and teach Sabbath school classes, how best to help the poor and to care for the sick, how to work for the unconverted. There should be schools of health, cooking schools, and classes in various lines of Christian help work. There should not only be teaching, but actual work under experienced instructors" (*The Ministry of Healing*, p. 149).

How can the typical pastor with limited training and resources train members? A few suggestions:

Use the trained. — Fit the program of the church to the training your members have. Adventists tend to educate themselves further than the general population.

Do not be frightened by the expertise and intelligence of strong people in your congregation. If you feel strong only so long as you are ministering to weaker parishioners, that may be a sign of an underlying insecurity with you. Don't delegate authority and power only to people you feel you can control, that is, to weaker people. You should minister to the strong as well as to the weak.

Use conference materials and personnel. — Use the conference/mission personnel and materials to train your members. Often departmental directors are underutilized by our churches. These persons are specialists and can provide valuable assistance in conducting seminars and training sessions.

Teach members to care. — Specific training and skill development in different areas of church work are important. But even more important is the ministry of caring. People who truly love people will find ways to help them effectively. Without love, all the seminars and all the certificates in the world profit nothing.

Train members to accept ministry from other members. — Sadly the sick and discouraged, the bereaved and lonely, too often feel ministered to by the church only if the pastor calls. It is embarrassing for elders and other church leaders to reach out to people only to hear them complain that the church is neglecting them only because the pastor has not been there. Ellen White observed, "The greatest help that can be given to our people is to teach them to work for God, and to depend on Him, not on the ministers" (*Testimonies*, vol. 7, p. 19). Train your congregations to understand that ministry is performed by the whole church community working together, rather than by the pastor alone.

CHAPTER 22

Pastoring Large Districts

Many Seventh-day Adventist pastors around the world are leaders of multichurch districts with as many as 20 to 30 congregations. Such leadership requires of the pastor special skills in delegation, training, and administration.

Pastoring a large number of congregations has some serious disadvantages. Pastors can be with a congregation for Sabbath morning service only a few times each year. They cannot relate to each congregation as intimately as they would like to. However, there are some decided advantages in multidistrict pastoring. Pastors find it necessary to train laypersons and delegate leadership responsibilities to them. In the pastor's absence, these leaders do most of the preaching, lead out in evangelism, care for nurturing the members of their congregation, and administer the various functions of the church.

Indeed, the more lay leaders become involved in church leadership, the more rapidly the church grows—a fact borne out in some world divisions by the striking correlation between the growth of the church and number of churches the average pastor serves.

Therefore, working with and training of local church elders are of primary importance to the success of a pastor, particularly of a multidistrict pastor. How can the pastor accomplish this task?

Three Secrets to Success

1. *Provide pastoral leadership and modeling to local church elders.* — With God's help pastors must be what their elders must become. Both need a burden for preaching, nurturing, evangelism, Christian education, and the care of church property. Pastors must be skilled in managing their time and planning their daily, weekly, monthly, and yearly itineraries. They should find ways to have personal contact with their members as often as possible. While doing this, they must carefully guard the time reserved for their own families.

Multidistrict pastors would want to locate their homes in a place that will be convenient for their ministry. Is the environment healthy?

Are the roads convenient all year round? Is public transportation available and easily accessible, particularly if pastoral visitation is dependent on it? How about living conditions and educational opportunities for the family?

2. Be involved in all the congregations. — Itineraries should be planned far enough in advance so each congregation knows when to expect you, and to plan for a preaching service that day. By doing this, the pastor will have more opportunity for personal contact with members. In some places the church may even provide a room on its premises for the pastor's overnight stay.

In large districts there will often be a baptism during these pastoral visits. Elders and laypersons have been sharing their faith during the pastor's absence. They have prepared the candidates thoroughly for baptism. The pastor would conduct the baptismal service, and encourage continued witnessing in preparation for the next visit one or two months later.

The pastor, of course, must be ready for emergencies such as funerals. Congregations will understand such interruptions to planned itineraries. However, attendance at weddings and other special services should be planned in advance and included in your regular itinerary.

3. Provide training in pastoral skills. — Local church elders need help in many areas:

> Conducting a committee meeting
> Sermon preparation and preaching
> Effective visitation program
> Strengthening the departments of the church
> Care of church property
> Deeper understanding of the Adventist message
> Care of new converts

The 1991 General Conference Annual Council recommended that local conferences/missions conduct a minimum of one training seminar for pastors and elders each year. If necessary, local congregations should cover the travel expenses of their elders attending this meeting.

Multidistrict pastors should also plan monthly or bimonthly meetings with all the elders in the district. These meetings will focus on planning for the district as well as each congregation. The plans will deal with evangelism, entering unentered areas of the district, sermon subjects, visitation, district and local congregation goals, pastor's itinerary, and plans.

Training can also be conducted during quarterly district meetings.

Quarterly District Meetings

The quarterly district meeting is being used with exceptional success in some parts of the world field. Where convenient, the entire district membership meets together for an entire weekend, in the spirit of a mini camp meeting. In districts where travel and distance is a problem the pastor may plan to conduct regional district meetings.

The quarterly district meeting aims:

1. To give pastors more exposure to the members of their district.
2. To provide fellowship opportunities for members from various congregations.
3. To develop coordinated evangelism plans for entering unentered areas of the district.
4. To share with each other joys and concerns of different churches.
5. To strengthen the work of church departments.
6. To plan for joint ventures such as helping a new congregation with the construction of a building, or supporting a new evangelistic outreach.

Under the district pastor's guidance, the members of the district will select leaders for their meetings. These individuals working with the pastor will plan for the programs. Schedules permitting, local conference/mission leaders may be invited to help, although they should not dominate the meetings. The pastor would also use the occasion to meet and plan with local church elders of each congregation.

In some parts of the world field, district associations have distinct identifications of their own, such as a name and a banner. During large conference/mission meetings, these banners are displayed. Conference leaders express appreciation for the work of congregations and districts in soul-winning evangelism, Global Mission, departmental support, and visitation.

CHAPTER 23

Church Growth

Finding New Members

Every pastor an evangelist. — Every pastor should be an evangelist. Promoting church programs is important, but adding new members is primary. "Ministers of God, with hearts aglow with love for Christ and your fellow men, seek to arouse those who are dead in trespasses and sins" (*Gospel Workers*, p. 35).

"The ministers are hovering over churches which know the truth while thousands are perishing out of Christ" (*Evangelism*, p. 381). "Instead of keeping the ministers at work for the churches that already know the truth, let the members of the churches say to those laborers: 'Go work for souls that are perishing in darkness. We ourselves will carry forward the services of the church. We will keep up the meetings, and, by abiding in Christ, will maintain spiritual life'" (*Testimonies*, vol. 6, p. 30).

The word "evangelist" is not to be understood only in terms of highly specialized evangelists. The itinerant evangelist is not the only evangelist. Some of Christendom's greatest soul winners have been pastors. Moody was always on the move, but Spurgeon remained in the same church for 35 years. We need Spurgeons as well as Moodys.

Every church an evangelistic center. — Outreach is the price a congregation joyfully pays for the privilege of calling itself Christian. Nothing is so inspiring as an enthusiastic, well-organized church led into evangelistic outreach by a true pastor-evangelist. You can measure the depth of a church's Christian love by how much of its time is spent in outreach.

Even a casual visitor can quickly tell whether or not a church has become a true evangelistic center. When it does, the worship service, the Sabbath school, and every other program of the church continuously keeps visiting nonmembers in mind. Everything said is first passed through a special soul-winning filter: "How will this sound to a nonmember? How will this be perceived by a non-Christian?" Only in such churches do members find it safe to invite nonmember friends to attend.

Every active member a witness. — Sheep enlarge the flock, not the shepherd.

The members of the New Testament church went everywhere telling the story of Jesus. Today too many seem to have joined the secret service; they keep very quiet about the good news of salvation; they end how Mark 16:8 ends: "And they said nothing to anyone, for they were afraid."

As a pastor, if you don't help your members to share their faith, you may be helping them to be lost. "In the great judgment day, those who have not worked for Christ, who have drifted along thinking of themselves, caring for themselves, will be placed by the Judge of the whole earth with those who did evil. They receive the same condemnation" (*The Desire of Ages*, p. 641).

A study of six rapidly growing Adventist churches showed that in these congregations members were exceptionally active at sharing their faith. Interestingly, this was not so much through church-sponsored programs as through spontaneous witnessing. Most souls were won through members relating to people at work and in their neighborhoods. "Let church members during the week act their part faithfully, and on Sabbath tell their experiences. The meeting will then be as meat in due season, bringing to all present new life and fresh vigor" (*Gospel Workers*, p. 199).

Every inactive member a concern. — In many congregations church attendance would double if inactive members could be reclaimed. Active members, especially elders and other officers, can be especially effective in reclaiming the inactive, because they have been friends in the past and understand something about the reasons for dropping out.

Those working for inactive members should be good listeners. They must be prepared to listen to pain without becoming either discouraged or defensive. People often drop out because of anxiety-producing events, either within or outside the church. Cries for help go unnoticed, and eventually they disappear. To reclaim them, the process must be reversed. They must first be heard.

We dare not expect that all who drop out will come back. However, about one fourth may return after one call by a well-trained team of lay visitors from their former church. The sooner you reach out to them, the greater the chances. Of members who are away for five years, about three fourths are unlikely to return.

Every avenue explored. — Look for souls everywhere. Jesus saw them in every place—even at a well in Samaria. Look for souls at every wedding, funeral, and social event. Watch for souls at every church worship service. Get names and addresses of visitors and see that they're followed up. Cultivate an evangelistic bias.

Organize stop-smoking, stress-control, weight-control, and cooking seminars. Subscribe to services giving names and addresses of new residents. Send them a letter welcoming them to the community. Include a list of services offered by the church and invite them to a worship service. Ask someone to look through the newspaper for birth and hospital announcements and send a greeting card in the name of the church.

Prepare and distribute a brochure listing occasions when people should call their pastor. Invite recipients to call the Adventist church during such times if they don't have their own pastor. Take members with you and train them as you give Bible studies. Utilize all the outreach methods that work best in your area. Above everything else, hold some form of evangelistic meetings or seminars on a regular basis. The fruit is always there, but it takes effort and an evangelistic bias to find it.

Preparing New Members *

Conversion before obedience. — "God would be better pleased to have six thoroughly converted to the truth than to have sixty make a profession and yet not be truly converted" (*Gospel Workers*, p. 370). Satan is not the least disturbed by our baptizing large numbers of people—if those we baptize are not thoroughly converted. For his purposes, the more unconverted persons brought into the church the better.

So there is much truth to the argument that we should concern ourselves primarily with whether or not candidates for baptism are converted—that we mustn't expect too much too soon of those just beginning the Christian life. If they're truly converted, the changes in lifestyle will come.

We might liken newly baptized members to fruit trees. Our desire that they bear fruit must take second place to ascertaining that they have been planted (converted and rooted in Christ).

Obedience before baptism. — Complicating the maintaining of balance between conversion and obedience is the fact that we humans can tell whether or not the tree is planted only by the fruit it bears. So while we cannot expect a lot of fruit in the prebaptismal life of the candidate, nevertheless some fruit must be visible. Surely this fruit should include Sabbathkeeping, church attendance, and refraining from the use of harmful substances.

On the other hand, no attempt should be made to require standards not adopted by the general body. It should always be clear that one does not earn salvation by conforming to rules and regulations, but when Christ dwells in the heart the life will be transformed more and more into His image.

Since baptism symbolizes not only the death, burial, and resurrection

---

* See *Church Manual*, chapter 5.

of Jesus, but also the death to and burial of the old life (Rom. 6:1-3), then there cannot be any insincere or incomplete laying aside of things of the world just for baptism. Death to the life of sin and worldliness must precede the burial in baptism. It is wrong to bury one who isn't dead.

Poorly prepared members make weak churches. "The accession of members who have not been renewed in heart and reformed in life is a source of weakness to the church. This fact is often ignored. Some ministers and churches are so desirous of securing an increase of numbers that they do not bear faithful testimony against unchristian habits and practices. Those who accept the truth are not taught that they cannot safely be worldlings in conduct while they are Christians in name" (*Testimonies*, vol. 5, p. 172).

Baptizing candidates who have not evidenced both conversion and obedience is unethical because of the burden it places on succeeding ministers. "A laborer should never leave some portion of the work undone because it is not agreeable to perform, thinking that the minister coming next will do it for him. When this is the case, if a second minister follows the first, and presents the claims that God has upon His people, some draw back, saying, 'The minister who brought us the truth did not mention these things.' . . . How much better it would have been if the first messenger of truth had faithfully and thoroughly educated these converts in regard to all essential matters, even if fewer had been added to the church under his labors" (*Evangelism*, p. 321).

Instruction before commitment. — Those seeking admittance to the church need to know the principles for which the church stands. They should not be asked to commit themselves without knowing what they are committing to. Prebaptismal instruction should include multiple exposure—personal reading and study, Bible studies, public meetings, baptismal class, etc. All instructional avenues, including visual aids, should be used. Different people learn in different ways.

One of the most popular and productive means of instruction in a church's evangelistic program is the pastor's Bible class. This usually combines the baptismal class and class for new members. If the pastor cannot teach it, an elder or another person earnest in soul winning should. The class often meets during the regular Sabbath school classtime. Only nonmembers, new members, or members bringing nonmembers should normally attend.

The class studies special doctrinal lessons. The same series can be repeated from time to time since class members, as they mature in their Christian experience, graduate into regular Sabbath school classes. Subjects should go beyond doctrine to include the spiritual life.

Theoretical instruction, on the other hand, is not adequate to prepare candidates for baptism. They must also experience a relationship with Christ and victory over sin. Therefore, someone should spend considerable time in counsel and prayer with each.

The world church in General Conference session has taken a firm stand supporting thorough baptismal preparation. You are obligated to give each candidate a baptismal certificate or profession of faith certificate that includes in unabbreviated form all the basic beliefs of the church exactly as printed in the *Church Manual* under Fundamental Beliefs of Seventh-day Adventists.

Although abbreviated forms of this may be used for public examination of candidates (see *Church Manual*, chapter 5), each candidate must receive a copy of the fundamental beliefs in full. The Ministerial Association has the proper certificates available.

Church approval before membership. — Final examination of candidates for baptism can be done before the entire church or a representative group such as the elders or church board. However the examination is done, it is unwise and theologically questionable for a pastor to take the sole responsibility. No person or group outside the congregation, not even the General Conference committee, has authority to add or drop a name from the church role. That responsibility rests solely with the local church body. The congregation will take its responsibility more seriously if it has more involvement than a mere raising of hands when a new member joins.

Sometimes members request rebaptism. If the original baptism did not truly represent to the individual a death to sin and new birth experience, perhaps rebaptism is appropriate. However, since baptism is a symbol of spiritual death, and since we die only once, we are usually baptized only once. Baptism is not the appropriate symbol for reconsecration; the Communion service (including foot washing) fills that place.

Children prepared before baptism. — Jesus' counsel to His disciples is His counsel to His ministry: "Let the little children come to Me, and do not forbid them; for of such is the kingdom of God" (Luke 18:16).

Young children should be encouraged to commit their lives to Christ and given assurance of salvation. "Children of eight, ten, or twelve years are old enough to be addressed on the subject of personal religion. Do not teach your children with reference to some future period when they shall be old enough to repent and believe the truth. If properly instructed, very young children may have correct views of their state as sinners and of the way of salvation through Christ" (*Testimonies*, vol. 1, p. 400).

"Never allow your children to suppose that they are not children of God until they are old enough to be baptized. Baptism does not make children Christians; neither does it convert them" (*Child Guidance*, p. 499).

On the other hand, there should be considerable maturity and preparation before baptism. "Baptism is a most sacred and important ordinance, and there should be a thorough understanding as to its meaning. It means repentance for sin, and the entrance upon a new life in Christ Jesus. There should be no undue haste to receive the ordinance" (*Testimonies*, vol. 6, p. 93).

The peak age for baptism of children is about 12 years. Twelve years was the age when a child began to participate as adult in worship services during the Old Testament times. It was the age when Jesus made His first pilgrimage to Jerusalem. From a psychological standpoint as well, 12 is a significant transitional age. There is some advantage in making this public commitment just before entering the difficult teen years. Many pastors begin prebaptismal instruction with children at ages 11 or 12.

Should children be approached concerning baptism? To Adventist parents, their child's baptism may be a sign of parental success; an exceptionally early baptism, a sign of exceptional success. Parents should be cautioned about urging early baptism. If a child is baptized at age 11 or earlier, it should probably be only at the child's choosing. A child who is not baptized by age 12, however, should normally be approached and encouraged, but never unduly urged.

In a Christian home parents should play a pivotal role in preparing children for baptism. "After faithful labor, if you are satisfied that your children understand the meaning of conversion and baptism, and are truly converted, let them be baptized. But, I repeat, first of all prepare yourselves to act as faithful shepherds in guiding their inexperienced feet in the narrow way of obedience. God must work in the parents that they may give to their children a right example, in love, courtesy, and Christian humility, and in an entire giving up of self to Christ" (*Ibid.*, p. 94).

One excellent plan is for parents to present prebaptismal lessons at home. Then, once a week, parents and children come to the church. There one person reviews the week's lesson with the children while another prepares the parents to teach upcoming lessons.

Too often children's baptismal classes lack interest. "Those who give instruction to children and youth should avoid tedious remarks. Short talks, right to the point, will have a happy influence. If there is much to be said, make up for brevity by frequency" (*Child Guidance*, p. 495). Use films or other visual aids if available. You probably will cover more and make a deeper impression.

If you have a church school you may be able to have a class at the school during school hours. Where there is no church school a class can be held at the church; or, children can join the pastor's Bible class during Sabbath school lesson time. Some additional options: You can make the class more effective and interesting by having short oral or written quizzes. Answers help you learn which child needs personal attention outside of class. Encourage children to take a correspondence course before baptism. When your program is over, give the children a set of review questions and let them know there will be a test before baptism. This helps the serious work harder and tests those who may be going along just because someone else is being baptized.

The goal of baptismal preparation should be not the indoctrination of the child, but becoming a new person in Christ Jesus. One way to encourage this is to ask each child at the end of the series to write a few sentences on "Why I Feel I Am Ready to Be Baptized."

Establishing New Members

Jesus told His disciples, "I have chosen you, and ordained you, that ye should go and bring forth fruit, and that your fruit should remain" (John 15:16, KJV).

The most miraculous thing about Pentecost is not that 3,000 were baptized in a day, but that "they continued steadfastly in the apostles' doctrine and fellowship" (Acts 2:42). With the Holy Spirit's aid it is possible to enjoy both quantity and quality in church growth.

Solving the apostasy problem is not a matter of personal preference, but of fulfilling Christ's commission. Jesus said, "Go and make disciples of all nations, baptizing them . . . and teaching them to obey everything I have commanded you" (Matt. 28:19, 20, NIV). In Greek "go," "baptizing," and "teaching" are all participles. They get their force from the verb "make disciples." Going, baptizing, and teaching are not ends in themselves; they are all means to the end of discipling. Jesus was saying that the church's business is making disciples.

Too many Adventist churches are like the fisherman who caught fish but had nothing to show for it because he put them in a sack with a hole at the bottom. God has blessed our church with success in fishing for people. But we're not keeping enough of what we're catching.

Sewing up the hole in the sack cannot replace fishing. A church that does not evangelize will fossilize. But we must realize more fully that our business involves both catching and keeping.

Give new members a high priority. — God has harsh words for shepherds who do not give priority to the weak in their flock. "Woe to the shepherds of Israel who feed themselves! Should not the shepherds feed the flocks? You eat the fat and clothe yourselves with the wool; you slaughter the fatlings, but you do not feed the flock. The weak you have not strengthened, nor have you healed those who were sick, nor bound up the broken, nor brought back what was driven away, nor sought what was lost; but with force and cruelty you have ruled them. So they were scattered because there was no shepherd" (Eze. 34:2-5).

New members tend to go through four crises:
1. The crisis of discouragement comes very quickly when they fail to live up to the high standards they committed themselves to at baptism.
2. The crisis of integration comes after months and occurs when they fail to replace friends from their old life with friends in the congregation.
3. The crisis of values comes probably later when study and family worship are neglected and the Adventist lifestyle is more and more compromised.
4. The crisis of confidence in leadership comes a year or two after baptism when they are given responsibility as leaders and, seeing the imperfect inner workings of the church, become disillusioned.

Pastors should watch for these crises, especially during the first two years of one's membership.

Have a friendship system. — Get new members close to someone they respect who cares about them. Note the three qualifiers. We need to get new members *close* to someone. By nature we tend to deal with new members' weaknesses by correcting or rejecting, by distancing ourselves. The Christian way is to get close enough to help bear them. Romans 15:1 counsels, "We then that are strong ought to bear the infirmities of the weak" (KJV). To "bear" a weak friend, you put your arm around and invite that person to lean on you. You must get very close before your strength can make up for your friend's weakness.

Get them close to someone they *respect*. Spiritual guardianship works well if the guardian is someone respected by, matched with, and attractive to the new member. But if the more successful, better educated members, longer in the church, refuse to give time to the rough-hewn new members, the new members seldom prosper.

Get new members close to someone who *cares* about them. People seldom choose to leave an environment in which they feel wanted, important, needed, loved. If the new members had felt loved elsewhere, chances are they wouldn't have come. If they don't feel loved here, chances are they won't stay.

Have some kind of guardian, sponsor, undershepherd, or friendship system whereby each new member is coupled with an experienced one. New members brought into the church by old members have an almost automatic guardian, and this is one significant reason that those coming into the church this way tend to stay.

The evangelist has been likened to the obstetrician, the pastor to the pediatrician, and the church members to the family. And it's the family that raises the baby. "Those who have newly come to the faith should be patiently and tenderly dealt with, and it is the duty of the older members of the church to devise ways and means to provide help and sympathy and instruction for those who have conscientiously withdrawn from other churches for the truth's sake, and thus cut themselves off from the pastoral labor to which they have been accustomed" (*Evangelism*, p. 351).

One way to operate a guardian program is first to meet with the guardians for training. They should probably commit themselves to the assignment for at least a year. Match members and guardians on Sabbath morning, before or after the baptism. Those baptized come forward and face the congregation. Their guardians come forward and face the new members. A charge is read for the new members and another for their guardians. A copy may be given to each. Guardians shake the hands of new members, which is the first official welcome into the church.

Guardians could be asked to report at least quarterly to the pastor or elder, showing which items on a new-member checklist have been accomplished. The items to which guardians are assigned might include: Go to new members' homes the day of baptism to extend a more personal welcome, perhaps delivering the baptismal certificate. Model Sabbathkeeping by inviting them to your home for Friday sundown worship and, at other times, for Sabbath dinner and afternoon. (New lifestyles are better caught than just taught.) Deliver specified books at appropriate times. Introduce new members to the church library. Make available the union paper, *Adventist Review*, and other periodicals. Show interest in their church attendance. Never let a meeting pass without saying a few friendly words.

Introduce new members to other members. (Research indicates that new members who make six to eight Adventist friends in the first six months almost always remain in the church.) Sit with them in meetings if they desire. After they've spent a maturing period in the pastor's Bible class, integrate them into your Sabbath school class.

Continue their instruction. — "As newborn babes, desire the pure milk of the word, that you may grow thereby" (1 Peter 2:2). Nobody ever ate enough at one banquet to last a lifetime. No evangelistic series or Bible study series provides enough spiritual food to last the rest of one's life. Continue instruction after baptism.

Family members usually don't eat right if they don't come to the table. At the very least, we must include Sabbath school and church attendance in our discipling formula. The absentee should be visited immediately and given the help and encouragement needed. The elder or pastor should be notified if the new member misses three consecutive Sabbath services.

A pastor's class or a new-member class ought to be part of every church program. If taught at Sabbath school lesson study time, it encourages the habit of attending Sabbath school and church. And such a class offers food that fits the new member's appetite and digestion.

Topics should include doctrines, Sabbathkeeping, worship, health, finance, studying the Bible for oneself, prayer life, family worship, family relationships, Christian education, and witnessing. Emphasize relational experience with Christ. Help the new members to know their Bibles. Provide time for sharing experiences and feelings.

A series of follow-up evangelistic meetings is helpful to review in greater detail and in a different setting the truths already presented. Give special attention to the prophetic truths of Daniel and Revelation.

Put them to work. — "When souls are converted, set them to work at once. And as they labor according to their ability, they will grow stronger. It is by meeting opposing influences that we become confirmed in the faith" (*Evangelism*, p. 355).

One of the surest signs that new members have been discipled is their beginning to disciple others. People may be more successful at soul winning when they are first converted than they will ever be again. While eventually friendships with those who are Adventists will predominate, at first their family and friends are for the most part non-Adventists. The combined effect of the new member's influence on old friends and the attractive example of a changed life make powerful soul-winning tools.

No wonder Jesus' first assignment to the former demoniac was "Go home to your friends, and tell them what great things the Lord has done for you, and how He has had compassion on you" (Mark 5:19).

Help new members discover their spiritual gifts and a ministry that fits those gifts. Organize a service opportunity committee whose assignment is to match the gifts of members with church work to be done. Invite new members to a soul-winning class. Take them with you when you give Bible studies or do other church work. Have a special sharing time during the worship hour when new converts give prearranged public testimonies of what the church is doing for them and what they are doing for the church.

Additional options. — Have a special social program the evening after baptism and feature the new members as guests of honor. Give each new member a packet listing and describing the programs and services of the church. Give a copy of the General Conference Ministerial Association pamphlet "In His Church," which introduces them to the church organization. Have a vegetarian food social. (Members bring vegetarian dishes along with recipes. New members bring salad, fruit, or dessert.)

Get the children into church school and Pathfinders. Give special attention to new members in your sermons. Encourage them to organize a support group of persons baptized in a given year—the class of '92. Ask officers to keep new members in mind when making simple work assignments. Keep a recreation program going.

Have an annual banquet featuring those baptized during the year. Ask the conference/mission to sponsor an annual new-member event, in which new members come to some central place to get acquainted with and be ministered to by the conference leadership.

An atmosphere of loving nurture can actually become a form of successful outreach. Nurturing congregations make members feel valued. Such members share this feeling with family and friends, and this attracts to the church those seeking a church home.

CHAPTER 24

Worship Service

Purpose of Worship *

Corporate worship emphasizes both the transcendence and immanence of God: God is great and God is here, God is above us and God is among us. Pastors must become specialists in leading congregations into this worship experience. Too often "we do not obtain a hundredth part of the blessing we should obtain from assembling together to worship God" (*Testimonies*, vol. 6, p. 362).

Worship is encounter. — Many of our pastors have used the same order of service, made the same announcements, sung the same songs, prayed the same prayers, and preached almost the same sermons year after year, decade after decade. We may respect differences in worship style when they result from differences in existing cultures. But we are fearful of adapting our worship to contemporary changes in society.

Some pastors are experimenting with new ways to worship. But these innovations have their problems too. Time may have drained some of the meaning out of traditional worship, but we must not replace it with gimmickry and entertainment. History shows that the church has sometimes lost its influence through failure to change, but it has also suffered because of people who became so obsessed by the need for change that they failed to preserve the distinctive message of the church.

Adventist ministers should not be afraid to experiment with new forms of worship, but we need some guidelines. There's no better place to find them than in that uniquely Adventist chapter, Revelation 14. Verse 7 insists we must be a worshiping people. It is our *worship* of our Creator that makes us unique. Adventist worship has three ingredients:

1. *Adventist worship should be awe-inspiring.* The first angel declares, "Fear God and give glory to Him." "Fear" suggests reverence, awe. Worship does involve having a good relationship with fellow-worshipers;

---

* See *Church Manual*, chapter 7.

a gospel of love cannot be realized in isolation. Worship also involves having warm feelings toward God. But these are no more than parts of the whole. Corporate worship must lead God's people into God's throne room.

The primary purpose of worship is not to feel good, but to see God. "Unless correct ideas of true worship and true reverence are impressed upon the people, there will be a growing tendency to place the sacred and eternal on a level with common things, and those professing the truth will be an offense to God and a disgrace to religion" (*Testimonies*, vol. 5, p. 500).

2. Adventist worship should be joyful. Revelation 14:2, 3 describes God's redeemed in worship: "The sound I heard was like that of harpists playing their harps. And they sang a new song" (NIV). This heavenly harp-playing and singing reveal that joy and feeling belong in worship. When we who are preparing for heaven worship as we will in heaven, our worship will be joyful. It will include our thoughts and our feelings, demanding clear heads and warm hearts. It will include the study of God, and studying God results in love and joy for knowing Him better.

Too many Adventist ministers have had the emotion educated out of them. They so fear emotionalism that they're afraid of any emotion at all. But we are wrong in presuming we defend our pioneers when we defend only the formal and the exclusively rational. Early Adventist worship included great quantities of relating and participating. And sometimes it was highly emotional.

3. Adventist worship should be experiential. Of the song the 144,000 sing, Revelation 14:3 declares, "No one could learn" it (NIV). Why? Because it is a song of personal experience. Nobody else can do it for us. Worship is experiential.

Worship is not a routine. It is not a tradition. It is not a passive, spectator sport. Worship is an event, a happening, a personal interaction between the Creator and the created. Worship is encounter.

Sometimes a worship leader needs to sit alone in the sanctuary, when the people are gone and the pews are empty, and ask the one question that counts: "Did they or did they not meet God today?" Worship is encounter.

Worship deserves planning. — "Is it not your duty to put some skill and study and planning into the matter of conducting religious meetings—how they shall be conducted so as to do the greatest amount of good, and leave the very best impression upon all who attend? You plan in regard to your temporal labors. If you learn a trade, you seek to improve year by year in experience, executing plans that shall show progression in your work. Is your temporal business of as much consequence as the service of God? . . . God is displeased with your lifeless manner in His house, your sleepy, indifferent ways of conducting religious worship" (Ellen G. White, in *Review and Herald*, Apr. 14, 1885).

Pastors have a direct responsibility for Sabbath worship services. However, they should share this responsibility with elders and possibly a worship committee. Such a committee might meet with the pastor about once a month and probe new ways to enhance the worship service.

As a pastor, prepare a Sabbath morning worship countdown sheet, with items you or your elder who serves as platform chair should check or arrange. Such items should include special music, sound system, platform personnel, platform arrangements, hymns for the platform party, and the order for going onto the platform.

The pulpit should not be given to ministers who do not carry valid, current denominational credentials.*

Parts of Worship

Ministering to children. — One significant consideration in determining parts of worship concerns children. Should time be set aside exclusively for them? Some say it is a must, to let children know they are important. Others argue that the whole service should keep children in mind, rather than giving them one small segment as though the rest of the service does not apply to them.

Many pastors include a children's storytime. Children come forward and sit together while a story is told. Congregations tend to enjoy this. It is, however, quite time-consuming, and does not always hold children's attention well. One help is for the platform party to sit with the children while the story is told. This shows their interest in them and helps the storyteller keep control.

Another good plan is to vary the program. Have the story some of the time, and at other times include children in other ways:

1. Prepare a handout with questions on the sermon and encourage the children to write their answers.
2. Address the illustrations in your sermon to children.
3. Take a child on the platform to read the Scripture text or give the benediction.
4. Plan the entire worship service around children once or twice a year, perhaps on Pathfinder Day.

---

* See *Church Manual*, chapter 9.

Some churches take a children's offering during the worship service and use the funds to support the youth program of the church. A child stands in front with a receptacle and children come down the aisle accepting money offered them by worshipers. Although congregations may be averse to more than one offering in the service, this program tends to be popular, because people love giving to children and watching them take the offering to the front.

Introduction to worship. — For the platform party, worship begins before they enter the platform. Platform duties should be quickly organized and the remainder of time spent in prayer. All elders, even if not serving on the platform, may well be present.

The announcement period can be a pastor's dilemma. Church leaders may feel unsupported if not allowed to make announcements. Church members may feel announcements interfere with their worship. Some churches feel announcements are not a part of worship, and therefore schedule them before the platform party goes on the rostrum. Others argue that only half the congregation hears the announcements if they are made between Sabbath school and church service.

To say that announcements cannot be a part of worship is to misunderstand worship. Most announcements have to do with service for the Lord, and leading members into service is a basic purpose of worship. Work for God is not out of place in the worship of God.

A good approach to announcements is to have them written down. Use the bulletin if you have one. Some cannot have bulletins and others choose not to have them so as to allow more spontaneity in the service. But find some way to have written announcements. Remember that good rule: for information, write it; for inspiration or emphasis, tell it.

A good worship leader can make an announcement period worshipful. Let the announcements create an atmosphere of warmth and fellowship. Make them a part of church life. Call them sharing time, body life, joys and concerns, king's business, or worship through service.

Beginning worship. — Although culture will cause considerable variation, here are some basic ingredients of a typical Adventist worship service.

Prelude. This means introductory music. Its purpose is to help people prepare their hearts for worship. Unfortunately, instrumental preludes often do not accomplish this. An option is to lead the congregation in singing.

Introit. This means entrance music. During this time the platform party enters and kneels. "When the minister enters, it should be with dignified, solemn mien. He should bow down in silent prayer as soon as he steps into the pulpit, and earnestly ask help of God. What an impression this will make! There will be solemnity and awe upon the people. Their minister is communing with God; he is committing himself to God before he dares to stand before the people" (*Testimonies*, vol. 5, p. 492).

It is a poor beginning when speakers enter and kneel without the congregation being aware the service has begun. One solution is to have the congregation stand as the platform party enters, and quietly sing a hymn (such as "We Would See Jesus"), thus dedicating themselves in song as ministers dedicate themselves in prayer.

Call to worship. This is a call from the pulpit inviting the congregation to worship. It can be formal, using an excerpt from the Psalms, such as "O come, let us worship and bow down." It can be informal, with words such as "Well, here we are again to worship God." It can be a litany (responsive reading), with congregational participation.

Doxology. This is a hymn praising God. The morning hymn may serve this purpose.

Invocation. The invocation invites or invokes God's presence. The pastoral prayer can include this purpose.

The purposes of these introductory parts to worship sometimes overlap. All parts are probably not necessary. If any is not meeting its purpose, it has become superfluous. Defend the purposes, but experiment with more effective ways of accomplishing them.

Music.* — The value of music in worship can hardly be exhausted, if we only understand all its potential effects. "Music should have beauty, pathos, and power" (*Testimonies*, vol. 4, p. 71). It is both unfortunate and understandable when musicians and pastors disagree over church music. The musician tends to be music-oriented, and the pastor audience-oriented. The first may ask if the music is well done, but the second asks if it was effective with the worshipers. Pastors must be patient with musicians, and so must musicians be with pastors. Pastor, let your musicians be the authority on music, and it will be easier for them to let you be the authority on worship.

Some worshipers can be led into worship by melody alone. Many,

---

* If yours is a small congregation with no instrument or instrumentalist, you may want to purchase the organ and piano accompaniment now available on compact discs for *The SDA Hymnal* through the GC Ministerial Supply Center.

however, need words; therefore, vocal music generally receives priority in worship. Even then, words of an unfamiliar piece sung by a soloist or a choir may be difficult to understand. Worshipers would appreciate having in their hands the words of such songs.

Choirs are a blessing in worship, yet they must not replace congregational singing. "The singing is seldom to be done by a few. The ability to sing is a talent of influence, which God desires all to cultivate and use to His name's glory" (*Evangelism*, p. 504).

Some suggestions to provide variation in music:

1. Have congregational singing during the intermission between Sabbath school and church service, and include at least one new song.
2. Feature Scripture songs instead of hymns from the hymnal.
3. Have youth choruses.
4. Rather than singing all the verses of a hymn, read a verse or every other verse to focus attention on the hymn's meaning.
5. Divide the church in groups and try some of the canons (rounds).
6. If there is no choir, let the congregation sing the introit and responses.
7. Conclude a sermon by inviting the congregation to stand, join hands, and sing as a symbol of commitment and unity.
8. Whenever a hymn is used in worship, note the date in your hymnal so you do not repeat some too often and use others too seldom.
9. Find other ways in your culture of incorporating acceptable traditional instruments of music.

Prayer. — It is a solemn thing to speak to the people for God. Is it not more solemn to speak to God for the people? If so, prayer may be considered the most significant part of worship. The Adventist tradition has been to have an elder or a member lead in prayer, and this has its advantages: the elder or the member represents the congregation in a very direct way. However, pastors are abdicating one of the most precious parts of worship leadership if they never lead their congregations in prayer. One solution is for the pastor to pronounce the benediction.

Posture. Kneeling is a most significant posture for prayer. Jesus "knelt down and prayed" (Luke 22:41). Numerous Bible passages indicate this posture (2 Chron. 6:13, Ezra 9:5, 6; Ps. 95:6; Acts 7:59, 60; Acts 9:40; Acts 20:36; Acts 21:5; Eph. 3:14). "Both in public and private worship it is our duty to bow down upon our knees before God when we offer our petitions to Him. This act shows our dependence upon God" (*Selected Messages*, Book 2, p. 312).

We must not, however, conclude that the Lord will not accept the petitions when minister and congregation remain standing, as during the invocation, benediction, or evangelistic service, or when all stand in consecration while prayer is offered. We find situations in the Scriptures in which, under certain circumstances, worshipers stood while a blessing or benediction was pronounced, as in 1 Kings 8:55: "Then he stood and blessed all the congregation of Israel with a loud voice."

Ellen White concurs: "It is not always necessary to bow upon your knees in order to pray" (*The Ministry of Healing*, p. 510). There are also circumstances when the condition of the floor or the seating arrangements make it difficult or well-nigh impossible for the congregation to kneel.

If prayer is the "opening of the heart to God as to a friend," then the position of the heart or mind is paramount over the position of the knees. Posture in prayer is important, but it is only symbolic. Scripture counsels, "So rend your heart, and not your garments" (Joel 2:13). God considers the inner attitude above the outer expression. Pride that finds our clothes too precious or our knees too tender for kneeling before our Maker is tragic irreverence. But pride that leaves us standing on the inside while kneeling on the outside is irreverence also.

Elements. Public prayer should be thought through in advance. It should be relevant to the needs of the congregation. We can think of prayer as including seven elements. Not all need to be in every prayer, but all should be considered as you plan your prayer. Their order is significant, based on the supposition that we must first show reverence for God and then get right with God before we ask anything else of God.

1. *Address to God.* Remember God's name is holy. Speak of it in prayer, but do not repeat it meaninglessly.
2. *Praise.* Adore God's name, and appreciate what He has done.
3. *Repentance.* Ask His forgiveness for the past.
4. *Dedication.* Ask His strength for the future. Commit yourself to Him before requesting things of Him.
5. *General intercession.* Intercede for God's work, world leaders, and your congregation, including the young, old, parents, ill, discouraged, etc.
6. *Specific intercession.* Remember special prayer requests, the meeting itself, and the speaker.
7. *Conclusion.* Affirm the right by which we approach the throne room: "In Jesus' name."

Length. "One or two minutes is long enough for any ordinary prayer" (*Testimonies*, vol. 2, p. 581). "Prosy, sermonizing prayers are uncalled for and out of place in public. A short prayer, offered in fervor and faith, will soften the hearts of the hearers; but during long prayers they wait impatiently, as if wishing that every word might end it" (*Gospel Workers*, p. 179).

Prayers tend to be long, not so much because we have so much to say, but because we say each thing forwards, backwards, then from the middle both ways. Having in your mind an outline such as the one above will eliminate that tendency. Requests for prayer announced publicly need not be individually repeated. Occasionally the pastor or elder having prayer should be required to hold a 2-year-old child while prayer is offered. It would shorten their prayers.

Additional suggestions.
1. Occasionally have five people share the prayer, each praying for one of the five central elements mentioned above. Even children could do this.
2. Instead of the person up front offering the entire prayer, the individual may "lead" the congregation by first addressing God, then suggesting topics for the congregation to pray silently. The prayer leader should pause after suggesting a topic.

Offering. — The offering appeal should be brief, intelligent, and worshipful. Giving is a direct part of worship. It has an overwhelming potential for teaching the basic Christian concepts of self-denial, sacrifice, and trust. Hence the offering appeal must emphasize a *spiritual* motivation. It should also explain the *financial* need. It should say why we give our money and where the money is going. People will give if they are spiritually motivated and are convinced of a practical need.

Scripture reading. — Scripture is central to Christian worship. Jesus began His public ministry in Nazareth by reading from Scripture. Paul instructed that his Epistles be read in the churches (Col. 4:16; 1 Thess. 5:27).

Passages chosen must be relevant to the emphasis of the day. Unfortunately, the congregation doesn't tend to perceive this relevance. Some pastors skip separate Scripture reading time and ask their congregations to turn to and possibly read aloud some passages during the sermon. This may require pew Bibles so everyone reads from the same version.

Passages must be well read. A well-prepared reading of Scripture can provide a moving experience. When the Levites officiated, "they read distinctly from the book," and "all the people wept, when they heard the words of the Law" (Neh. 8:8, 9).

Encourage audience participation. Use responsive readings. Vary the ones reading Scripture and thus reflect the diversity of the congregation. Have a shut-in read the Scripture on videotape when you visit, then replay it on Sabbath. Prepare an illustrated Scripture reading. Many Psalms lend themselves to illustration through nature slides, video, etc.

Have a church school teacher or Sabbath school division leader work with children to dramatize the Scripture. This, when thoughtfully and reverently done, can become a highlight of the service. The entire sanctuary service in Israel was drama, an illustration of how Jesus saves. As a people who emphasize the sanctuary we should not be afraid to use the same teaching technique.

The portrayal can be as simple as each participant taking the part of a person in the Scripture and reading that individual's words. It can be mimed. Scenes depicted can be reenacted as they must have taken place, or they can be contemporized. This can be an excellent device to involve youth, not only in the worship service, but in understanding how the Bible applies to life as they live it.

Preaching. — Too often preaching tends to be negative. Your first calling is not to denounce sin, but to announce salvation. The word "gospel" means good news. If you're not preaching good news, you're not preaching the gospel!

Preach the Bible relevantly. Adventist preaching must always be Bible-centered. Our people want to know and they must know what the Bible teaches. Stories, sociological or philosophical discourses, with the Bible scarcely opened, will not feed the soul or produce revival and reformation.

The truly biblical sermon does not just include the Bible. It begins with the Bible. Biblical preachers come to the Bible first in their sermon preparation. As nearly as possible, they come with a blank mind, knowing nothing but their passage or topic. They don't open the Book looking for something that agrees with what they want to say. They open it to find what it wants them to say.

When you begin biblically, you have an inexhaustible supply of sermon material. Your well is guaranteed never to run dry. Having published more than 3,000 sermons, Charles Spurgeon declared, "After 35 years I find that the quarry of Holy Scripture is inexhaustible. I seem hardly to have begun to labor in it."

When you begin biblically, you don't get bored with your preaching. Why? Because you are continually learning rather than continually repeating over and over what you already know.

Make the Bible relevant, but do not let relevance replace the Bible. Relevance is absolutely essential, but it can have a rather deceptive influence on our preaching. For example, some preachers tend to oust guilt-producing sermons, and preach only self-esteem-building sermons. In the quest for relevance, let not the Word and its salvation theme suffer.

Plan annually. To bring a new enthusiasm to your preaching, try yearly pulpit planning. Once a year—possibly in the summer, when church activities tend to slow down—plan your preaching for the next year.

Planning requires looking in both directions, so first list the sermons you have preached in the past year—or even better, in the past two or three years. Look for what you have neglected or overemphasized. Then, on the basis of your findings, the denominational and secular calendar year, the needs of your congregation, and your particular interests and concerns, select the topics and passages for next year's preaching.

Yearly planning saves time. It takes much less time than what you would spend through the year if you depended on picking sermon topics helter-skelter.

Yearly planning disciplines you to grow. You will be pulled away from preaching only on favorite areas, and you will be pressed toward wrestling with some you have neglected.

Yearly planning produces balanced preaching. Preachers who love their people provide them with food that's not only tasty and nutritious but also varied. When you have been feeding the congregation an unvaried diet based on whatever you like best, the process of planning a sermon year will practically force you to face the fact.

Heresy does not so often come from preaching what is false, but from an incomplete presentation of the gospel. It results from an overemphasis upon one truth of the gospel at the expense of other truths. Yearly planning produces balanced preaching, and balanced preaching produces balanced Christians.

Prepare early. Do your Bible study and reading the first days of the week. Keep at it until you feel you know about what God wants said. But you still won't quite know how He wants you to say it. The ideas need to soak in your mind. You must find illustrations and practical applications.

Now go about your other duties. Let the sermon wander through your mind, floating somewhere between the conscious and subconscious. Starting your sermon early produces these dramatic rewards:

It eases the pressure and increases creativity. Creativity despises deadlines. Last-minute sermon preparation produces first-rate ulcers and second-rate sermons. The brain's filing system tends to jam when pressed too hard. But if you take off the pressure, it may produce profusely.

It saves time. Instead of gazing at the ceiling trying to come up with a story or poring over books of old illustrations, let illustrations come out of your week. Both consciously and subconsciously your sermon will grow as you are working.

It makes your sermons practical and interesting. Sermons that grow out of the present fit the present. As you visit, as you counsel, as you face moments of trauma that engulf your congregation, as you relate to your own family, ask, "Could my sermon help here?" or "Is there something here that could illustrate my sermon?" The sermon whose illustrations and practical applications grow out of ministry to your congregation is bound to fit your congregation.

Stay close to Christ. Preaching is overflowing. You cannot overflow an empty cup. If you are a discouraged preacher who can't seem to come up with anything to preach, you are looking at the empty cup of your own soul and trying to get it to pour out on others what it does not have. First fill your own cup. Only then are you ready to overflow.

On the other hand, the cup that is overfilled has to overflow. When you are filled with Jesus, it is easier to speak about Him than to be quiet. You can hardly wait for your next sermon. The Water of Life floods your congregation.

Order of Worship

"For God is not the author of confusion. . . . Let all things be done decently and in order" (1 Cor. 14:33-40). Every feature of the worship service must be related to the whole, move toward an objective, and culminate in congregational response. It should be planned so as to progress toward a point of commitment.

Congregational participation. — We tend to think of worship as consisting of: preacher as actor, God as prompter, and congregation as audience. Actually, true worship consists of: congregation as actor, preacher as prompter, and God as audience. "Much of the public worship of God consists of praise and prayer, and every follower of Christ should engage in this worship" (Ellen G. White, in *Signs of the Times*, June 24, 1886). Thus, for each worshiper, worship must become a participating event.

Litany (responsive reading). Responsive reading fits well for the call to worship, Scripture reading, offering dedication, or sermon response. The reading may be placed in the bulletin or read from the hymnal, but the centrality of the Bible in worship is emphasized when people read directly from Bibles. However, this involves a little training of the congregation and providing pew Bibles so everyone has the same version. The reading can be divided in many imaginative ways, such as: leader, women, men, choir, left side, right side, balcony, all, etc.

Singing. Congregational singing works well for the introit, prayer response, and benedictory response. An effective offertory is the congregation singing "We Give Thee but Thine Own." Many hymnal songs work well for these responses; so do such informal songs as "We Have This Hope," "Father, We Love You," "Because He Lives," "Hallelujah," etc.

Many pastors use the time between Sabbath school and the church service for congregational singing. Sometimes a small group may lead out in the singing, with music from either the hymnal or other sources.

Audience movement. There is both psychological and physical purpose in planning properly spaced audience movement (usually standing or kneeling) throughout the worship service. The psychological purpose is to get worshipers actively involved in the service. The physical purpose is to keep the blood circulating. For the latter reason, it is ideal to have the congregation on their feet shortly before the sermon begins.

Audience movement may include inviting worshipers with special prayer requests to come forward and kneel together for the morning prayer.

Sample worship formats. — Pastors often list worship items in their bulletins under general divisions, such as:

1. Praising, Praying, Preaching.
2. We Gather, We Praise, We Proclaim, We Respond, We Return.
3. Adoration, Proclamation, Dedication.
4. Church at Work, Church at Worship.
5. Worship Through Praise, Worship Through Giving and Receiving, Worship Through the Word, Worship Through Dedication.

Sample worship formats are included in the *Church Manual*, (chapter 7). Here are additional formats:

LONGER FORMAT:

Prelude	Instrument or congregational singing.
Introit	Music by choir, instrument, or congregation.
Call to worship	If included in bulletin, congregation can participate.
Doxology	Not necessary if congregation sang introit.
Invocation	
Hymn of praise	
Prayer	Response by choir, instrument, or congregation.

WORSHIP SERVICE

Welcome and announcements May include personal ministries.
You may want announcements earlier, but the entire congregation won't be present. Another option is to place the announcements just before prayer and conclude the announcements with prayer requests. Soul-winning experiences and interviews should be included somewhere. This could be during announcements or while the offering is taken.

Offering If the offertory doesn't hold worshipers' attention, use this time to have testimonies and interviews, or invite the children to make their way forward for children's story. Congregation may sing as offering is brought forward and dedicated, thus emphasizing giving as an act of worship.

Scripture reading

Music Special music or a pulpit hymn introducing the sermon.

Sermon

Hymn of invitation/dedication

Benediction Response by choir, instrument, or congregation.

Postlude

SHORTER FORMAT:

Prelude

Introit Congregation standing for silent prayer or singing as speakers kneel.

Hymn Congregation remains standing.

Prayer Includes invocation of God's presence.

Announcements May include lay activities.

Offering

Sermon

Benediction

Additional suggestions. —
1. Have on the platform people from different groups within the congregation—youth, parents, grandparents, young marrieds, singles, etc.
2. Let a family comprise the platform party.

3. Attempt to represent the congregation's age spectrum every week.
4. Use graphics and visual aids. Do a little study into the different sensory types—audio, visual, kinesthetic. This will lead you to look for new and different ways to reach people. Since all don't learn the same way, worship should include several different ways of reaching worshipers.
5. Have special Sabbaths, high days, days when members invite visitors and come anticipating an extraordinary blessing.
6. Train your congregation to expect an appeal at the end of every sermon. You might print "invitation" or "appeal" as a separate item in your bulletin. Remind listeners at the beginning of your sermon that they will be asked to respond. They will listen differently.

Don't follow a format just because it's expected, but because it works in bringing your congregation into a meaningful encounter with God. Worship is encounter.

CHAPTER 25

Prayer Meeting

Importance of Prayer

Churches should emphasize the ministry of prayer. It follows that churches should also emphasize prayer meeting. "Seek every opportunity to go where prayer is wont to be made. Those who are really seeking for communion with God will be seen in the prayer meeting" (*Steps to Christ*, p. 98).

Why is prayer meeting not well attended? Are members too busy, too far away, or just too lethargic? Or is it because the pastor places a low estimate on it?

We may consider many ways of strengthening the prayer meeting, but we must begin with one emphasis: however the midweek service is planned, it should give high priority to prayer. Call it at a more convenient time or place—but pray. Name it Fellowship Hour, Prayer and Praise, or Hour of Power—but pray. Pray in small groups, focus on a prayer list or prayer box, pray conversational or burden prayers in which each prays about only one special item—but pray. Prayer meeting is for praying.

Ways to Increase Attendance

Create a dynamic atmosphere. — Hold prayer meeting in an appropriate room. A small group in a large room reduces intimacy, dampens fellowship, and infers defeat. Have the temperature comfortable before people begin arriving. Let them enter a well-lighted room. Have some music as people come, even if it must be recorded music. Start on time; don't wait for all to arrive; begin with something that doesn't demand everyone's presence.

Be dialogic. — Prayer meeting is more for teaching than preaching. Presentations should usually be no more than 20 minutes. Cultivate a

---
See *Church Manual*, chapter. 7

purposeful plan for dialogue.

Prayer meeting tends to attract a Bible study-oriented group. Plan a series based on discussing together a Bible book, Bible chapters, Bible characters, Adventist beliefs, prophecy, etc.

Save time by relating prayer meeting to your next Sabbath's sermon. Give the principal passage of your upcoming sermon in the bulletin the Sabbath before and invite people to study it before prayer meeting. Present a brief exegesis of the passage at the prayer meeting, and then ask small groups to discuss how it applies to their lives. Have each small group share a summary of their discussion with the full group. Use this feedback in preparing your sermon for Sabbath.

Emphasize fellowship. — People are invariably attracted to any place where they feel a warm fellowship. Prayer meeting should include time for testimonies, reflections, and sharing.

Keep testimonies short—and current. Ask "What has the Lord done for you this week?" "What prayer has been answered this month?" "What soul-winning experience have you had this year?" Restrain the dominant and encourage the timid. Assign testimonies: favorite Bible text, how they became Christians, etc.

Encourage relational testimonies. "I" centered testimonies are generally wearisome. Those that testify to what other individuals or the church as a whole have done create the fellowship atmosphere.

Have a church night. — How helpful it would be for busy families, including the pastor's, if weeknight programs could be coordinated so families could spend more evenings together. A church night does this. Begin a fellowship hour early in the evening with a soup supper. Then for the remainder of the evening hold prayer meeting, Pathfinders, committee meetings, choir practice, recreation, etc.

Additional suggestions. —
1. Hold a Testimony Countdown or some other seminar-type program.
2. When conducting your last meeting of a baptismal class, suggest, "Now, prayer meeting will take the place of our next regular meeting."
3. Let an elder who has a particular gift for it specialize in planning and leading prayer meeting.
4. Hold prayer meeting as small study groups in the homes of members—possibly elders.

CHAPTER 26

Visitation

Pastoral Visitation

Importance of house calls. — In most cultures a homegoing preacher makes a churchgoing people. Home visitation is important for both pastors and their people: for people because they need to know that their pastors care; for pastors because they need to know how their people live during the week. As someone said: "The road from study to pulpit runs in and out of houses and hospitals, farms and factories."

Ellen White comments: "Remember that a minister's work does not consist merely in preaching. He is to visit families in their homes, to pray with them, and to open to them the Scriptures. He who does faithful work outside of the pulpit will accomplish tenfold more than He who confines his labors to the desk" (*Testimonies*, vol. 9, p. 124).

Problems of house calls. — In many countries clergy are the only professionals still making house calls. This fact in itself should indicate some problems involved in house calls. These include:

Absence. Because husband and wife often work away from home daytime visitation is often difficult.

Distance. Many ministers pastor large churches or large numbers of churches. Some have very limited transportation available.

Inaccessibility. In most cities high-rise apartments often cannot be entered except by special invitation.

Safety. In many cities it is unsafe for the pastor to visit some streets at night, and people are afraid to open their doors to someone they don't know.

Time. Visitation is very time-consuming. Under some circumstances pastors spend more time on the road getting to a home than in the home, and they wonder if they are using their time efficiently.

Suggested solutions to the problems of house calls:

1. When you first come to the district, visit every member. Prove at the beginning that you care. After that, let elders and other members do much of the regular visitation while you emphasize specialized visiting as outlined below.

2. Give high priority to visiting those in special groups. A busy pastor overburdened with regularly visiting everybody may neglect those who need help the most. Special groups include: evangelistic interests, spiritually discouraged, sick, grieving, beginning marriages, failing marriages, new parents, parents whose children are leaving home, etc. Many in these groups can be visited in the daytime, saving precious evening hours.

3. Train and encourage members to contact the church. Prepare and distribute a handout, "When You Should Call Your Pastor," listing special occasions such as:
- Before going to the hospital.
- When a baby is born.
- When there is a death in the family.
- When there is a prolonged reaction to grief.
- Before giving up on your marriage.
- When you would like to talk or pray about a difficult situation.
- When you are spiritually depressed.
- When you know of someone in need of spiritual help.

4. Visit by telephone. It may be only half as effective, but if you can make 10 times as many calls per hour, you have accomplished five times as much good.

5. Make yourself available at church, especially on Sabbath. This kind of visiting with people is by far the most economical of both time and money. Be in the church foyer a half hour before Sabbath school. Encourage your spouse to do the same if possible.

Visiting people as they come in gives you more time with each than just a handshake as they leave. Don't miss Sabbath school, but visit in the foyer for 30 minutes before it begins. As Sabbath school ends, and if you find time, visit those who arrive for the church service only. You need especially to befriend and encourage these people.

Purpose of house calls. — The purpose of the pastoral call is not social, is not utilitarian, and is not to prove you've been in every home. Although social interest, increasing church attendance, or raising money may be involved in the pastor's visit, the primary purpose of the pastoral call must always be spiritual.

Planning of house calls. — *Before the visit.* Have a card file. People needing special attention should be flagged. Remove from the file the cards of those you wish to visit. This avoids the necessity of recopying information.

Some pastors plan by territories; scheduling all visits in the same area in one time frame saves time. Others prefer visiting by groups of people. For example, they would choose to visit one day the recently bereaved; this allows them to prepare themselves and their thoughts especially for that group. Still others designate at least one day a week to visit prospective members.

Visit by appointment. In many parts of the world, to show up at a home without prior arrangement is not only ill manners, but could well be a waste of time, for you may be knocking at the door when no one's home. However, you don't have to spend your own time making appointments. A church volunteer can do this by contacting people at church on Sabbath or by the phone, if it's available. A retired person or a shut-in may have just the gift and time to be involved in this ministry

During the visit. A pastoral visit has three basic parts, in the order given below.

1. Be a friend. Begin on a social level. Talk little and listen much during this part of the visit. As Will Rogers said: "Everybody is ignorant—only on different subjects." Sit in genuine ignorance and awe as people tell you about their interests. Most men want to talk about their work and most women about their families.

Don't compete with the TV or radio if you can avoid it. It may be discourteous to ask that it be turned off, especially if children or nonmembers are listening. Try lowering your voice so it can't quite be heard above the radio or TV. Often someone will voluntarily turn it off.

2. Be a Christian friend. When a natural opening comes, move the conversation in a spiritual direction. Whether or not the Bible is read may depend on the home, the culture, and your personality. Many pastors are most comfortable with a pocket Bible. They keep this out of sight when arriving so as not to appear too sanctimonious to non-Christians. Yet it can be brought out when appropriate.

3. Be a praying Christian friend. Nearly always pray. Kneel if appropriate. Seldom ask permission to pray; it embarrasses people by inferring that prayer may be out of place in their home. Do invite the children or others present to join the group. You should have every name memorized by this time, and pray for each individually. Include the non-Christians, if any, in the home. Pray for the absent members. Always pray a blessing on the home.

Leave almost immediately, while the spiritual tone of the prayer prevails. Don't let anyone take your coat when you arrive. You then lose control of your leaving. They can keep you there as long as they keep your coat and the visit ends on a mere social note.

Most pastoral visits should be 10 to 20 minutes in length. Occasionally 30 minutes may be acceptable, especially if you're just getting acquainted. Longer visits tend to become social calls. Don't give members the idea that you've nothing to do but sit and talk all day.

On the other hand, don't spend the entire time on the edge of your seat as though you can hardly wait to get away. Sit back, relax, listen, but only for a limited time. You're on the King's business, and you must leave the impression that His business is both thriving and demanding.

If, in spite of all your planning, no one is at home, write a personal note on the back of a calling card. It's half as good as a visit. It proves you came. It shows you care.

After the visit. Go down the street and around the corner, stop and update your card. Write down names if you didn't already have them. Note where absent children are. Record the family's concerns and your impressions. Remembering these details on subsequent visits convinces the family of your genuine interest.

Lay Visitation

Every member of your congregation should probably receive a home visit from the church every year—but not always by the pastor.

Parish plan. — Inaugurate a parish or undershepherd plan, organizing your members into parish zones, probably on a geographical basis. An elder, assisted by a deacon and a deaconess, could be in charge of a parish zone. The elder would lead out in planning visitation as well as other programs that build spiritual strength of the group. It is unfair, however, to assume that every elder, deacon, or deaconess has the gift or interest for such a ministry. Each must be allowed to fight in his or her own armor.

Match. — Visitors properly matched with those they visit bring strengths surpassing what the pastor's visit might bring. Those who have gone through bereavement may visit the bereaved. Singles visit singles, etc.

Train. — Offer specialized visitation training. You could offer brief classes in each of the following types of visiting: general membership, new contacts, inactive members, shut-ins, nursing homes, hospitals. Let members choose their class and a specialized visitation that fits their experience, interests, and gifts.

"On-the-job training" is best. Take someone along when you visit—especially elders, who in turn will train others to visit. Show them how a visit should progress from social, to spiritual, to praying levels.

Be creative. — Use the church bulletin board creatively. Try placing a notice: "Visit a shut-in today. Turn over the card of the one you will visit." Hang a card on each hook placed in the board. One side of each card says "Visit me" and contains the name and address of a shut-in. The other side of the card says "Thank you."

Make Communion Sabbath a day for elders, deacons, and deaconesses to visit and share Communion with those who would have attended church if they were able.

Teach your congregation to accept ministry from each other. Members should be helped to see that a spiritual visit from another church member is a "pastoral" visit.

Help your people learn to care. Any organizational plan will break down if your members don't really care about others. On the contrary, it is amazing how much visitation gets done with how little organization when members simply love people.

Hospital Visitation

Guidelines for a hospital visit. —
1. Turn gossip into a gift. Assign members who always seem to know everything that goes on the responsibility of notifying you when a member is hospitalized.
2. Go immediately. Hospital stays are getting shorter and shorter, and people feel neglected and even rejected if someone representing the church doesn't visit.
3. Go afternoons if possible. In the evening there are likely to be other visitors, which may interfere with a spiritual visit. Save evenings for work that can't be done during the day.
4. Check at the nurses' station as a courtesy to the caregivers. Also, you can learn a little about the patient's illness and make sure a visit is not out of order. This is especially important in an obstetrics ward, where special rules may apply.
5. Befriend others in the room.
6. Don't wake the patient. To rest is difficult in a hospital. Write a sentence or two on your calling card and leave it by the bed.
7. Don't sit or lean on the bed. This can bring serious discomfort to a sore body.
8. Do touch with a lingering handshake as you begin your visit. It shows you care.
9. Be cautious in asking about illness. It is better to have gotten this information at the nurses' station. However, the direction of your visit somewhat depends on why the patient is there, and the nurse may not be available or willing to tell you. The patient may be facing immediate surgery or a serious diagnosis, such as malignancy. You might ask, "Are you in for something very serious?" or "What has been happening to you?" You'll learn whatever the person wants to share about the illness. Or ask, "How are you feeling?" The answer will give you clues as to how you might minister and how long you should stay. Leave

almost immediately if the patient is in pain.

Be sensitive to pretended feelings. Some think really good Christians should not experience fear or worry. They pretend, especially to the pastor, a courage and bravado they don't genuinely feel.

10. Be positive. The hospital is not a place for frivolity. Hurting patients want their negative feelings respected, but bring a little sunshine.
11. Listen much and talk little. But let patients know you have heard and understood them. Your mere presence reminds patients of what you have already taught them.
12. Read a Scripture text if appropriate. Carry a pocket Bible.
13. Be brief. A 5 to 10 minute visit is usually adequate.
14. Pray. Take the patient's hand and pray specifically for the needs expressed. Pray a special prayer with new mothers, blessing their babies.
15. Leave almost immediately, while the aura of prayer prevails.

Scripture readings. — Keep, in the flyleaf of your pocket Bible, scriptures that fit various visitation situations. For hospital visitation, such Scriptures might include:

General Scripture texts:
  Ps. 23; 46; 103; 121
  Jer. 30:17
  Matt. 11:28-30; 15:30, 31
  Rom. 5:3-5; 8:16-39
  James 5:13-16
  3 John 2

Before surgery:
  Ps. 91; 103:1-5
  Isa. 43:1-3; 58:8, 9

In pain:
  Isa. 26:3, 4
  Matt. 11:28, 29
  John 14:27

Facing death:
  Ps. 23; 90:1-6, 10
  Isa. 56:11
  John 3:14-16
  John 14:1-4, 25-27
  Rom. 8:35-39
  2 Cor. 5:1-4

On recovery:
  Ps. 34:4-8; 107:1-9
  Luke 17:12-18

Birth of child:
  Matt. 18:1-6
  Mark 10:13-16
  Luke 1:46-49

CHAPTER 27

Counseling

In the general population, of those who experience emotional difficulties, 40 to 50 percent will first seek a minister or religious leader for help. The percentage among churchgoers, of course, is higher. The pastor can usually deal adequately with about 80 percent of cases.

Counseling Limitations

Ministerial ordination bestows neither omnipresence nor omniscience. As ministers, we must know our limitations.

Limited time. — Our principal business is to preach the gospel. Everything else, including personal counseling, must be secondary. Pastors do have to respect and deal with the emotional problems of their parishioners, but Bible-based, Christ-centered preaching, emphasizing hope and forgiveness, will prevent many of the difficulties for which people seek counsel.

Prevention is better than cure. Pastors major in prevention when their ministry centers on the assurance of salvation through Christ. Churches major in prevention when they sponsor such programs as marriage enrichment, which prevent or help cope with problems.

In counseling, pastors need to keep in mind certain cautions. More than other counselors, pastors are continually confronted with chronic complainers. Some seek only sympathy and attention rather than help. They come because pastors are sympathetic—and they're free. Some counselees go from pastor to pastor seeking one who will be conscience for them. Finding one who would approve what they want to do, they'll quote that pastor the rest of their lives as an excuse for their behavior. Pastors sometimes become susceptible out of kindness, lack of counseling expertise, or because of their own egos—they need to be needed.

Love those seeking sympathy or wanting your approval, but don't let them dominate your time. Limit your counseling to four or five sessions at most, making your time and expertise available to more people.

Limited expertise. — Know when to refer. Pretending a counseling expertise that you really don't have may not only be harmful to the counselee, but even lead to legal difficulties for you and the church.

Consider the following factors when deciding whether or not to refer: How *strongly* is the counselee experiencing grief, anger, jealousy, guilt, loneliness, resentment, or bewilderment? Is the person so overwhelmed by these feelings that he or she cannot function in a normal way? Or is it only a concern that the individual is struggling with while still able to function normally? Has the problem arisen recently, or is it a long-term pattern?

Watch for such inappropriate responses as illogical verbalizing, uncontrollable emotions, staring into space or inattentiveness, extreme depression, inability to make simple decisions, belief that others are out to get them, and loss of control in eating and other habits. These can be psychotic symptoms, and people who exhibit these should be referred to a professional counselor or psychiatrist who is trained in treating severe conditions.

Be aware ahead of time what resources are available in your area so you can refer cases you are not qualified to handle. You can usually find help by inquiring at your local mental health department or hospital chaplain's office.

Crisis Counseling

Most counseling for most pastors should be limited to short-term or crisis counseling. Five suggestions for crisis counseling:

1. *Learn to listen*. — Listening flatters. It shows the counselee you care. Talking clarifies the problem for the counselee and is in itself excellent therapy. By putting their feelings into words, people move from the emotional to a more rational level, where they begin finding answers for themselves.

Listening clarifies the problem for the counselor. While you're talking you're not learning. When you concentrate too much on coming up with answers, you may misunderstand some of the questions. The one word that likely does more good in counseling than all other words put together is "Uh-huh." It shows you're listening and encourages the speaker to continue.

Be totally accepting and unshockable in what you hear. Be as nonjudgmental as Jesus was toward the woman caught in adultery.

Hear both sides. In any relational problem, never assume that what you hear from one side is completely accurate—or that the person is deliberately lying. More likely, it's a case of being right in one's own eyes. The implied flattery that comes with you being selected as the counselor tends to bias your thinking in favor of the counselee. After all, anyone who had the good sense to seek your counsel couldn't be too far wrong! Never try to make a judgment without hearing both sides.

2. Concentrate on solutions. — Spend most of your time on solutions, not problems. Some people go over and over a problem wanting only sympathy and refusing to work on a solution. If they solved their problem, they wouldn't feel important any longer. They'd lose the excuse for coming. Not only are you wasting your time with such people; you are hurting them by over sympathizing with them. You will become their crutch and may prevent their ever walking.

Don't try to solve people's problems. Help them to define what the problem really is and then let them work through it.

3. Help them choose a plan. — Counselees find it easier to concentrate on solutions if they can see various options. Help them decide which option seems best, and form a plan for putting it into operation. Some counselors draw up a literal written contract at this juncture. The pastor's task is largely to encourage them to implement their own decision. If counselees don't follow through on their plan, you should question spending great amounts of additional time with them.

4. Know when to refer.

5. Practice strictest confidentiality. — For pastors this is both an ethical and a legal requirement.

Pray with your counselees. Prayer focuses attention on the surest, most lasting source of help—God.

Lay Counseling

Surprisingly, research indicates that caring lay counselors, trained or not, are as helpful to most counselees as professionals.

Spouse. — The spouses of pastors make effective counselors. They often have the sensitivity to understand relational issues better than their partners. Make a bargain with your spouse that if your spouse will help with counseling, you will spend an equal amount of extra time with your family.

Professionals. — Sometimes your congregation will have persons with training in some area of counseling. The pastor must tap this expertise and not allow it to cause professional jealousy or competition between pastor and member. Use such persons not only for referring your counselees, but also for training members willing to share the counseling load.

Congregation. — Members counseling members is a Christian duty: "Bear one another's burdens, and so fulfill the law of Christ" (Gal. 6:2). Pastors may organize a healing "clinic" based on the assumption that some in the congregation have already faced and conquered the problems counselees now have. If pastors can identify these people, give them a little training, and get them together with those having problems, they not only provide help where needed, but make the church a truly healing community.

Support groups can be organized where people with similar needs not only share and seek solutions to their problems, but pray for and support each other. The church can also establish a resource center. A small library of books and pamphlets with practical information and guidance on how to cope with typical problems can be most helpful.

CHAPTER 28

Church Fellowship

Unity

The shepherd's first business is to keep the flock together. People need fellowship. If they don't find it in the church, they'll go looking elsewhere.

Christianity demands love and unity. "We know that we have passed from death to life, because we love the brethren. He who does not love his brother abides in death" (1 John 3:14). "By this all will know that you are My disciples, if you have love for one another" (John 13:35).

Unity empowers the church. "Now when the Day of Pentecost had fully come, they were all with one accord in one place" (Acts 2:1). "When there is harmonious action among the individual members of the church, when there is love and confidence manifested by brother to brother, there will be proportionate force and power in our work for the salvation of men" (*Testimonies to Ministers*, p. 188).

Christian love produces unity despite differences. "And above all things have fervent love for one another, for 'love will cover a multitude of sins' " (1 Peter 4:8). The fire of Christian love dissolves the dross of class hatreds, race clashes, social ruptures, and minor theological controversies.

Seeds of disunity and disloyalty, on the other hand, scatter easily. If you as pastor are not loyal to conference leadership, you are likely scattering seeds that will take root in your own congregation and produce a church not loyal to your leadership. Until you learn how to help your members confront and cope with forces that keep them pulling in different directions, they cannot move the church.

Communicating With Members

Fellowship grows when people hold much in common. The word "communicate" comes from the same root as "common." Good communication between members facilitates better understanding and commonality between them. This increases fellowship. Here are some ways for your church to communicate:

Church bulletin—weekly communication. — Some information in a church bulletin is standard and does not need weekly change: church name, address, and phone; pastor; key officers; statement of basic beliefs; tear-off for pastoral information.

Other information generally falls into three parts: "A Church That Studies" (Sabbath school), "A Church That Worships" (worship hour), and "A Church That Serves" (upcoming activities, finances, etc.).

Church newsletter—monthly communication. — Most churches having newsletters distribute them by mail. This helps the regular members, the absentees, and the visitors from the area who sign the guest registrar to keep in touch with the church program, plans, and activities. It also provides a way of sharing those items that some feel are too secular for Sabbath morning presentation.

Have a mailing bee to care for the mailing of the newsletter. You might encourage especially the older members to come. They have the time, and they need the fellowship.

The church newsletter helps: (1) to inform, (2) to promote, (3) to save announcement time from the worship hour, and (4) to foster fellowship. To emphasize the latter, highlight names in the newsletter. If you have several churches, use only one newsletter, but assign portions of it to each church. This creates fellowship between the churches, and the churches also would have a better appreciation of how busy the pastor is.

Suggested items to include in the newsletter:

Pastor's corner. This is your column to speak your heart. Remember especially the nonattenders. Here is one significant way you can communicate with them. You might also include, without bragging, a report of your activities for the month: number of sermons, evangelistic meetings, Bible studies, pastoral visits, etc.

Schedule. Have a calendar spread-out, listing church activities for each day. Some members will post the calendar at home so as not to miss church events. You might even include your Sabbath morning sermon titles; sometimes a title will entice an inactive member to attend.

News items. Include special church services and church socials. Emphasize personal events: weddings, births, baby dedications, baptisms, graduations, anniversaries, illnesses, deaths. You might make a special listing of upcoming birthdays and wedding anniversaries. Encourage members to send personal greetings.

Feature a family of the month. Let the editor interview a church family. Learn about their background, careers, children, interests, and what the church means to them. Don't hesitate to interview single people for this column.

Youth items. Emphasize your interest in young people by devoting a portion of the newsletter to youth activities. Include a children's page with Bible quizzes, puzzles, and games. Have children or youth write a few paragraphs sharing how they feel about the church.

Church directory—annual communication. — A church directory can be a very effective tool in communicating and encouraging fellowship within the church community. Just having the names of all members of the church in their hands will enable members to become better acquainted with each other. An occasional pictorial directory would also be helpful.

The ideal time to prepare a church directory is after the church elections and planning for the upcoming church year. The directory can, then, be used to outline the year's program. Features might include:

- Mission statement of the church.
- A brief historical sketch of the church.
- Pastor's message. This could include special objectives for the new year.
- A schedule of Sabbath services, including Communion Sabbaths.
- Special seminars and programs and when they'll be conducted.
- Names of officers.
- Committees, and times they meet.
- Birth dates of members, beginning with January 1. (Omit year of birth.)
- Pastor's daily and/or weekly schedule, including day off for family. (Assure availability at all hours for emergencies.)
- Telephone numbers frequently called: church office, pastor's home, school, conference office, youth camp, Adventist Book Center.
- Names of conference officers and departmental directors.
- Addresses and phone numbers of local businesses, services, or institutions operated by Seventh-day Adventists.

Other communication ideas. — Encourage fellowship among members through such plans as:

Congregational survey. Communication, after all, occurs when those involved both talk and listen. Church leaders mustn't do all the talking. A congregational survey is a device for listening. Such a survey yields best results if taken on a Sabbath morning. Ideally, the survey should be taken as the annual planning process begins.

Pass out a form asking two or three questions (including an open-ended one) about each of the areas of the church's program, such as: worship, preaching, lay activities, Sabbath school, youth, prayer meeting, socials, etc. Anonymous responses may produce more frank answers, but you should have some way of determining sex and age of respondents.

New-member packet. Give such a packet to each new member. The packet should include a welcome letter from the pastor, a floor plan of the church indicating various facilities, and, if available, a church directory and newsletter. Each department should be encouraged to prepare a leaflet describing the department's program in such a way as to interest new members.

Membership profile. Organize a visitation program and complete a profile for every member and family. Include in the profile family background, membership background, names, birth dates, baptismal dates, occupations, special interests, and church leadership interest and/or experience. (Computer software for this kind of information is available at the General Conference Ministerial Association Supply Center.)

Pew registration card. Place cards in the pews encouraging worshipers to register attendance, report an illness, request a pastoral visit for themselves or a friend, ask for baptism, membership transfer, etc. This information can also be requested on a tear-off attached to the bulletin.

A more complete system is to have a large card at the end of each pew, possibly in a folder. Every person present is asked to register. All write their names and check whether they're members, visitors, have some special request, etc. When the card has gone the length of the pew, it is sent back, and each person is encouraged to look at each name and get acquainted with everyone worshiping in their pew that morning.

Telephone. Form a phone committee, made up especially of the aged, handicapped, or others usually at home and unable to participate in many church programs. Whenever there is a special problem (eg., illness, death, etc.) facing the congregation, committee members contact those assigned to them and share the concerns.

Another plan is to use a phone answering machine. Get a special line and call it a care-ring number. A brief recording is updated daily, after which callers may leave their message. This method can also notify members of special announcements, such as schedule changes, an emergency hospitalization, arrival of children from camp, or an emergency board meeting.

Special-occasion cards. Keep a supply of cards in your office to be sent for members' birthdays, anniversaries, graduations, and hospitalizations. Cards need not be expensive, but a little personal note from the pastor will make them meaningful.

Letters. Write a letter addressed to each newborn child, dated on the day of the child's birth, welcoming him or her to the big world and affirming his or her wonderful parents. Invite the baby to get acquainted with Jesus early in life, and make Him the best friend. That first letter is almost certain to go into the baby's memory book.

Write a letter on the first anniversary of a death. By now everyone else may seem to have forgotten the loss, but the surviving loved one hasn't. It'll mean a lot for that person to know you haven't.

A wife of a pastor can write a letter addressed specifically to the women of the congregation, sharing her interest in and love for them. This may be especially effective in a new pastorate, and even more so if a spouse is a little shy and reticent in meeting people.

Small Groups

Moses organized Israel into groups of 10 (Ex. 18). Jesus chose a group of 12 and spent most of His ministry with them. He often taught in private homes (Matt. 13:36, 17:25; Mark 9:33; 10:10). The New Testament church centered its activities on small groups, in fellowship, study, sharing, praying, and eating together (Acts 2:42, 46). Acts has nine references to Christians worshiping in homes.

Ellen White emphasizes, "The formation of small companies as a basis of Christian effort is a plan that has been presented before me by One who cannot err. If there is a large number in the church, let the members be formed into small companies, to work not only for the church members but for unbelievers also" (*Evangelism*, p. 115).

The 10 largest Christian churches in the world have grown to their present size through small groups. In fact, a large church loses many of its disadvantages if subdivided into small cell groups. Picture the congregation as a large circle. Inside are smaller circles representing small cell groups. Members who are part of one of the smaller circles seldom leave the large circle. One pastor of a large Adventist congregation was pleasantly surprised when studying the spiritual health of recent converts to discover that not one who had been involved in a small group had left the church.

The life of the body is in its cells. If the cells die, the body dies. If the cells are healthy, the body is healthy. When the cells multiply, the body grows. A study of church movements shows that every major revival has been influenced by a ready access to the Bible and the gathering of believers in small, intimate groups.

Our time and our society are known for massive mobility and migration. People get uprooted from family and friends, many of them moving to distant cities. Loneliness is a key word of our age. The small group becomes a substitute family, and it meets a special need. Strangers are accepted regardless of cultural, ethical, or religious background. They are loved regardless of sin or skin.

Home groups. — *Purpose.* Home study groups aim to both revive members and attract nonmembers. They provide an excellent means of reclaiming inactive members. Research shows that most people attend church, not so much for doctrinal reasons, but because church attendance offers them a Christian support system. Conversely, most people stop attending church, not because they disbelieve the church's doctrines, but because they do not find in that church the support they need. And one of the most time-tested Christian support systems is the home cell group.

A strong emphasis of such groups is fellowship. Both the small size and the home setting are more conducive to fellowship than the regular church setting. Even those not ready to identify with a church feel comfortable in the nonthreatening atmosphere of a home group.

Format. Groups should probably be no smaller than 4 or larger than 15. Most meet weekly. Meetings last about an hour and are typically divided into three parts:

1. Sharing. Most home groups have their sharing time at the beginning of each meeting. The sharing of joys, blessings, and disappointments is a natural way to begin a meeting. It relieves tensions, provides honest affirmation, and creates a warm group spirit. Dialogue is the key to success. No one must be allowed to dominate the group.

2. Study. Preferably Bible study. The group may choose a book of the Bible. Members study it alone during the week, and discuss it with the group at the weekly meeting. The leader probes for answers to such questions as "What does the author say in this text?" and "What does God say to me through this passage?"

3. Prayer. Keep a prayer list. Ask members to remember each member of the group by name every day in private devotions.

How to begin. The pastor need not be a permanent member of any one group. In fact, your presence may impede open dialogue. You may visit around from group to group. Your greatest contribution is in recruiting and training group leaders. The leaders would invite members living near them as they form the groups. The first meeting is usually given over to prepare a group covenant. This might include an agreement to:

- Meet weekly for a given number of weeks.
- Attend every meeting in the series unless ill or out of town.

- Do the appointed study for each meeting.
- Protect confidences.
- Refrain from negative statements about other people or organizations.
- Invite others into the group.

Those unable to support the covenant agreed upon at the first meeting should be allowed to withdraw gracefully.

Church groups. — Small groups can, of course, meet at the church and be made up of those having special interests or needs. For example:

Seminar groups. People show much interest in attending a church after marriage, birth of a child, change of residence, divorce, death of a loved one, etc. Thus, a church may want to sponsor a regular program of seminars to attract those with such special interests. Try family life seminars, parenting classes, coping seminars, Bible study classes, and a range of seminars covering physical, mental, and spiritual health.

Integrate special programs with Sabbath worship. For example, on Father's or Mother's Day, preach a sermon on the home and announce the beginning of a parenting class.

Support groups. Organize an ongoing family life or marriage enrichment support group. Consider support groups for singles, women, senior citizens, and for those recovering from grief.

Conducting such ministries exclusively as "bait" to lure people into church membership is manipulative and un-Christlike. But it is equally irresponsible to conduct such programs without the clear purpose of building a strong and caring fellowship within the congregation.

Sabbath school groups. A small Sabbath school class, properly taught, has an almost unlimited potential for good. Unfortunately, too few Sabbath school classes really work. Keep the classes small, and train your teachers to be relational Bible discussion leaders.

Social Events

People are four-sided beings. The church is interested in their developing not only spiritually and mentally but also physically and socially. Social events assist this kind of balanced development. The church also seeks balance between the young and the old. They may not always be attracted to the same events, but both need social programs. We must never neglect our youth, but mustn't ignore the older folk, either. Many are alone and have almost no fellowship except through the church.

Socials help you get to know your people. Human nature shows up differently at a social function than at a church service. Socials attract family and friends of members to church functions.

Socials create shared experiences, and shared experiences create bonding. Groups that meet for study or witness can also plan for social get-togethers. When people do things together, they feel close to each other.

Additional Fellowship Options

Sabbath morning suggestions. — Sometimes visitors get more attention than they feel comfortable with. Sometimes they get none at all. Visitors are important; when they come to the church, they are looking for something, and it's the church's business to help them find it. Every church service ought to be planned with the assumption that visitors will be present.

Have someone greet visitors in the parking lot. Assign somebody to take visiting children to their Sabbath school divisions. Have a greeter in the foyer. Get visitors' names in the guestbook and read them from the pulpit as part of the welcome. Allow time in the worship service for people to exchange greetings and welcome visitors. Asking visitors to stand can be embarrassing in some cultures. Some would love it, but others may not.

In a sense, warmth cannot be organized. Fake fellowship is repulsive. No formally organized greeting will likely make a strongly positive impression. The best greeting is one from a member who is not doing an assigned job, but who simply cares about people. Encourage members who have the gift of hospitality to approach visitors informally. They should begin, not by awkwardly reminding them they're visitors, but by sincerely wanting to know them. Don't ask unwelcome questions, yet try to learn their situation by a simple introduction and a pleasing inquiry: "My name is _____. What brings you to _____?" This will help the visitors to share whatever information they want to share. If they don't wish to share much, respect their right to privacy. Let social instincts take over from there.

Most churches don't really know whether they're friendly or not. Oddly, those whose members feel the warmest fellowship with one another often seem coldest to visitors. Members are enjoying each other so much they don't realize how excluded this makes a visitor feel. Ask someone to visit your church unannounced and fill out a checklist reporting reactions to: parking, greeters, ushers, the worship service, members' personal greetings, etc.

Put postal-sized cards in the pews. You might call them "Encouragement Cards" (see Heb. 10:24, 25, RSV). Place names of the sick and shut-ins in the bulletin. Invite members to write an encouraging note to one or more of them and turn it in. Some member can make it a special ministry to hand-deliver or mail these.

Make the acceptance of a new member a big event. If the elder has to ask from the pulpit whether or not the person is present, it tells them and everyone else that joining the group isn't very important to the group.

Sing an appropriate song (such as "Blest Be the Tie") as church leaders welcome new members. Have them stand by an elder at the door after church, where they can be personally introduced to and welcomed by the congregation. Do not ask them to stand there without a host. If they are timid, people will forget and go by without a greeting, and you've done more harm than good.

Some Sabbath, ask the congregation to sing or the instrumentalist to play "Jesus Loves Me." Invite adults to seek out the children, greet them, and let them know how much they love having children in the church.

Have an annual memorial service. Read names of members who died during the year. Ask relatives to stand and receive a flower. Preach on the Christian's hope in the resurrection.

Two or three times a year, have a special recognition day when appreciation is expressed for members who have given long and exemplary service to the church.

Now and then choose a family of the week. Have an insert in the bulletin dedicated to a biographical sketch of the family. Sing their favorite hymn, remember them by name in the morning prayer, and have them stand by the door as people leave.

Interview someone in the congregation about his or her conversion, profession, outreach, etc. If someone has had a special prayer answered, if something especially good has happened, let that person share the joy with the congregation.

Videotape members at home or at work, telling how they share their faith on the job. Videotape shut-in members sharing their hope in Christ despite difficult circumstances. Audiotape worship services and deliver copies to shut-ins.

Plan Sabbath fellowship dinners.

Miscellaneous suggestions. — Put a "dial-a-ride" phone number in the bulletin for those who need emergency transportation to a church function. You may have some in the church who don't do much else for the church, but would excel at providing transportation.

Invite a photography-minded member to take pictures of church events throughout the year. Once a year at a social (or better yet, at a business meeting), show these on the screen to encourage the church over the good things they've accomplished together.

Learn members' names. You can't convince people you care about them if you don't know their names. Make your own album of church members. Give each family a sheet of paper for them to provide the information you need and a family picture. Put these sheets in a notebook. Use the album in learning more about your members.

Make a big event of significant occasions in the life of your members, such as a fiftieth wedding anniversary. At such celebrations you may want to give a special plaque honoring those involved.

Discipline

Importance of discipline. — In church discipline two extremes are often practiced: neglect on the part of some, harshness and severity on the part of others. And yet Scriptures teach that church discipline is essential for preserving the integrity of the church.

- Matthew 18:15-20 teaches that a sinning member is to be
  1. confronted,
  2. reproved, and
  3. excluded from the church if refusing to repent.
- Acts 5:1-11 illustrates
  1. the seriousness of sin within the church,
  2. the sensitivity of the Holy Spirit to sin, and
  3. the quick judgment of God upon sin.
- First Corinthians 5:1-5 teaches that in the event of persistent, unrepentant sin, the church is to
  1. grieve,
  2. deliberate,
  3. judge the sin, and
  4. exclude the unrepentant member.
  (See also 1 Thess. 5; 2 Thess. 3; 1 Tim. 5; Titus 1; 3.)

Breakdown of discipline is a major precursor to the decline of a church or denomination. Why be part of a group that doesn't stand for anything that makes a difference? And yet who is responsible for church discipline?

Ministers have a discipline responsibility. God calls the minister a spiritual watchman. He declares that if "you do not speak to warn the wicked from his way, that wicked man shall die in his iniquity; but his blood I will require at your hand" (Eze. 33:8).

Congregations have a discipline responsibility. "God holds His people, as a body, responsible for the sins existing in individuals among them" (*Testimonies*, vol. 3, p. 269).

Church discipline requires both backbone and balance. "We must guard against undue severity toward the wrongdoer, but we must also be careful not to lose sight of the exceeding sinfulness of sin. There is need of showing Christlike patience and love for the erring one, but there is also danger of showing so great toleration for his error that he will look upon himself as undeserving of reproof, and will reject it as uncalled for and unjust" (*The Acts of the Apostles*, pp. 503, 504).

Purpose of discipline. — What are to be the church's purposes in disciplining members? Five need mention:

1. *To honor Christ.* "Brethren, if a man is overtaken in any trespass, you who are spiritual restore such a one in a spirit of gentleness, considering yourself lest you also be tempted. Bear one another's burdens, and so fulfill the law of Christ" (Gal. 6:1, 2). Gentle restoration honors Christ. However, the disciplining process involves certain temptations: the temptation to harshness, hypocrisy, judgmentalism, and impatience.

2. *To restore sinners.* The word "discipline" comes from the same root as "disciple." The purpose of discipline is to disciple. The Good Shepherd gave first priority to the one sheep missing. He went after it, not to shame it, not to hurt it, but to bring it back. The act of discipline is meant to be the beginning of a way back for one who has wandered.

3. *To maintain purity.* One identifying mark of Christ's special people just before His return is that they "keep the commandments of God" (Rev. 12:17). We dare not take lightly our responsibility to honor and uphold Christ's commandments.

Sin, shrugged off, affects the entire church adversely. "Do you not know that a little leaven leavens the whole lump? Therefore purge out the old leaven, that you may be a new lump, since you truly are unleavened. For indeed Christ, our Passover, was sacrificed for us" (1 Cor. 5:6, 7).

4. *To discourage others from sinning.* One purpose of rebuking those who are sinning is "that the rest also may fear" (1 Tim. 5:20).

5. *To show care.* To discipline anyone you cannot love is unchristian. Discipline must always be preceded by extended thought, discussion, prayer, and self-examination: Do we have any spirit of vengeance? Are we being tempted by love of authority? Are we holding others to standards we are not following ourselves? Is our ego tricking us into putting others down to lift ourselves up? A church that disciplines without loving is committing a sin worse than that of the offender.

On the other hand, true love does not negate, but rather requires discipline, as every parent knows. God says, "As many as I love, I rebuke and chasten" (Rev. 3:19). While true love sometimes necessitates chastening, loving must precede chastening.

There are uncritical lovers and unloving critics. The former cause stagnation in the church: "I accept you, but I won't take undesirable actions in order to help you." The latter causes hurt: "I could help you, but I can't accept you." What the church needs is critical lovers who first accept sinners, then sacrifice themselves to help them.

Administering discipline. — The *Church Manual* deals extensively with church discipline, giving definitions, causes, and procedures. These need not be repeated here. However, here are seven helpful suggestions to pastors in the process of administering discipline:

1. *Depend on the* Church Manual. The *Church Manual* represents both our church's understanding of biblical principles of discipline and its wisdom hammered out through practice and discussion. It cannot be changed by anyone but the world church, meeting in General Conference session. To ignore it is to set yourself above the collected wisdom of the world church and is an act of disloyalty to your church. More than that, you lose a tool that can be your guide and protection.

2. *Emphasize forgiveness.* Some accuse the Christian army of being the only one that shoots its own wounded. This must not be so. People being disciplined may see it as rejection, and those who feel rejected react with hostility. They may feel the church's punishment far more than its forgiveness. They may find it difficult to believe that God forgives them when church members apparently cannot. Thus, any act of discipline must be accompanied by an overwhelming emphasis on forgiveness.

Forgiveness is central to Christianity. Christ insisted, "But if you do not forgive men their trespasses, neither will your Father forgive your trespasses" (Matt. 6:15). Again: "If your brother sins against you, rebuke him; and if he repents, forgive him. And if he sins against you seven times in a day, and seven times in a day returns to you, saying, 'I repent,' you shall forgive him" (Luke 17:3, 4). Paul urged the congregation to extend forgiveness to an offender the moment the first sign of repentance was seen (2 Cor. 2).

Ellen White emphasizes, "If your brethren have erred, you must forgive them. You should not say, as some have said who ought to know better, 'I do not think they feel humble enough. I do not think they feel their confession.' What right have you to judge them, as if you could read the heart?" (Manuscript 11, 1888).

3. *Discipline biblically.* Jesus provided us the procedure for dealing with sin (Matt. 18:15-17).
    a. Go to the person individually.
    b. Go with one or two witnesses.
    c. If nothing happens, take the matter to the church.

d. If the person won't hear the church, consider the individual as outside the church. Of course, the way we treat those outside the church is to try to win them to the church.

"No church officer should advise, no committee should recommend, nor should any church vote, that the name of a wrongdoer shall be removed from the church books, until the instruction given by Christ has been faithfully followed" (*Testimonies*, vol. 7, p. 262).

In a court of law, the accused are presumed innocent until proven guilty. The church cannot act differently. "When anyone comes to a minister or to men in positions of trust with complaints about a brother or sister, let them ask the reporter, 'Have you complied with the rules our Saviour has given?' and if he has failed to carry out any particular of this instruction, do not listen to a word of his complaint. Refuse to take up a report against your brother or sister in the faith. If members of the church go entirely contrary to these rules, they make themselves subject of church discipline and should be put under the censure of the church" (E. G. White Manuscript 11, 1888).

4. *Discipline early—yet patiently.* Persons committing a serious sin are often sorry for it immediately afterward. Confronting the sin soon may lead to repentance. Many pastors and churches, however, because they find the confrontation so distasteful, do nothing until months and even years later. Then, often when the individual asks for transfer of membership, the recommendation to transfer is denied on the basis of what happened long ago. The church, unwilling to act when the sin becomes obvious, should be very embarrassed to act later. Such action proves not only its negligence but its lack of forgiveness.

On the other hand, discipline should not be applied impetuously. "In dealing with the erring, harsh measures should not be resorted to; milder means will effect far more. After the best means have been perseveringly tried without success, wait patiently and see if God will not move upon the heart of the erring" (*ibid.*).

5. *Discipline voluntarily.* If discipline seems unavoidable, the offender, if given opportunity, may choose to withdraw voluntarily. Under some circumstances this may save unnecessary public discussion of the issue and embarrassment to the individual. When a name is to be dropped at the individual's request, discourage discussion of details. A person volunteering to withdraw hopefully feels less rejection than when forced to do so.

6. *Discipline impartially.* Discipline must never depend on how many friends or how much power an offender has in the church. Persons involved in the offender's problem or closely associated with him or her should be excluded from deciding the case. There is good reason that only a business meeting should make final discipline decisions. Church boards might be tempted to treat someone from their own group

preferentially. Pastors live with the perpetual temptation to be partial toward one who comes to them for counsel and against one who doesn't.

7. *Protect confidentiality.* A good general rule is "The larger the group, the fewer the details." In business meeting, members have a right to ask detailed questions. Usually, however, they will allow embarrassing details to remain with a smaller group, such as the church elders. The pastor, of course, should not choose to be alone in knowing the full story. Matthew 18 stipulates that, between the one-to-one encounter and the church group encounter, there should be a small group encounter, "that by the mouth of two or three witnesses every word may be established" (verse 16).

Public confession has a place if the offense has been public, but the church must receive this in a spirit of forgiveness and acceptance rather than punishment. Careless discussion or disclosure could lead to legal, ethical, or relational difficulties. These can be avoided if the *Church Manual* is followed.

CHAPTER 29

Church Finance

Spiritual Giving

Money-raising essential. — Pastors are primarily spiritual leaders, shepherds of the flock. Most enjoy "feeding" the sheep, but some speak disparagingly of "shearing" them. They want to give *to* them, not take *from* them, because their first concern is the health of their sheep. Unsheared sheep, however, are unhealthy. They need wool, but are overburdened and overheated if they have too much. Pastors must raise money, but they must do it for the spiritual health of their members, not just the financing of programs. Finding funds to support the church's program is one of the major problems pastors face. It ranks next to that of finding sufficient volunteer personnel. Often church financial headaches are symptoms rather than the primary problem. If financial difficulties keep recurring, it is usually because the methods used to correct them treat the symptoms rather than the problem.

Pastors who do not have strong business instincts should rely on business-minded members to handle church finances. Ministers need not always assume the role of fund-raisers. However, the one responsibility they cannot escape is stewardship training and education—an absolute essential, not only for the financial stability of the church, but for the spiritual growth of its members.

Wrong money-raising methods. — *Giving to get.* Self-centered money-raising methods may seem productive in the short term but actually encourage more selfishness than liberality. "We do not propose to appeal to the lust of appetite or resort to carnal amusements as an inducement to Christ's professed followers to give of the means which God has entrusted to them. If they do not give willingly for the love of Christ, the offering will in no case be acceptable to God" (*Welfare Ministry*, p. 289).

Project giving. Although useful under emergency circumstances, fund-raising through projects relies too much on continuous talk about money and does not provide continuity of financial support engendered in systematic giving. Planned annual giving ensures sound financial management of a church. "Making urgent calls is not the best plan of raising means" (*Testimonies*, vol. 3, p. 511).

External compulsion. Raising funds through coercion of any kind, public or private, is not acceptable for a church. "Systematic benevolence should not be made systematic compulsion. It is freewill offerings that are acceptable to God" (*ibid.*, p. 396).

Right money-raising methods. — Christian stewardship is a biblical principle. It teaches us to see life as a divinely appointed opportunity for learning to be faithful stewards in temporal matters, thus showing our readiness for a higher stewardship in eternal matters. Tithe is a voluntary recognition of God's ownership. Offerings become a physical measurement of our love to God and our desire to see His work prosper. Pastors should present continually the reasons for Christian giving. Four principles:

Gospel motivation. People will give if they're motivated by the gospel. "Even so the Lord has commanded that those who preach the gospel should live from the gospel" (1 Cor. 9:14). The expenses of the church should be met by those whose hearts have been changed, not by human persuasion, but by the gospel—the good news about Jesus.

An act of worship. People will give if they see giving as an act of worship. The center of Old Testament worship was not preaching, praying, or singing. The typical invitation to worship was "Let us sacrifice to the Lord our God" (see Ex. 3:18; 5:3, 8; 8:27; 10:25). If people have wrong attitudes toward giving, perhaps it is because pastors have not helped them understand the vital relationship between sacrifice and worship.

A mission to support. People will give if their church has a mission. If the church has a program its members believe in, they'll pay for it. As one man said, "I don't mind putting gas in the car if it is going somewhere, but I don't want to waste my money just to keep the motor idling in the driveway."

A systematic plan. People will give if their church has a giving plan. The best programs usually include someone's visiting each home each year to explain the systematic giving plan and the need for it, and inviting participation. Members may then turn in anonymous commitment cards on Sabbath. The commitment can be taken in the home, but this brings pressure to bear on members. It can be done by mail, but this does not have the personal touch and the opportunity for discussion.

Long-term church stewardship plans should include instruction on wills and trusts, probably by your conference/mission trust services director. Members ought to be encouraged to leave some of their money to the church.

Handling Church Money

Of all people, pastors should recognize that money given to God should be managed in a way He would approve. When members perceive poor financial management in the church, giving invariably declines. On the other hand, when the pastor is seen as a careful steward, both confidence and giving increase.

Internal control. — Internal control provides for a system of checks and balances to prevent theft. A good system of internal control reduces the risk of assets being stolen, removes unnecessary temptation, improves the accuracy of financial records, and protects treasurers and pastors from false accusations.

Every offering should be counted by two people and recorded separately by each. All money should go through the treasurer's books. Never "borrow" from the offering. All payments of money should be initiated by a written request describing the reason for the request, which fund is to be charged, and to whom it is to be paid.

Church treasurer. — Treasurers should receive appreciation more often and be changed less often. The work of some church leaders is in public, but the work of the treasurer is mostly out of sight, and too often out of mind.

The treasurer's first responsibility is to the church board, not the church pastor. The board may vote certain funds to be used at the pastor's discretion, but pastors must not pressure treasurers to give them money without church board approval. This is both unfair and unethical. Good pastors will not ask, and if they do, good treasurers will not give.

Budget preparation. — The annual church planning program should precede the preparation of the annual budget. This protects the budget from being based on "circular progress"—using last year's program and budget to determine next year's program and budget. Typically, the local budget of a church might equal about 30 to 50 percent of the tithe. If there is a church school, about half the local budget goes for Christian education.

The budget should be voted at a business meeting where all have opportunity to share their views and accept ownership of the plan. (A sample church budget is shown in the *Church Manual*.)

Church indebtedness. — Long-term debt tends to bring

discouragement to the pastor and a stalemate to the congregation. How can a church press forward when most funds are earmarked for what was done in the past?

Further counsel on raising and dispensing funds is available in the *Church Manual*, chapter 11.

CHAPTER 30

Church Campaigns

Many members and some ministers bristle at anything in the church that sounds promotional. Pastors don't want to become "holy salespersons." Yet without promotion mission offerings diminish, evangelism fails, and even socials go unattended. That which gets promoted gets supported.

The issue is not *whether* we should promote, but *how* we should promote. Here are five suggestions that help take the "pain" out of a campaign:

1. Keep it on the calendar. — Each year, review the church's program of the past year and make plans for the upcoming year. Counsel with the church board and prepare a calendar that includes the major campaigns for the year. Have the calendar voted by a business meeting so that every member has input and the opportunity to know what's coming.

Promote only one major campaign at a time. Every department at every level, including the local church, wants to use the pastor and the church service to promote its projects. You owe some loyalty to all these good programs, but you don't have the time and your congregation doesn't have the patience to give each the emphasis the program sponsors desire.

Promote strongly those programs you, your church, and your conference/mission give highest priority and find some way to make mild mention of the rest. For example, some churches allow only one piece of promotional material to be handed out per week, and make other materials available on a table in the foyer.

2. Keep it short. — Short and intense campaigns create much more enthusiasm and satisfaction than those that are long and lackadaisical.

3. Keep it visible. — Many people are reached more readily through seeing than hearing. Details are better understood when written down where they can be reread. Written materials get into members' homes as ongoing reminders. Make your information visible through your bulletin, newsletter, or even a goal device.

4. Keep it simple. — Use the Bible plan of subdividing the church into small working bands. You can often organize a campaign better by using existing entities such as Sabbath school classes than by setting up a new organization.

Some campaigns can center on the telephone. Shut-ins need church work to do and someone to talk to. Organize them to telephone a message to every member.

5. Keep it spiritual. — Sabbath morning is for worship. Church work, however, is a natural and necessary outgrowth of worship. Promotion must never crowd out spirituality, but involvement in church activities is a necessary, practical application of the spiritual experience. It puts worship to work.

Pastors should not allow inactive members' complaints to deter them from promoting programs that encourage members to get involved in the work of the church or press it forward in its spiritual mission.

CHURCH 31

Church Facilities

When you first arrive in a new church or district, be cautious about assessing and criticizing church facilities. Those were built with the congregation's efforts—not yours. The older the building, the more it is stained through with memories of births, baptisms, marriages, funerals, and spiritual nurture. Until you become sensitive to a building's history, you cannot understand some members' reluctance to redoing or replacing it.

You will likely move away eventually, and whatever church facilities you leave behind will remain for the members and their children to worship in—and possibly pay for. All these are strong arguments for respecting the congregation's desires for improving facilities and for insisting that a highly regarded local leader chair a building committee.

The *Church Manual* contains important counsel about financing new facilities. Here are some practical suggestions regarding church buildings:

Locating

The old real estate caveat applies to church buildings as well: "In building a building, three factors are of prime importance: the first is location, the second is location, and the third is location." At least five issues should be considered in choosing a church location:

1. Centrality and accessibility. — Study demographics. Is the land centrally located among the people the church plans to win and serve? A church's location should center more on the people to be won than on the present members being served. Is the neighborhood stable, or are people moving away and demographics changing? Is transportation readily available?

Of all public buildings, churches are probably the most underutilized. The right location might make church facilities usable on weekdays for a day-care center, medical clinic, seminars, counseling, etc.

2. Visibility. — An attractive building, visible from a busy thoroughfare, is a perpetual, positive advertisement for the church and what it stands for.

3. Cost. — Price is important, but it is shortsighted to allow cost to outweigh all other considerations. Inexpensive land is often inexpensive because water, electricity, sewer, gas, good roads, etc., are not readily available. Too many churches have been built in poor locations because land was donated or purchased cheaply. It costs just as much to put up the building on a poor piece of land as on a choice one, and it may be worth only half as much when finished.

4. Size. — Too small a lot leaves no room for expansion. Too large a lot is expensive to maintain. The unused portion may become a community eyesore. What are the long-term plans of the congregation? Should it become large, or should it swarm and begin other congregations as it grows? Will there be need for a church school or other facility on the same land?

5. Restrictions. — Is the property zoned to allow a church building? Is there a clear title or deed? We have lost millions of dollars' worth of property during the brief history of our church because of careless titling of property. Pastors must cooperate with their conference/mission to make certain that deeds to all church properties are in the name of the legal association set up for the purpose.

Designing

Four questions ought to be asked about the design of church facilities.

1. Is it attractive? — Seventh-day Adventists extol simplicity. We are reluctant to divert money from missions to build beautiful buildings. At the same time we find that God ordered a significant display of beauty in the wilderness tabernacle and seemed to bless in the building of rather lavish Old Testament temples.

How should the pastor answer when confronted with these divergent viewpoints while leading a congregation in their design of a church facility? Ellen White offers balanced counsel: "Do those who are ready to complain of this house of worship consider for whom it was built? that it was made especially to be the house of God; to be dedicated to Him; to be a place where the people assemble to meet God? . . .

"Many of our people have become narrowed in their views. Order, neatness, taste, and convenience are termed pride and love of the world.

A mistake is made here. Vain pride, which is exhibited in gaudy trappings and needless ornaments, is not pleasing to God. But He who created for man a beautiful world, and planted a lovely garden in Eden with every variety of trees for fruit and beauty, and who decorated the earth with most lovely flowers of every description and hue, has given tangible proofs that He is pleased with the beautiful" (*Testimonies*, vol. 2, pp. 257, 258).

2. Is it functional? — What functions other than Sabbath morning worship will be held in the building? Is ample provision made for meeting the social and outreach needs of the church as well as the needs of children and youth? Good architects will save the church a sum greater than their fee by designing a building that is both beautiful and functional.

3. Is it flexible? — *Seating should be flexible.* Immovable pews and sloping floors make it very difficult to use the sanctuary for any kind of small group activity. Choir loft pews inhibit use of the space for other purposes.

Size should be flexible. A small crowd in a large room dampens enthusiasm and makes the meeting look like a failure. The spirit of a meeting is greatly enhanced when room size matches audience size. The ideal sanctuary has portions that can be opened or closed depending on the crowd. Study should be given to providing smaller rooms for smaller crowds. These can usually double as Sabbath school rooms.

Sound should be flexible. Music and preaching tend to compete with one another in their sound needs. Acoustics should be live enough so music is bright and people will sing well, yet deadened enough so speaking does not create an echo. A good sound amplification system increases flexibility.

4. Is it intimate?. — Until recent years, church sanctuaries tended to be long and narrow, separating the worshipers from each other and from their worship leaders. One minister likened the resulting task of the preacher to that of a suitor sitting on one side of a river and trying to win a maiden on the other side by bawling out his love at the top of his voice.

A part of worship is fellowship—people getting together with one another and together with God. Ideally, sanctuaries should be shaped so worshipers are close to one another and close to, if not surrounding, their worship leaders.

The pulpit is usually located in the center of the platform to emphasize that the preaching of the Word is central to Adventism and Adventist worship.

Maintaining

Most unattractive churches are unattractive, not so much because they are old or poorly built, but because they are poorly maintained. Neatness, cleanliness, and tasteful interior decorating are not expensive. It's amazing how much difference a little paint can make.

Congregations can become so comfortable in their church surroundings that they no longer notice the deficiencies. Deacons and other church leaders should periodically view the building as though they were visitors getting their first impression. A checklist may help their evaluation of: yard, sign, exterior paint, foyer, interior decorating, restrooms, fire protection, etc.

Church facilities should, of course, be insured in accordance with conference/mission policies. It's presumptuous to expect God to protect us from our own indolence.

Renting

Long-term rental of our buildings to other churches or organizations should be approached cautiously. Such rentals may lead to misunderstandings, cause extra wear on the building, and always increase maintenance and utility costs. Sabbath school leaders grow impatient over strangers rearranging their rooms. Members may not like the difference in methods of worship and messages preached. Congregations that rent their church in order to raise additional income are almost invariably disappointed.

However, if another church group has lost their place of worship, letting them rent your church for a time may be the Christian thing to do. If you do rent, put every part of your agreement in the most precise written document possible, to help prevent hard feelings later. The conference/mission may insist that their executive committee approve this document.

CHAPTER 32

Christian Education

Importance of Christian Education

It was said of Michelangelo that he could look at a block of marble and see an angel's form waiting to be released. Pastors should be able to look at their congregation's children the same way.

What the church does about its children is of paramount importance to Christ. He taught, "And whoever causes one of these little ones who believe in Me to stumble, it would be better for him if a millstone were hung around his neck, and he were thrown into the sea" (Mark 9:42).

Ellen White wrote to the church, "In the highest sense the work of education and the work of redemption are one" (*Education*, p. 30). "Wherever there are a few Sabbathkeepers, the parents should unite in providing a place for a day school where their children and youth can be instructed" (*Testimonies*, vol. 6, p. 198). No wonder the Adventist Church has established more than 5,000 schools in more than 100 nations—one of the largest educational programs of any Protestant denomination.

Practical Suggestions

1. Have an annual Christian education Sabbath. — Shortly before the beginning of the school year, center an entire worship service on Christian education. Invite teachers from your church school to the platform and have a special prayer of dedication for them. If desirable, church school children and their parents may be included in the dedication. You can dedicate youth going off to boarding schools. Even if you don't have a church school, you can still promote the importance of Christian education.

2. Support your teachers. — Pastors and teachers are partners in

---

For more on the Adventist philosophy of Christian education, and for help in running a school program, see the *Church Manual*, chapter 8.

ministry. Pastors should be involved with the school, but must not interfere with or override the teacher's program.

Parents of church school children sometimes feel they have special authority over teachers. Their tuition pays the teacher's salary. Some sit on the board that hires the teacher. As church members, they feel they own the school. The pastor, along with the school board, must protect teachers from parental harassment. And that's doubly true for the pastor who is also one of the parents.

When a boarding school sends home a student under discipline, never take that student's or the parents' word as final on what really went wrong at the school. Get the school's response as well before deciding what really happened.

3. Spend time at the school. — Offer to take worship, perhaps once a week. Schedule it so you include some time on the playground. You may get closest to both teacher and students there. If you have athletic ability, the respect you earn on the playground will add impact to the messages you present in clasroom and pulpit. Your success in changing people's attitudes toward Jesus depends less on what you say about Him than on what they think of you while you say it.

4. Consider day care. — Many parents are looking for a well-qualified, trustworthy place to leave children while they are at work. Your church may already have facilities usable for this purpose, or the program may be affiliated with your church school. The project can be evangelistic; you may win parents to Christ through resulting friendships. Also, the children might continue right on into church school.

5. Consider complementary religious education. — Adventists prefer running their own schools. Where this is impossible, consider some structured program that brings children together before school, after school, or on week-ends to get the Bible instruction and spiritual nurture they would receive if church school were available.

SECTION FOUR

The Minister and Special Services

33. Baptism
34. Child Dedication
35. Church Dedication
36. Communion
37. Funeral
38. Ground Breaking
39. House Blessing
40. New Parish Induction
41. Prayer for Sick
42. Wedding

CHAPTER 33

Baptism

Importance of Baptism

Baptism symbolizes not only Christ's death for us, but also our death to sin and new birth in Him. It affirms joining the family of God, and sets one apart for a life of ministry.

Baptism a big event. — Research has shown that the retention rate of new members is directly proportional to the receptivity of their local church. To create, for candidates, a pleasant memory of their commitment to Christ and to maximize the bonding process between them and the church family, baptism should be made a big event in the life of the church.

For the same reason, baptizing the children of the church should not be taken less seriously than that of candidates from outside the church. Baptism is a rite of passage for the church's children. They may have grown up in the church presuming they weren't considered of much importance because they were only children. But with their baptism they hope to be treated a little like adults, as though they really matter to the congregation. If the church does not give adequate importance to the baptism of these children, the children may soon decide that the church is not important to them.

We normally want our families and friends present for the biggest events of our lives. They ought to be invited to one's baptism. Some churches have wedding-type invitations printed that say something like "For Christians, Bible baptism signifies new birth—a new beginning. Just as marriage symbolizes the joining of human lives, so baptism symbolizes our joining with Jesus and His church family. You are cordially invited to witness this beautiful celebration of renewal in the life of _____." The candidate's name, followed by time and place of baptism, is written in by hand. Thus, one printing of the invitation fits all. Candidates are encouraged to invite their family and friends and are given as many as they choose to use.

Baptism a local event. — Ideally, baptism should be an event of the local church. Understandably, conference/mission leaders may be enthusiastic about camp meeting and youth camp baptisms. They want to see fruit for their labor. People tend to enjoy mass baptisms climaxing evangelistic meetings, and there is probably a place for them. Unfortunately, however, baptisms held away from the local church sometimes fail to bond the new members with the congregations they join.

In the case of church youth, when they are baptized elsewhere it can be an affront to the local church pastor, Sabbath school or church school teacher, or Pathfinder leader who has spent a lot of time helping them learn to love Jesus.

Two commitments are made at baptism. The candidates commit themselves to Christ and His church. The congregation commits itself to loving, befriending, enfolding, and training the candidates. Since it is at the baptism that these commitments are made, candidate and congregation ought to be together for the event. As in a physical birth, it's best if the family that's going to raise the baby is involved in its delivery.

When conducted as part of the Sabbath worship service, baptism should be given major importance rather than the appearance of a hastily added appendix. When conducted as a separate service, it should be preceded by a short address on the meaning of the ordinance. Between immersions of candidates, instrumental or choral music is appropriate. The congregation may also choose to sing and thus play a more active part in the event.

Baptism a frequent event. — Frequent small baptisms are usually preferable to occasional large ones, because:

1. This keeps soul winning perpetually before your congregation.
2. Fruit should be picked when ripe and not held back for long periods.
3. Each baptism encourages someone in the audience to take the same step.

As you plan your program for the year, set and announce monthly or at least quarterly dates when baptisms are planned. Deacons and deaconesses who prepare the baptismal facilities will appreciate the advance notice.

Authorization to baptize. — The *Church Manual* stipulates, "In the absence of an ordained pastor, the elder shall request the president of the conference or local field to arrange for the administration of the rite of baptism to those desiring to unite with the church." No local church elder may officiate in the baptismal service, even if the circumstance is unusual, without first obtaining permission from the conference/mission president.

Before Baptism

Baptismal facilities. — Masonry baptistries often crack. Metal baptistries rust, unless wiped dry after each use. Some kind of fiberglass baptistry is probably most ideal. Corners and underpinnings must be built exceptionally strong to withstand the immense weight of the water. Where water is extremely scarce, a barrel may be used.

Water should be warmed if possible. The shock of cold water may cause a nervous candidate to suck in the breath and take in water. Some methods of warming will leave the bottom cold unless the water is stirred.

If a microphone is used, it should be kept out of reach of participants in the baptistry. An electric shock can be fatal to someone standing in water. The mike should be turned off between candidates so the minister can whisper to candidates and put them at ease.

Outdoor baptisms provide an effective evangelistic witness to the public. Make certain, however, that the water is not polluted. When baptizing in a river, baptize so that the candidate's head is upstream. The current thus draws the person toward you rather than away from you.

Handicapped people can be carried into the water and even immersed while sitting in a chair, whether the baptism is indoors or out. In extreme medical emergencies, the service may take place in a home or hospital. In one such situation Ellen White advised, "Arrangements will be made to fulfill the aged man's request for baptism. He is not strong enough to go to ―――― or to ―――― and the only way in which the ceremony can be performed is by getting a bathtub and letting him into the water" (*Evangelism*, p. 315).

Baptismal assistants. — Deacons normally prepare the baptistry and assist male candidates. Deaconesses prepare the robes and assist female candidates. Robes should be checked regularly for missing fasteners and hem weights. Baptismal assistants need to be not only competent, but gracious and thoughtful, able to encourage and comfort nervous candidates.

If the baptistry has no curtain, a blanket should be placed around the candidates as they step out of the water. Even heavy robes may cling immodestly and portray an unfortunate picture of immersion baptism, especially to non-Christian family and friends present. The blanket also provides warmth and reduces nervous shivering. A practical plan is for deacon or deaconess to wring out the bottom of the robe as candidates leave the water, take them to a private place, then invite them to step into a tub and drop their baptismal robe. This keeps floors less slippery and easier to clean up.

Where a member or assistant pastor has been especially instrumental in winning a soul, invite that person to help the candidate in and out of the baptistry and thus play a significant part in the baptism.

Baptismal attire. — If possible, the church should make provision for culturally appropriate baptismal attire such as robes. "In every church, baptismal robes should be provided for the candidates. . . . The robes should be made of substantial material, of some dark color that water will not injure, and they should be weighted at the bottom. Let them be neat, well-shaped garments, made after an approved pattern. There should be no attempt at ornamentation, no ruffling or trimming" (*ibid.*, p. 314).

Notice that dark robes are suggested. Since white is more revealing when wet, white robes may need to be double-layered. Heavy material increases modesty. Hem weights prevent embarrassment from the robe bottom floating when entering the water.

If robes are used, candidates should bring underclothes to wear beneath. A swimsuit is less revealing under the robe and thus ideal. Some may wish to wear stockings and a shower cap. A handkerchief to be held over the nose and a towel for drying should be brought if these are not furnished by the church. If baptismal robes are not available, candidates should, if possible, bring a complete change of clothing so that clothing may be worn for the baptism and dry clothing put on after.

Fishing boots, reaching from the feet to just under the arms, are ideal for the minister's attire. You need carry no clothes to the church, and changing is much quicker. You simply remove your coat and shoes, roll up your sleeves, step into the boots, and put on the robe. You can dress or undress in less time than it takes the congregation to sing a hymn. Be certain, however, that the boots come high under your arm, or the immersion process may scoop water into them.

Putting the candidate at ease. — Candidates should probably witness a "dry run" in preparation for their baptism. Explain the process and show them how the minister will hold them. Assure heavy candidates that they will be light in the water. (If a candidate is large and you are small, use deeper water.) It may be wise to assure participants they don't have to speak in the baptistry, that you will be in charge, and they need not really remember anything. Details about holding the breath, bending the knees, etc., are probably superfluous.

Encourage them to concentrate on their spiritual commitment and let you take care of the physical details.

Examining and receiving into membership. — Pastors, evangelists, or Bible workers should not take sole responsibility for the doctrinal examination of candidates. Public examination tends to convince the church they have been properly prepared. On the other hand, going into doctrinal details may sound odd to visitors, since the examination is mostly a formality and no one is likely to voice reservations in public.

A less public appraisal of candidates' spiritual commitment and doctrinal understanding can be conducted by the church board, elders, or some other small group designated by the church. Pastors and evangelists must remember that they come and go. New members should be approved and welcomed by members who will stay by to nourish them. (For more on teaching and examining new members, see chap. 23; also the *Church Manual*.)

Voting candidates into membership may be done before or after the baptism. If before, the vote is subject to baptism. A brief litany can be effective:

Leader:	Do you as a congregation open your hearts, your families, your spiritual and emotional resources to these new family members today?
Congregation:	We do.
All:	We are all now members of the body of Christ. You are now our brothers and sisters. God is your father and ours. Jesus is your brother and ours. The Holy Spirit is our mutual comforter and sustainer. We accept you and celebrate your entrance into the family of God.

Candidates may be asked to step to the front when being voted into membership. After the vote, the minister and local elders seated on the platform usually step down, give each a baptismal certificate, and, in behalf of the congregation, extend the right hand of fellowship, welcoming them into the church family.

During Baptism

If members of the same family are to be baptized at the same service, it is ideal for them to come into the water together. The father, as spiritual leader of the home, is usually baptized first.

Introducing the candidate. — As candidates enter the baptistry, make certain the bottom of the robe does not float. Then, before you speak to the congregation, position them and ask them to take hold of you and be prepared for their immersion.

You may want to ask family and/or those who helped win the individual to stand. If the candidate is a child from the congregation, be sure to mention Sabbath school and church school teachers, Pathfinder leaders, etc. Individualize each baptism by saying just a few words about the candidate's background and how he/she was won to Christ.

An optional plan is to ask candidates to spend a thoughtful evening before their baptism writing out a brief testimony as to what their baptism means to them. Encourage them to mention people who have helped bring them to their decision. Someone especially involved with winning them can be asked to read this from the pulpit while candidate and minister stand in the baptistry.

Immersing the candidate. — Candidates usually enter the water carrying a handkerchief or facecloth. If you are right-handed, take this cloth in your left. You want your stronger arm reserved for placement behind candidates to carry their weight. Have them take hold of your left wrist with both hands, one under your wrist and one over. This gives them something secure to hold on to.

Now, you speak to the audience, ending with a well-planned sentence, the first part of which addresses the candidate's personal commitment. For example, "And now, _____, because of what Jesus has done for you and because you have given your life to Him and want to be a part of the family of God [raise your right hand], I gladly baptize you in the name of the Father, and of the Son, and of the Holy Ghost. Amen."

Place the handkerchief over the candidate's face with the heel of your left hand under the chin to keep the mouth closed, and gently pinch the nostrils closed between your thumb and fingers. Place your right hand between the candidate's shoulders, holding a piece of the robe in your closed hand so the person cannot slip out of your grasp in the water. Take one step to your right as the candidate is immersed.

Baptize tenderly. Immerse candidates slowly and raise them gracefully to the standing position, disturbing the water as little as possible. Wipe the candidate's face gently with the handkerchief. Share a hug or handclasp. At this juncture, some pastors pray a prayer of blessing and commissioning to a life of Christian ministry.

Appeal and announcement. — When the last candidate has left the baptistry, announce the time of the next baptism and give an invitation for those who want to be included to stand, raise their hands, or fill out a card, etc.

After Baptism

Baptism should be followed by a reception—an expression of bonding between candidate and congregation. Some suggestions you might consider:

1. Invite candidates to stand with the pastor at the front door to be greeted by members. Place a winsome elder or other church leader with them to introduce them to members.

2. If the congregation is not too large, invite members to join hands in a circle around the perimeter of the sanctuary, singing "Blest Be the Tie" or "I'm So Glad I'm a Part of the Family of God." After the benediction the circle can become a receiving line, with each member giving a personal welcome to the newly baptized.

3. Prepare a congratulatory card for each candidate. Send these through the congregation and have each member write a note, favorite text, etc.

4. Give a separate card to each member and ask each one to write a note. Make these into a baptismal scrapbook for the candidate.

5. Hold a reception or fellowship meal fully dedicated to the new members. Ask them to come forward to receive flowers and sit on the platform. Have them introduced by someone close to them. Include an interview, asking why they chose to become Seventh-day Adventists and what they hope to contribute to the growth of the church.

6. Encourage the families of converts to have some kind of celebration on their own to underline their interest and joy. This is especially meaningful to children of the congregation.

For more suggestions for welcoming and nurturing new members, see chapter 23.

CHAPTER 34

Child Dedication

Biblically Appropriate

Dedication of children to God, especially the firstborn, was practiced in Old Testament times. Hannah dedicated her child, Samuel, to God and to the service of His house (1 Sam. 1:27, 28).

Mary and Joseph brought the infant Jesus to the Temple in "Jerusalem to present Him to the Lord" (Luke 2:22). Ellen White says of this: "The priest went through the ceremony of his official work. He took the child in his arms, and held it up before the altar. After handing it back to its mother, he inscribed the name 'Jesus' on the roll of the firstborn" (*The Desire of Ages*, p. 52).

Although the New Testament does not command such a ritual, the way Jesus related to the little ones encourages dedicating children to God. From the incidence of Jesus blessing the children (see Matt. 19:13-15; Mark 10:13-16; Luke 18:15-17) we may note six significant points:

1. Jesus blessed the children. "And He took them up in His arms, put His hands on them, and blessed them" (Mark 10:16).
2. Blessing the children was a profound event. All three Synoptic Gospels tell the story.
3. Infant children were included. "Then they also brought infants to Him" (Luke 18:15).
4. Jesus neither commanded nor initiated the blessing. Matthew records, "The disciples rebuked them" (Matt. 19:13). It is unlikely the disciples would have opposed the blessing if Jesus had initiated it.
5. Jesus encouraged the blessing when parents requested it. "Let the little children come to Me, and do not forbid them" (verse 14).
6. Jesus was displeased with those opposing the blessing. "The disciples rebuked those who brought them. But when Jesus saw it, He was greatly displeased" (Mark 10:13, 14).

Ellen White counsels, "Let ministers of the gospel take the little children in their arms, and bless them in the name of Jesus. Let words of tenderest love be spoken to the little ones; for Jesus took the lambs of the flock in His arms, and blessed them" (*Evangelism*, pp. 349, 350).

It is understandable, however, that child dedication would be questioned by those whose background leads them to associate it with churches that practice infant baptism. For this reason, in the Seventh-day Adventist child dedication service there are no godfathers or godmothers and the name is not formally given. It is not a christening service, and should not appear as such.

The service should be organized to emphasize its four basic purposes:

1. To thank God for the miracle of this birth.
2. To covenant the parents to raising the child to love Jesus.
3. To commit the congregation to providing the facilities and support for assisting the parents in their task.
4. To bless the child and dedicate it to God.

If a minister is not available, an elder may officiate during child dedication. However, an elder should not officiate without the local church pastor's approval.

Planning the Service

Place. — Some cultures encourage a "baby presentation" in the home. However, in most circumstances the ideal is to have the baby dedication as part of the Sabbath morning worship service. Since commitment of the congregation is one of the purposes of the dedication, it should be held when the largest possible representation from the congregation is available.

Time of year. — The annual church calendar should include dates when baby dedications are planned. Two a year may be sufficient. The most ideal times are probably Mother's Day, when parental training is being emphasized, and early in the Christmas season, when emphasis is on the Christ child. Announce the dedication date a few weeks in advance, inviting the parents to plan for the service. Make the event evangelistic by encouraging participants to invite their family and friends.

Information card. — Since you want to individualize each child's dedication, and also prepare a certificate to be presented at the dedication, it is well to have a simple information card filled out by each family ahead of time. Include such items as: baby's full name, date of birth, place of birth, weight at birth, father's name, mother's name,

CHILD DEDICATION

other children in the family, and any item of special interest connected with the baby.

Age. — Babies may be dedicated at as young an age as parents are prepared to bring them to church. Children after school age are seldom dedicated. An exception may seem appropriate in the case of children of new church members.

Conducting the Service

The typical dedication service has four parts.

1. Parents called forward. — Make the baby dedication an important family event. Encourage non-SDA spouses to attend when their children are dedicated. Involve other siblings, who may feel a bit left out by all the attention the baby is getting, to join the dedicatory service. Grandparents may wish to be included. Occasionally a grandparent will bring the baby even if parents are unwilling to attend, although this is not ideal.

Invite parents to come forward during the singing of the opening hymn, chosen to fit the dedication. Such hymns include: "Gentle Jesus, Meek and Mild"; "Happy the Home"; "I Will Early Seek the Savior"; "Jesus, Friend of Little Children"; "Jesus, Son of Blessed Mary"; "Lead Them, My God, to Thee"; and "Love at Home."

Using the morning hymn in this way not only introduces the dedication, but saves time, since a morning hymn would have been sung anyway. The last stanza of the hymn could be sung after the dedication as parents leave the platform.

The entire dedication should take no more than four to five minutes. The homily must be very brief. Homilies before events such as weddings, baptisms, or child dedications are usually not very effective: anticipation of the upcoming event is so strong that people hear little of what is said beforehand.

Parents are also fearful their baby will cry. Five minutes seem to them like an age. If the homily is more than one or two minutes, it can be given while parents are still in the congregation, perhaps on the front row.

2. Homily. — Parents should stand facing the congregation. There is some spiritual significance in the father, as spiritual leader, holding the child. On the other hand, the mother might do better at keeping the child quiet. It may be best to let the parents decide.

The homily should emphasize the covenanting or charging of the parents and the commitment of the congregation. A thought may be brought from such passages as:

Deut. 6:4-7	"Teach them diligently to your children."
1 Sam. 1:27, 28	"For this child I prayed . . . I also have lent him to the Lord."
Ps. 127:3-5	"Children are a heritage from the Lord."
Prov. 22:6	"Train up a child in the way he should go."
Isa. 8:18	"Here am I and the children whom the Lord has given me!"
Jer. 13:20	"Where is the flock that was given to you?"
Matt. 18:2-6, 10	"Take heed that you do not despise one of these little ones."
Matt. 19:13-15	"Then little children were brought to Him that He might put His hands on them and pray."
Mark 10:13-16	"Let the little children come to Me, and do not forbid them."
Luke 1:46-55	The Magnificat.
Luke 2:22-38	"They brought Him [Jesus] to Jerusalem."
Luke 18:15-17	"Then they also brought infants to Him."
Eph. 6:4	"Bring them up in the training and admonition of the Lord."

Ellen White's counsel may also be included in the thoughts presented:

The Ministry of Healing, pp. 40, 41: "They thought these children too young to be benefited. . . . One mother with her child had left her home to find Jesus. On the way she told a neighbor."

Ibid., p. 351: "No work entrusted to human beings involves greater or more far-reaching results than does the work of fathers and mothers."

Ibid., p. 394: "The spirit that prevails in the home will mold their characters."

The Desire of Ages, pp. 511-517: "Blessing the Children."

The Adventist Home, pp. 159-276: "Heritage of the Lord"; "The Successful Family"; "Father, the House-Band"; "Mother—Queen of the Household."

Close your homily with remarks such as the following:

"Parents, before setting your child apart in dedication, I invite you to enter into a covenant with God. In bringing this little child for Christian dedication, you are accepting before God the sacred responsibilities of fatherhood and motherhood. By this symbolic act you seek to express your belief that this little one is not only your child but God's.

"The congregation joins you in dedicating this precious one to God, assisting you in working toward the day when this act of dedication shall be followed at an appropriate age by baptism, thus entering into full and happy membership in this church family.

"You, therefore, as parents promise to do all in your power to bring this child up in the nurture and admonition of the Lord. Do you so covenant?"

Parents answer: "We do."

3. Prayer. — Pastor and parents should kneel for the dedicatory prayer. The congregation usually remains seated. It is important that an individualized, relational atmosphere prevail during the dedication. One way to accomplish this is for the pastor to hold the baby while praying. If you do this, and the baby smiles, you'll likely be glad you did. If the baby cries, you'll wish you hadn't.

An alternate method is for the parents to hold the children and you lay your hands on the head of each child in turn as you mention each one's name in prayer. If the group is large, elders may join in the laying on of hands.

The four purposes of a child dedication, included above, should be mentioned in the prayer. Ideally, each child and parent should be mentioned by name. You could lead into the Lord's Prayer, with pastor, parents, and congregation joining their voices in consecration.

4. Certificate and congratulations. — Certificates are usually given to parents after the dedication prayer. Typically, these include enrollment in the Sabbath school cradle roll, and you may want the leader of that division to assist you in congratulating parents and giving the certificates. Certificates can usually be obtained at Adventist bookstores or through publishing houses.

Litanies

Litanies such as the following may be used to increase participation of parents and congregation in the dedication. They would normally replace most of the homily and lead into the dedication prayer.

Litany 1

Pastor: "If it be your intention to present this child to the Lord, please answer 'We do' to the following questions:

"Do you here this day recognize this child as the gift of God, and give heartfelt thanks for God's blessing?

Parents: "We do."

Pastor: "Do you here this day dedicate this child to the Lord?"

Parents: "We do."

Pastor: "Do you here this day pledge as parents that you will use home, school, church, and every other means available in helping this child learn to love Jesus?"

Parents: "We do."

Pastor to congregation: "Do you here this day promise to support these parents through your prayers, church programs, and a nurturing church atmosphere?"

Congregation: "We do."

Litany 2

If the group is large, and at the same time you wish to individualize the service by including parent and congregation, have each read a few sentences. The first set of parents reads something they, or they and the pastor, have prepared. Then the congregation replies. Both statements should include the child's name. Then the second set of parents does the same, and again the congregation replies. For example:

First parents: "We are here to bring _____ to the Lord. We ask God's special blessing on us as we train him/her to be a loving Christian. We ask for special wisdom. And we thank God for this unique opportunity."

Congregation: "We support you in the holy calling of training _____ and join you in praying for insight and wisdom as we share his/her life with you."

Second parents:	(Some similar, individualized statement.)
Congregation:	(A reply uniquely fitted to that statement and pledging the congregation's support.)

Litany 3

A dedication litany at Christmas season should include something about the Incarnation. For example, parallel the miracle of Jesus birth with the birth of these children:

Pastor:	"Do not be afraid, for behold, I bring you good tidings of great joy which will be to all people. For there is born to you this day in the city of David a Savior, who is Christ the Lord' " (Luke 2:10, 11).
	"The Incarnation of God shows His high regard for children."
Fathers:	"And as God the Father gave His son for us, we bring our children this morning as a gift to Him."
Mothers:	"God has given many gifts. We praise Him today for giving us the gift of creating this new life that we now dedicate to Him."

Additional Suggestions

Here are some alternate suggestions for a child dedication:

1. Have a children's choir or a children's division of the Sabbath school sing as parents come forward for the dedication.
2. Look up the meaning of the baby's name and base your homily on a Bible text or thought that amplifies the meaning.
3. When handing the child back to its parents after holding it for the prayer, or as you congratulate parents and give the certificates, say to each, "Take this child, nurse it, and train it for the Lord."
4. If your spouse has the inclination or gift, share the homily. Let the husband speak to the fathers, and the wife to the mothers.
5. Prepare a special church bulletin for the dedication, with a picture of the baby being dedicated. Do not show favoritism by giving such treatment only to special families.
6. Have a photograph taken of the dedication. Provide one copy for the parents and one for the church bulletin board.

CHAPTER 35

Church Dedication

A church dedication should be one of the most carefully planned services a pastor does. It offers a valuable opportunity to place the Seventh-day Adventist Church into the community spotlight. To the congregation, it represents the celebration of a difficult project successfully accomplished.

Guests play an important part in a dedication service. City officials and community pastors are often invited to attend. Conference/mission officials and former pastors should be invited to participate. For these reasons, set the date far in advance after consultation with conference/mission leaders.

Order of Service

A typical order of service would be:

Hymn
Opening prayer
History of the church
Scripture reading
Special song or hymn
Dedicatory sermon
Act of dedication (optional)
Prayer of dedication
Hymn or special song
Benediction

Hymns. — Appropriate hymns for church dedication include: "The Church Has One Foundation"; "Glorious Things of Thee Are Spoken"; "Christ Is Made the Sure Foundation"; "Built on the Rock"; "Lead On, O King Eternal"; "Blest Be the Tie That Binds"; "Praise God, From Whom All Blessings Flow."

History of the church. — In view of the fact that their direct relationship with the congregation usually tends to be short, pastors and conference officials should not dominate the dedication service. Church facilities belong more to the congregation than to the clergy. An elder or other local leader whose roots go deep into the history of the church can do a better job of telling its story.

Charter or lifetime members should be recognized and honored. Proper appreciation ought to be expressed to those most directly involved with the present building.

Give special recognition to the pastor who led out in the building program. Often this pastor, who worked so hard and was so directly involved in the building, has moved on before the debt is paid and the building dedicated. In fact, the conflict created in the difficult process of building sometimes necessitates the pastor's moving. The sacrifice involved should be recognized.

The history can climax with announcement of upcoming plans and programs for serving the community. The church must not emphasize its past without also projecting its future.

The service is not to be used as an occasion for raising money toward church indebtedness. All debts incurred in the building's purchase or erection must be paid before its dedication.

Scripture reading. — Appropriate Scripture readings could be chosen from 2 Chronicles 6:14-42 or 1 Kings 8:23-53 (Solomon's prayer dedicating the Temple). Other passages often used at church dedications include:

Ex. 40:33-35	"The glory of the Lord filled the tabernacle."
1 Chron. 29:10-16	"All this abundance that we have prepared to build You a house . . . is all Your own."
2 Chron. 2:4	"I am building a temple, . . to dedicate it to Him."
Neh. 4:6	"So we built, . . . for the people had a mind to work."
Neh. 6:16	"They perceived that this work was done by our God."
Neh. 12:27	"Celebrate the dedication with gladness, both with thanksgivings and singing."
Ps. 27:4, 5	"That I may dwell in the house of the Lord."
Ps. 48:9-14	"Your lovingkindness, in the midst of Your temple."

Ps. 84	"How lovely is Your tabernacle."
Ps. 100	"Enter into His gates with thanksgiving."
Ps. 122	"I was glad when they said to me, 'Let us go into the house of the Lord.'"

Dedicatory sermon. — The sermon should be brief for many reasons:

1. Time is limited because of the full program.
2. The speaker is addressing an "anticipating audience." The people have come, not to hear a sermon, but to witness the act of dedication.
3. Church dedications are usually held on Sabbath afternoon. People have already had a sermon in the morning.

Any of the texts mentioned above can be developed into a dedicatory sermon. Employ a good introduction, such as likening the occasion to the mountain climber who has worked so long and hard, and finally stands at the top enjoying the view and celebrating the accomplishment.

In addition to leading toward the dedication of the church building, the sermon should address another important question: "Will this be a dedicated church?" A church is not a building, but a group of people. The congregation has come to dedicate itself, not just its building (see Rom. 12:1, Ps. 127:1).

Act of dedication. — The dedication itself takes place during the dedicatory prayer. To increase audience participation, have a responsive reading of a litany or poem before the prayer (suggested litanies are given below).

A burning of the mortgage, or a piece of paper symbolizing it, could take place here or during the history portion of the service. This can be a climactic event, especially if the church has been in debt for some time and has recently sacrificed significantly to become debt-free. It may be very appropriate to sing the doxology as the mortgage burns.

Prayer of dedication. — The dedicatory prayer deserves much thought and preparation. The ideal model is probably that of Solomon in 2 Chronicles 6. The prayer may include the following:

- Thanks to God for putting in His people's hands the means and in their hearts the desire to build.
- Confession of sin and plea for the outpouring of the Holy Spirit upon the congregation.
- A blessing for each guest present.

Now comes the precise moment of dedication. The prayer could conclude like this:

"We now dedicate this building to You, O God,
    as a light in this community,
    as a house of prayer for all people.
For the worship of God,
    for the conversion of sinners,
    for the preaching of Christ and His Word,
    for the fellowship of the family of God,
    for the saving of our children,
    for the dwelling place of God,
we now dedicate this house, in the name of the Father, and of the Son, and of the Holy Spirit. Amen."

Dedication Litany

Minister: To the glory of God, our Father, by whose favor we have built this house;
To the honor of Jesus, the Son of the living God, our Lord and Saviour;
To the work of the Holy Spirit, minister of life and light,

Congregation: We dedicate this house, O God, to Thee.

Minister: For worship in prayer and song,
For the preaching and teaching of the Word,
For the celebration of the holy ordinances,

Congregation: We dedicate this house.

Minister: For comfort to those who mourn,
For strength to those who are tempted,
For help in Christlike living,

Congregation: We dedicate this house.

Minister: For sanctification of the family,
For the guidance of children and youth,
For the salvation of men and women,

Congregation: We dedicate this house.

Minister: For the defense of liberty,
For the training of conscience,
For the defense of Christ and His holy law,
For aggressive warfare against evil,

Congregation: We dedicate this house.

Minister: For the help of the needy,
For the relief of the distressed,
For hastening the coming of Christ,

Congregation: We dedicate this house to Thee, O God.

Minister: As a gift of gratitude and love from those who have experienced the gift of Christ's grace, we bring this house as a freewill offering to our God.

Congregation: We, the people of this congregation, now consecrating ourselves anew, dedicate this entire building to the cause of Christ and to the service of humankind.

Dedication Poems

Thou, Whose Unmeasured Temple Stands

Thou, whose unmeasured temple stands,
Built over earth and sea,
Accept the walls that human hands
Have raised, O God, to Thee.

And let the Comforter and Friend,
Thy Holy Spirit, meet
With those who here in worship bend
Before Thy mercy seat.

May they who err be guided here
To find the better way;
And they who mourn, and they who fear,
Be strengthened as they pray.

May faith grow firm, and love grow warm,
And pure devotion rise,
While round these hallowed walls the storm
Of earth-born passion dies.

—William Cullen Bryant

This We Ask

God bless all those whose membership is here;
Thy people, Lord, who love Thy house and Thee,
And may we find in Thy great book at last,
Each name recorded for eternity.

God bless the strangers gathered in our midst;
Lonely, perhaps, and far from home, they need
The blessed comfort of their Father's house,
The proffered bread of life on which to feed.

God bless the one who here propounds Thy truths,
Be in his heart, speak through the words he speaks,
That every listening, eager one may find
The wisdom and the comfort that he seeks.

And when at last, the benediction said,
May we go, strengthened for the days ahead.
—Grace Noll Crowell

Dedication Weekend

A church dedication can, of course, be held at any time, including Sabbath morning. However, because it is a special event in the life of the congregation, you may include several weekend services. For example:

Friday evening— "Our church in consecration." This could include a Communion service and special musical program.

Sabbath school— "Our church at study." Use special participants such as longtime members or former pastors.

Worship hour— "Our church at worship." Have a guest speaker.

Sabbath afternoon— "Our church in dedication." The dedication service.

Sabbath evening— "Our church in fellowship." A social event.

Dedication Booklet

A dedication booklet becomes a precious memento to church members. Some churches sell extra copies to pay for printing. If you have one, include the following:

Order of service for each meeting of the weekend.
A picture of the new building, perhaps on the cover.
The litany to be used during the act of dedication.
Names of present and former pastors, if possible, with pictures and dates served.
Names of conference/mission representatives participating.

Names of church dedication committee.

An abbreviated history of the church to include pictures of former church buildings.

Names of architect, builder, building committee.

Facts about the building—dates of groundbreaking, beginning construction, first meeting, etc; seating capacity; cost; diagram of the floor plan, identifying the purpose of each room.

Poem.

Church Opening

Since Seventh-day Adventists dedicate only debt-free buildings, congregations often move into a new church home before it is finished and long before its dedication. It is appropriate, however, that there be some special program for this event, although it should not be considered as significant as the dedication. Music, of course, should play a large part in such a happy experience.

There can be a ribbon-cutting. Some congregations march from the old premises to the new. People love entering a new building but hate leaving the pleasant memories of the old. One bridge from the old to the new is to include in the church opening some items brought over from the former building.

Both the church dedication and the church opening are newsworthy events in most places. The occasions should be used to achieve favorable community attention to the church and its program.

CHAPTER 36

Communion

Importance

Communion is an occasion of solemnity and heart-searching, of rejoicing and anticipation. Properly planned and conducted, it brings encouragement and spiritual renewal to the congregation. Conducting Communion service is, therefore, one of the most sacred duties of a pastor or elder. "Everything connected with it should suggest as perfect a preparation as possible." "This ceremony is not to be performed listlessly" (*Evangelism*, pp. 277, 278).

When held. — The *Church Manual* stipulates, "In the Seventh-day Adventist Church the Communion service customarily is celebrated once per quarter." The word "customarily" needs to be emphasized. Paul's statement, "For as often as you eat this bread and drink this cup" (1 Cor. 11:26) infers that the Bible does not determine the frequency of Communion.

The Communion, in addition to the quarterly services, may be observed at special times. Some congregations plan Communion for an occasional evening candlelight service, or a New Year's service, or a special service just for the young people. Foot washing should always be included.

The regular Communion service should be held as part of the Sabbath worship hour. It is too important to relegate to any smaller gathering. Limiting Communion participation to only those willing to come to a specially called meeting is admitting the church's failure to make this sacred service meaningful to the membership at large.

Communion should be announced at least a week in advance so members can prepare themselves and deacons and deaconesses can prepare the emblems and equipment.

Who officiates. — Ordained ministers or elders should conduct the Communion service. Deacons assist by distributing the bread and wine.

Who participates. — Jesus' example of including Judas at the first Communion proves that participation should not be limited to only exemplary Christians. "Christ's example forbids exclusiveness at the

Lord's Supper. It is true that open sin excludes the guilty. This the Holy Spirit plainly teaches. But beyond this none are to pass judgment. God has not left it with men to say who shall present themselves on these occasions. For who can read the heart?" (*The Desire of Ages*, p. 656).

Paul does say, "Whosoever eats this bread or drinks this cup of the Lord, in an unworthy manner will be guilty of the body and blood of the Lord" (1 Cor. 11:27). However, he is not speaking of unworthy people who participate, but of an unworthy manner in which they participate. In the case of the Corinthians this included bitter contentions (1 Cor. 1:11), quarreling factions (1 Cor. 3:3), drunkenness (1 Cor. 11:21), and overemphasizing Communion as a social occasion.

Point this out to those whose overactive sense of guilt discourages their participation. In announcing the Communion service, emphasize the opportunity it provides for members to renew their faith in Jesus and their fellowship with other believers.

Seventh-day Adventists observe open Communion. Adults who feel they have committed their lives to Christ may participate. "But let a man examine himself, and so let him eat of that bread and drink of that cup" (verse 28).

Children, however, should not participate until they are mature enough to have received formal instruction in the meaning of the service and committed themselves to Christ in baptism.

Problems

Attendance on Communion Sabbaths tends to be lower than other Sabbaths. Some see Communion as a tedious obligation rather than an exciting privilege. Some sincere members stay away, saying, "I just don't feel worthy." Even some leaders absent themselves with "I already took part someplace else." Why do people feel bored with Communion? Here are four possible reasons:

1. Lost meaning. — Time tends to drain the meaning from any ritual or tradition. Eventually it may be repeated more for tradition's sake than for its spiritual significance. Each church needs to restudy its Communion traditions and revitalize interest in its celebration. "Why do we do the way we do?" If the answer is not a truly spiritual one, it may be time for some careful, prayerful innovation.

Caution! Moving traditions back toward their original spiritual intent is dangerous. People resist change. Solid, dependable Christian people especially resist change. And they resist change in church most of all.

Change must never be for the sake of change, nor for the sake of convenience. Innovation that tends to make the sacred common must be discouraged. However, encourage change if your church's practice attracts attention to the celebration itself rather than to the spiritual lessons Jesus meant it to teach.

Innovations suggested in this chapter and in the *Church Manual* (1990 ed.) are meant to encourage change only to keep spiritual understanding perpetually above meaningless tradition.

2. Social embarrassment. — Aggressive, extrovertive people have difficulty understanding it, but shy members find the choosing of a foot-washing partner a socially embarrassing experience. They fear the rejection of being turned down. Make sure that understanding leaders are around to help participants find partners.

3. Excessive length. — The Communion service lasts longer than other worship services. To some individuals and in some cultures this is no issue: the beauty and spiritual significance of the service make the time problem insignificant. However, pastors must be sensitive to the feelings of all their members. Are parents having difficulty with restless little ones because of a lengthy service? Do children get bored because of the limited relevance of the service to them? Are some ill at ease because their nonattending or non-Christian family members are impatiently waiting at home for lunch?

4. Cultural differences. — Several cultural factors influence the way Communion is celebrated. What is interesting in one culture may not be so in another. Cultural variations in conducting a Communion service need not be discouraged so long as they effectively teach the spiritual lessons Jesus intended. Local leadership can give better counsel about what is appropriate in a given culture.

Sermon

Traditionally the Communion sermon is given just before separating for the foot-washing service. One variation is to give a brief homily at that point, introducing foot washing. Save the remainder of the sermon for the beginning of the Lord's Supper. Two advantages: 1. Fewer people will leave church at the time of separating for foot washing. The service has been so brief they've hardly worshiped and will be more inclined to stay by and participate. 2. Placing the principal sermon just before the Lord's Supper will increase its spiritual impact on that part of the service.

Total sermon time should probably not exceed 10 minutes. Communion is not a preaching service. A few suggested passages for Communion service sermons:

John 13:3-17
Matt. 26:26-28
Mark 14:22-24   Jesus instituting foot washing.
Luke 22:19, 20   Jesus instituting the Lord's Supper.

Matt. 16:24	"Deny himself, and take up his cross, and follow Me."
Mark 14:18, 19	"'One of you . . . will betray Me.' . . . 'Is it I?'"
John 6:53-56	"Unless you eat the flesh of the Son of Man and drink His blood, you have no life in you."
1 Cor. 10:16, 17	"One body; for we all partake of that one bread."
1 Cor. 11:23-26	"You proclaim the Lord's death till He comes."
Gal. 6:14	"The world has been crucified to me, and I to the world."
1 Peter 2:21	"Christ also suffered for us, leaving us an example."

See also *The Desire of Ages*, "A Servant of Servants" and " 'In Remembrance of Me'."

Foot Washing

Foot washing is a powerful symbol. Some might be able to take part in the Lord's Supper without much personal impact. But it is practically impossible to offer one's feet for washing or to kneel and wash the feet of another without learning something about humility. Perhaps that is why this portion of the service is most difficult for some.

Do not accept that washing the feet at home replaces this ordinance. Discourage holding foot washing between Sabbath school and church, relegating it to a minor position. Any deemphasis of foot washing would gradually lead toward participating in the Lord's Supper only. This has happened in other churches that once practiced the ordinance of humility, but eventually dropped it as being inconvenient.

Before separating for foot washing, make an appropriate announcement, inviting the visitors to participate or observe. Urge the members to participate.

Men separate to one room and women to another. Make certain to provide for the handicapped. You may want to reserve a room for family foot washing. The *Church Manual* states, "In places where it is socially acceptable and where clothing is such that there would be no immodesty, separate arrangements may be made for husband and wife or parents and baptized children to share with each other in the foot-washing ceremony."

Foot washing is a time for making wrongs right, for reaching out to those with whom you have differed, and this should be emphasized. This kind of alienation takes place quite often between husband and wife or between parents and teenage children. Communion day can become a beautiful time for uniting families.

Do not, however, emphasize family foot washing to the neglect of those who are in church without marriage partners.

Deacons and deaconesses should have prepared basins and water, preferably warm. Sufficient towels ought to be provided so that each person has a clean one. Basin, soap, and towel should be provided so that all may wash their hands after the ceremony.

Hymns may be sung or background music played as feet are washed. Each participant, before washing the other's feet, may offer a short prayer. Both feet should be washed. Partners sometimes conclude with an embrace.

Participants return to the sanctuary when finished. When the group is small, they could form a circle, join hands, perhaps sing a song such as "Blest Be the Tie That Binds," and pray before returning to the sanctuary.

Deacons and deaconesses should participate in the foot washing service, but preferably they should have done so earlier, perhaps when setting up the equipment. The congregation should not have to wait for deacons and deaconesses to be served after they've finished waiting on others. Fifteen precious minutes of worship time may be lost to poor planning of the transition between foot washing and the Lord's Supper.

If the sanctuary is emptied during foot washing and if visitors are welcome to remain there, some plan for continued reverence should be followed. Music can be played. Conduct a story time for unbaptized children. Designate someone to tell stories illustrating the lessons of Communion. Make the Communion service a time for children to feel especially included, rather than thoughtlessly excluded.

Lord's Supper

Immediately after the foot washing is over, have someone lead in the singing of a hymn, such as "Jesus Invites His Saints" or "Thy Broken Body, Gracious Lord." Such singing creates a proper spirit as the congregation assembles again in the sanctuary. The hymn can also serve as introit for minister and elders as they take their places at the Communion table, followed by the deacons, who take their seats in the front row.

Emblems on the Communion table should be covered before and after the service. Individual covers are sometimes placed on the bread and the wine receptacles, or the entire table may be covered. Two deaconesses may be invited to come sit in the front row to remove and later replace the cloth covering the table, although this custom has no direct relevance to the upper room experience or the lessons Jesus was teaching.

The officiating minister or elder uncovers the bread and reads an appropriate text, such as 1 Corinthians 11:23, 24. The congregation remains seated with bowed heads and those at the table kneel as an officiating elder asks God's blessing on the bread.

Rising from their knees, minister and elders symbolically break a portion of the bread. (Most should have been broken before the service.) The bread is given to the deacons, who distribute it to the congregation.

When the deacons return from serving the congregation, elders and minister serve them and one another. The one officiating repeats an appropriate phrase, such as the words of Jesus in 1 Corinthians 11:24, and leads the congregation in the partaking of the bread, followed by silent prayer.

The leader covers the bread, uncovers the wine, and then reads a text such as 1 Corinthians 11:25, 26. An elder offers a prayer of blessing on the wine, and the distribution process is repeated. The leader repeats a phrase such as the words of Jesus in 1 Corinthians 11:25, and leads the congregation in the partaking of the wine, followed by silent prayer.

The deacons then recover the glasses and return them to the table, where the leader covers them. The deaconesses cover the table.

If this method is followed, deacons pass up and down the aisles six times, all of which tend to draw attention away from rather than toward the spiritual lessons of the Lord's Supper. There is, however, a much briefer and simpler way to serve the emblems without diminishing any spiritual symbolism. The deacons can carry both bread and wine on the same tray and serve them at the same time. They can place the trays on a special table in the rear. The glasses may be left in the seats or in racks mounted on the rear of the pews. Blessings, reading of scriptures, and partaking of the emblems can follow the usual order. This brief distribution order helps to abbreviate the extraneous and concentrate on the spiritual.

During distribution of emblems, have some special music, centered on lessons of the Lord's Supper. Other options include Bible reading, testimonies, a hymn, or instrumental music. Little time should elapse between a worshiper's receiving the emblems and partaking of them.

Communion should always end on a high note. Wrongs have been righted. Sins have been forgiven. Hope has been restored. It's a time for rejoicing. Close with bright, joyful music, such as: "Praise God, From Whom All Blessings Flow"; "Redeemed! How I Love to Proclaim It!"; or the "Hallelujah Chorus."

After the closing hymn the congregation is dismissed, either by benediction or by silent prayer. As the congregation leaves, deacons may stand at the door and take up an offering for the poor.

Following the service, deacons and deaconesses dispose of leftover bread or wine in a respectful manner. In no case should either be eaten or drunk.

It is recommended that our churches use individual Communion cups. This enables the entire congregation to partake of the wine in unison, and also provides protection against the health hazard of the common cup.

Additional Suggestions

1. Preach on Communion the Sabbath before. Perhaps one reason congregations lose sight of the spiritual lessons of the Communion service is that there is little time in the Communion sermon for instruction. Use the Sabbath before.

2. Include an "invitation to the table" litany. Something like the

following could be incorporated into the service at the beginning of the Lord's Supper:

Leader: "We enter now into a time of special blessing."
People: "We come anticipating that blessing."
Leader: "When we eat . . .
People: "We remember the broken body of Christ."
Leader: "When we drink . . .
People: "We remember the spilled blood of Christ."
Leader: "Reveal Yourself to us now, our Lord, as You revealed Yourself to Your disciples then."
People: "Grace our table with Your presence, and give us a foretaste of the feast to come."
All: "Come, for all is ready."

3. Include a "partaking" litany. As participants partake, each saying his/her own name:

Leader: "This is my body . . .
People: "Which is broken for _____ ."

• • • • •

Leader: "This is my blood . . .
People: "Which is shed for _____ ."

4. Serve church shut-ins. Organize your elders and deacons to take Communion to those physically unable to attend the service. This guarantees every shut-in four visits a year. Foot washing is usually not included, because of the handicapped being unable to wash another's feet.

5. Have an extra Communion for youth. Invite your youth to a special service, perhaps in your home. Plan a program that both teaches the spiritual lessons of Communion and leaves with your young people a memory of the service as being something special. This should not replace youth participation in the quarterly service.

Recipes

Only unleavened bread and the unfermented juice of the grape should be used in the Lord's Supper. Where it is impossible to obtain grapes, grape juice, or grape concentrate, the juice of raisins may be used. In isolated areas where none of these are readily available, the conference or mission will provide advice or assistance.

Recipe for Communion bread

1 cup fine-ground flour (preferably whole grain)
1/4 teaspoon salt
2 tablespoons cold water
1/4 cup olive or vegetable oil

Method: Sift flour and salt together. Pour the water into the oil, but do not stir. Add this to the dry ingredients and mix with a fork until all the flour is dampened. Roll out between two sheets of waxed paper to the thickness of thick pie pastry. Place on an ungreased, floured baking sheet, and mark off with a sharp knife into bite-size squares, being careful to prick each square to prevent blistering. Bake at 450 degrees Fahrenheit for 10 to 15 minutes. Watch carefully during the last five minutes to prevent burning. Serves 50 persons.

Alternate recipe for Communion bread

1 cup fine-ground flour (preferably whole-grain)
1/4 teaspoon salt
3 tablespoons pure vegetable oil
4 1/2 tablespoons cold water

Method: Put oil in a bowl and add salt. Slowly add water, beating constantly with a fork until the ingredients make a thick, white emulsion. Quickly add the flour and mix lightly into a dough. Turn out on a floured board. Fold over and over and pound with a wooden mallet or potato masher until elastic (five or six minutes). Roll to the thickness of pie crust, place on an oiled baking sheet, and mark with a knife into bite-sized squares. Bake at 400 degrees Fahrenheit. Brown only slightly, as browning gives a strong flavor.

Unfermented wine. — Secure good grapes, strip them from the stem, and stew them in an enameled saucepan until they come to the boiling point. Strain through a coarse cloth, then boil for 15 minutes. Just before the juice boils, skim off all the scum that rises. When the juice is at the boiling point, pour into strong bottles that have been sterilized and kept warm so they will receive the hot juice without breaking. Fill to within one-half inch of the cork, and cork immediately. Cut off the cork close to the bottle, and seal with sealing wax. Set aside in a dark place, and do not move the bottles unnecessarily.

CHAPTER 37

Funeral

At a baptism, people look for the candidate being baptized. At a wedding, they look for the bride being married. But at a funeral, people look for God. Don't dread funerals. Proper as it is to abhor death, you ought to take fullest advantage of any occasion where people are looking for God.

Respect the traditions of local culture while dealing with death and funerals—but only to the extent they are not contrary to Christian principles and the biblical teaching on death. Move your people away from cultural traditions that infer immortality of the soul and the necessity of appeasing the spirits.

Respect the traditions of your congregation. Each church tends to establish funeral customs. For example, some deliver food to the homes of those in mourning; others provide a meal at the church after the funeral. Some have funerals at the church; others use funeral parlors. Some schedule viewing the body as people enter the church for the funeral service, some just before leaving, others not at all. Learn the funeral traditions of your new congregation before conducting your first funeral.

Because cultures and congregations vary so widely, only basic guidelines are given here. They may require considerable adaptation to fit local situations.

Before the Service

Visiting the family. — *Go immediately, if possible.* Don't say too much. People are in shock. Minds are numbed. This is no time for a theological discourse. Mourners remember very little of what is said during this time of initial shock, but they will remember the nonverbal evidence that you cared. They will remember that you dropped everything to come. They will remember a heartfelt hug. A caring wife can often be more effective with grieving women than can her pastor-husband. Joining hands in a prayer circle is generally appropriate.

Offer the assistance of the church. Mourners seldom make use of the suggestion "Let us know if we can be of help." They don't want to presume and may not be thinking clearly enough to know what to ask for. Therefore, make specific suggestions of how the church might help: notifying relatives and friends, answering the phone or door, taking the children into a member's home for a day, providing food, or cleaning the house in preparation for company.

Do not, however, attempt to relieve mourners of all the work to be done. To be kept fairly busy is one of the best antidotes for grief. Removing work increases depression. The bereaved should be allowed to carry on as many usual activities as possible during the period of crisis.

Offer your assistance as pastor. Always begin by assuming the family might want someone else to conduct the funeral. Ask, "Have you contacted the minister you would like to have conduct the service?" The family may also have preference regarding those who sing, serve as pallbearers, or assist their minister in the service.

If you are ever the guest minister invited to conduct a funeral in another pastor's district, work closely with the local pastor. Encourage the family to have their pastor assist you.

If the family asks you to conduct the service, you should then talk over the necessary details and plan a funeral that fits their specific wishes. Remember, however, that funeral directors are paid to handle many of the details of a funeral. Don't do their work for them.

Beware of giving too much advice. People should make their own decision regarding choice of funeral director, cost of funeral, place of interment, etc. If asked, pastors usually recommend that funerals be in the church. Stay out of family squabbles. There may be cases in which unfair advantage is being taken of a widow and wise pastoral counsel is necessary.

Who officiates. — Usually no license is required for conducting a funeral. In the absence of a minister, an elder may lead out. This should not be done, however, without the pastor's approval. An elder or friend of the family may be called on to assist the minister in the service by giving the obituary, scripture, prayer, etc.

In some places the pastor or the elder who conducts the funeral must make sure he or she has the proper death certificate from civil authorities before interment.

Seventh-day Adventist ministers are paid by the tithe. It is not their practice to receive a fee for conducting funerals unless a large travel expense is involved.

Viewing the body. — Viewing the body tends to be emotionally healthy, for it actualizes death. Without facing the body, some bereaved people tend to deny the reality of their loved one's having died. The viewing almost invariably leads to tears, but tears cleanse the soul. Don't discourage bearable pain. In grief, pain must precede healing. The sooner the pain is faced and felt, the quicker the recovery.

The wisdom of many cultures underlines this fact. Sometimes family and friends are invited to the funeral parlor for viewing. Sometimes the body is kept at home and a wake is held there. Sometimes religious services are held around the casket every evening until the burial. In whatever way the viewing is practiced, it serves a useful purpose. Death must be faced before recovery can begin.

At the funeral service the body may be displayed so that people pay their respects as they enter. The casket is then sealed permanently. With tears having been shed, the funeral service focuses on hope and is not dampened by a final viewing afterward.

Other cultures and congregations insist that viewing afterward can be a positive experience. They place the mourners in the first row during the service. Afterward, people file by to view the remains, then those who know the family well share a handshake, hug, or word of encouragement. This makes the final viewing for them a rich, church family experience.

Typical Funeral Service

The funeral director. — The funeral director is in charge of funeral arrangements. The minister is in charge of religious features. You are a specialist in religion. He/she is a specialist in funerals. You need not pretend you know everything about funerals. Depend on his/her expertise, especially when moving to a new area. Even proper clergy dress varies from place to place. Seek his/her counsel. The funeral is conducted as a team.

Arrive for the funeral early. This is one service that seldom starts late. Besides, you need to talk through with the funeral director, musicians, and your assistants the details of the service.

Meeting the mourners. — Mourners are typically brought together in a side room before the funeral service begins. Ask the funeral director to take you to them as soon as they have assembled. Again, this is not a time for saying much. You are there to learn, so that what you say during the service will better fit the situation.

What is the emotional condition of the principal mourners? Kneel down and grasp the widow's hand. This may be your first chance to meet the entire family. Are some especially moved? Do some seem to come without the Christian hope? A funeral is an excellent place to spot evangelistic interests to be followed up later. Many a wayward son or daughter thinks serious thoughts at Dad's or Mother's funeral.

The beginning preacher may assume mourners suffer from almost uncontrollable grief. Visiting them just before the funeral will help you know before the service that this isn't always so.

If death was preceded by a prolonged illness, the family has gone through much of the grieving process already. The deceased may have become a cantankerous nonperson during the long process of dying, and the family may feel relieved that their loved one is finally freed from pain. Death may bring more a sigh of relief than a wail of sorrow.

All this will affect the service you're about to conduct and the sermon you're about to preach.

Order of service. — A simple order of service might be:

1. *Ministers enter* as the funeral director gives the signal to begin.
2. *Scripture reading and prayer.* The Scripture might be taken from those listed below, perhaps combining several together. The prayer should include thanksgiving to God for the life He has given the deceased, comfort for those who mourn, and the hope of eternal life through Christ. Since non-Christians are usually present, the one praying usually stands and the audience remains seated for the prayer.
3. *Solo or hymn.* Congregational singing doesn't work well if many are emotionally disturbed.
4. *Obituary.* The family may wish to prepare the obituary, although this carries problems. It might be too long, poorly written, or unrealistically laudatory. The death of a loved one leaves family members feeling guilty for not having treated him/her better. This guilt ought not to be assuaged by an obituary that portrays a life far more perfect than the audience finds believable.
5. *Sermon and prayer.*
6. *Solo.* This should be a song that ends the service on a note of assurance and hope. The ending of the song provides an excellent signal for the funeral director to take charge.

Move to the head of the casket. If there is to be a viewing, remain there until after the audience and family have passed by. Give strength by your presence more than by your words. When the funeral director is ready, lead the way as the casket is placed in the hearse. The general protocol is that you do not leave the casket from this point until after the interment. The funeral director will likely direct you to ride either in the hearse or in a car preceding it.

Sermon. — *General principles.* A funeral sermon (1) should be Bible-based and Christ-centered, (2) should be short—usually about 15 minutes in length, (3) should not be a doctrinal exposition—this is no

FUNERAL

time for heavy proof or hard reasoning, and (4) should include both thanks for this life and hope for the life to come.

Your file ought to include at least one folder marked "Funeral Sermon Garden." Keep dropping into that file ideas that could be developed into a funeral sermon. Two things you can depend on: funeral sermons always come, and they must often be prepared on short notice.

Personalize the sermon. A funeral sermon should not talk just about death, but about this death. The easiest way to do this and the shortest way to prepare a sermon is to wait until at least some of the family have gathered, then go to the home and get the family talking about the deceased. Ask about work, group associations, hobbies, personality traits.

Pick one or more good traits that are generally known, and emphasize them in your sermon. Even the most wicked woman may have been good to her children. Even the least gifted man may have been admirably loyal. The family will likely flood you with stories about the loved one's strengths. The best of these will make excellent sermon illustrations.

Don't build the dead up unrealistically. The audience knows the dead too well. If what your sermon says about the deceased isn't credible, what it says about Christ won't seem credible either.

Ask to see the deceased's Bible. You may learn much about the person's devotional life. Look for underlined texts, poems, notations, etc. You might even preach the funeral sermon from this Bible.

Never assume the deceased to be eternally lost. However, if they are not known to be Christians, never assume they are saved. Rather, talk about God's love for them, that in God's hands they're in better hands, more loving hands than ours could ever be. Talk about how anxious and able God is to save. Talk about lives in your audience still being lived, races still being run, and how, through Christ, everyone present can have the hope of life after death.

Scripture. — Sermons and scripture readings might be drawn from the following:

Job 14:1, 2, 14, 15	"You shall call, and I will answer you."
Ps. 23	"Yea, though I walk through the valley of the shadow of death, I will fear no evil; for You are with me."
Ps. 27	"Wait on the Lord; be of good courage, and He shall strengthen your heart."
Ps. 46	"God is our refuge and strength, a very present help in trouble."
Ps. 90	"Lord, You have been our dwelling place in all generations."

Ps. 91:1, 2, 11, 12	"I will say of the Lord, 'He is my refuge and my fortress; My God, in Him I will trust'."
Ps. 121	"My help comes from the Lord."
Isa. 33:15-17, 24	"And the inhabitant will not say, 'I am sick'."
Isa. 35:3-10	"Then the eyes of the blind shall be opened, and the ears of the death shall be unstopped. . . . And sorrow and sighing shall flee away."
Isa. 40:28-31	"But those who wait on the Lord shall renew their strength."
Isa. 43:1, 2	"When you pass through the waters, I will be with you."
John 14:1-6	"I will come again and receive you to Myself."
Rom. 8:14-39	"All things work together for good to those who love God."
1 Cor. 2:9, 10	"Eye hath not seen, nor ear heard."
1 Cor. 15:20-26	"The last enemy that will be destroyed is death."
1 Cor. 15:51-55	"This mortal must put on immortality."
Phil. 3:20, 21	"For our citizenship is in heaven."
1 Thess. 4:13-18	"Lest you sorrow as others who have no hope."
1 Thess. 5:1-11	"Whether we wake or sleep, we should live together with Him."
Heb. 4:14-16	"For we do not have a High Priest who cannot sympathize with our weaknesses."
2 Peter 3:8-14	"Not willing that any should perish but that all should come to repentance."
Rev. 7:15-17	"They shall neither hunger anymore nor thirst anymore."
Rev. 14:13	"Blessed are the dead who die in the Lord."
Rev. 21:1-4	"And God will wipe away every tear from their eyes."
Rev. 22:1-5	"They shall see His face."

Funeral of child

2 Sam. 12:16-23	David's grief. "I shall go to him, but he shall not return to me."
Mark 10:13-16	"For of such is the kingdom of God. . . . And He took them up in His arms."

Funeral of youth

Eccl. 11:6-10	"Rejoice, O young man, in your youth."

FUNERAL

Eccl. 12	"Remember now your Creator in the days of your youth."
Luke 7:11-15	Nain widow's son. "Young man, I say to you, arise."

Funeral of godly woman

Prov. 31:10-31	"Who can find a virtuous wife? For her worth is far above rubies."
Matt. 26:10-13	"Wherever this gospel is preached in the whole world, what this woman has done will also be told as a memorial to her."
Acts 9:36-42	Dorcas. "This woman was full of good works."

Funeral of elderly

Gen. 5:24	Enoch. "And he was not, for God took him."
Gen. 15:15	"You shall be buried at a good old age."
Matt. 11:28	"I will give you rest."
2 Tim. 4:6-8	"I have fought the good fight, I have finished the race, I have kept the faith."

Poem. —

What must it be to step on shore, and find it—heaven;
To take hold of a hand, and find it—God's hand;
To breathe a new air and find it—Celestial air;
To feel invigorated, and find it—Immortality;
To rise from the care and turmoil of earth
Into one unbroken calm;
To wake up and find it—Glory.

Typical Graveside Service

If the graveside service includes the military, or if a lodge is participating, plan with them beforehand so your programs can be coordinated. Encourage them to do their part first. Such services often infer immortality of the soul and Adventists present are offended if the last words spoken over a loved one are about his/her being in Paradise.

If the weather looks threatening, come to the graveside prepared. You can slip a piece of clear plastic into your pocket to cover your Bible as you read in the rain or snow.

Stay by the casket while the pallbearers prepare to carry it from the hearse to the graveside. Ask the funeral director what route should be taken to the grave and where the deceased's head will be.

Lead the casket to the grave. Avoid walking on other graves. Stand at the grave near the head of the deceased. Wait for the funeral director's signal to begin the graveside service. The use of music at the graveside is determined by local custom or by family wishes.

Informal committal. — The graveside service should be very brief. Probably there has already been a service. People are grieving, and are standing. The weather may not be cooperative. A simple, informal committal may consist of only a scripture and prayer:

Scripture. An ideal graveside scripture is 1 Thessalonians 4:13-18: "But I do not want you to be ignorant, brethren, concerning those who have fallen asleep, lest you sorrow as others who have no hope. For if we believe that Jesus died and rose again, even so God will bring with Him those who sleep in Jesus. For this we say to you by the word of the Lord, that we who are alive and remain until the coming of the Lord will by no means precede those who are asleep. For the Lord Himself will descend from heaven with a shout, with the voice of an archangel, and with the trumpet of God. And the dead in Christ will rise first. Then we who are alive and remain shall be caught up together with them in the clouds to meet the Lord in the air. And thus we shall always be with the Lord. Therefore comfort one another with these words."

An alternate scripture is 1 Corinthians 15:51-55.

Prayer. The prayer should end on a positive note with an appeal to your audience to so live that when death comes it will be met with the certain hope of life again through Christ.

Formal committal. — If a formal committal is desired, it fits well between the scripture and the prayer. Interment customs vary. In some places the minister drops a handful of earth or flower petals on the casket as the committal is read. Some feel "earth to earth, ashes to ashes, dust to dust" is a rather crude reminder that the corpse will decay, and so eliminate this portion of the committal.

A sample committal for a Christian:

"Forasmuch as God in His infinite love and wisdom has permitted our dear brother [sister] to fall asleep in Christ, we do tenderly commit his [her] body to the ground, [earth to earth, ashes to ashes, dust to dust] in the sure and certain hope of a joyful resurrection when our Lord shall return in glory. Then this body of our humiliation shall be changed and made like unto His glorious body, according to the mighty working whereby He is able even to subdue all things unto Himself."

A sample committal for one not known to be a Christian:

"Forasmuch as God in His goodness and the outworkings of His providence has permitted this our friend [brother/sister] to lay down the burdens of this life, we do lovingly commit his [her] body to the ground; [earth to earth, ashes to ashes, dust to dust] remembering, as we do, that all the issues of life are in the hands of the everlasting Father of love and compassion, and that He has promised eternal life to those who love Him."

After the service. — Following the prayer and the end of the service, walk directly to the immediate family and greet each one briefly. If your spouse is present and feels comfortable doing it, the spouse can join you and add that special touch that's so meaningful at such times.

Do not rush away. Use the occasion to meet informally people you may never see in church. When the family begins to leave, you are free to go.

Additional Suggestions

Interment before funeral. — A less traditional approach is to have the interment before the funeral, perhaps as a private service for the family. From the graveside the family goes to the church, where a public service is held. The casket has been faced for the last time. The death has, in a sense, been buried. Now the service concentrates on the celebration of a life rather than the mourning of a death.

Audience participation. — An intimate, informal service may include an invitation from the minister something like this: "You have come here because you knew and loved _____. Each of you has unique and special memories of him [her]. If you can muster enough courage, I believe you will find that sharing those memories in one or two sentences from where you are seated will help yourself and his [her] family."

Cremation. — Cremation will likely become an increasingly acceptable way to handle the dead. It is less of a financial burden on the family. In crowded areas, space for burial is becoming increasingly difficult to find.

Seventh-day Adventists take no theological stand against cremation. We believe that God will be no more dependent on preexisting matter at the resurrection than He was at Creation. Local culture and the local congregation may, however, discourage its use.

Ministering to the Grieving

Six suggestions for successfully ministering to the grieving after the funeral:

1. Be present. — Doctors expect new mothers to suffer from postpartum blues after the birth. Ministers should expect mourners to suffer from "postpartum blues" after the funeral. Their adrenaline is drained, the immediate crisis is over, the company is gone. At the funeral they confronted their loss. Only after the funeral do they confront their loneliness. They may be more depressed a few days after the funeral than before.

Unfortunately, society and even the church tend to overlook all this. They sympathize before the funeral, but forget and neglect afterward. The pastor, as a professional, must understand this unfortunate fact and realize that ministering to the grieving only begins with the funeral and should continue for many months after. Teach your church the importance of developing some kind of support system for an ongoing ministry to the grieving.

Make a pastoral call soon after the funeral. As a nice gesture, take as a gift a tape recording of the service.

A long-term plan is to mark a calendar in your office so you are reminded to send a note of encouragement on each anniversary of the death.

2. Be patient. — Grieving takes time. Sleeplessness, anxiety, fear, anger, and a preoccupation with self and with sad thoughts may continue on and off for a year or more. Unrealistic expectations that those bereaved should "snap out of it" may leave them feeling anxious and guilty and make the process of grieving more difficult.

Be patient with the bereaved who express anger at God. Anger is a natural part of the grieving process. Though anger against the God who could have prevented the death is unfair and hopefully temporary, it is only natural.

3. Listen. — Talking is an effective means of releasing emotions and undergoing healing. The grieving may be uncomfortable sharing their pain and may even prefer to be left alone, but sharing brings healing. Friends may talk about everything except the death; the minister must not. Ask, "Would you like to talk about it?" or "Tell me how things are."

Actually, the bereaved usually enjoy talking about their lost loved one once you get them started. It brings up precious memories. Knowing you feel the deceased's life story is worth listening to induces contentment.

The Christian faith brings great comfort and hope to those who mourn. You will be most helpful, however, not by insisting what their faith *should* be doing for them, but by probing for and listening to what it *is* doing for them.

4. Discourage denial. — Some bereaved Christians, believing it is wrong to have ongoing grief feelings, deny them. Others may simply want to avoid the pain of grief. But in grieving, the old adage holds true: "no pain, no gain." Memories, of course, are precious and important. In a sense, however, people must say goodbye to the past before they can enjoy the present or look forward to the future.

Be sensitive to indications of denial such as refusal to talk about the death, inability to part with the deceased's personal effects, and ongoing use of medication to mask the depression.

5. Encourage activity. — Grieving is important. It is necessary. But it also tends to be self-centered. As soon as possible, the grieving should commit themselves to some regular activity of benefit to others.

Becoming active in a grief support group may be a beginning. For example, the widows in the church might form a group to support one another and to perform other ministries for the church.

6. Make peace with your own death. — Christians in general and Christian preachers in particular have a belief system that gives strong support when facing death. That does not mean that you have faced the inevitability of your own death and made peace with it. Until you do, you may never be comfortable around death, and of limited help to those grieved by it.

CHAPTER 38

Groundbreaking

A groundbreaking service encourages congregational involvement and unity in supporting a building project. It engenders enthusiasm, especially if the church has been planning, praying, and giving for the building over a long period of time. At last something tangible is happening.

Planning the Service

Setting the time. — Groundbreaking is not entirely a religious service and thus does not belong on Sabbath. Sunday is often an ideal time.

Inviting the guests. — Conference/mission representatives should be invited. Local political and other community leaders might attend. Pastors from other churches will sometimes come. The news media ought to be notified and encouraged to give liberal coverage.

Preparing the site. — The site should be cleared. Perhaps a platform needs to be erected and a sound system installed. If the service is going to be long, chairs may be needed.

Architectural drawings of the building should be prominently displayed. A mock-up of the proposed structure will help people visualize it.

If the ground is to be broken with shovels, several should be provided. Sometimes the shovel blades are painted gold or silver. Alternatively, an earth-moving machine may be used to turn over the first dirt.

Another plan that includes congregational participation is to provide a plow. A long rope is attached to the plow, and the congregation pulls the plow through the ground—a beautiful symbol of a congregation pulling together in the building project. If the building has been marked out ahead of time, a furrow can be plowed around its perimeter and the building easily visualized when the groundbreaking is finished.

Order of Service

The order of service suggested below may be used when the audience is comfortably seated and when you have planned for a regular service. However, the service could be abbreviated, depending upon local circumstances.

Opening song	Many congregations do not sing well outdoors. For that reason, congregational singing may be omitted, especially if the group is small.
Prayer	Involve a non-Adventist pastor or a leader in the local congregation to offer the prayer.
Special song	
Sermonette	This should be very brief. It should consist mostly of a scripture reading and a litany in which everyone can participate. Texts and litanies listed under chapter 35 could be useful.
Special song	
Speeches	Special guests may be invited to speak briefly, but in view of the full program they should be few in number. Have someone narrate the history of the church or of the present building project, and talk about the immediate plans for beginning the building.
Groundbreaking	Special participants in breaking the first ground usually include the pastor, head elder, building committee chairperson, and representatives from the conference/mission and community. A child should be included as a representative of the church of the future. If the building is a school, include the school board chairman, principal, and a teacher.
Special song or hymn of dedication	
Benediction	

Stonelaying

A stonelaying service may take the place of groundbreaking. It is held after the building has begun and features the laying of a stone to become part of the foundation. The service can follow the same general order as for groundbreaking.

Recommended texts include: Ezra 3:10, 11; 6:14; Matthew 21:42; Acts 4:11; 1 Corinthians 3:9-11; and 1 Peter 2:4-8.

CHAPTER 39

House Opening

Purpose

The practice of house blessing varies according to culture and the wishes of each individual family. The world church does not have any regular tradition for such services. Some families may request the blessing when they purchase or build their first home, some when they pay off the mortgage and the home is truly theirs. Still others ask for a house blessing whenever they move to a different home.

Typically, the house blessing is held after the house is completed, the furniture installed, and probably the family moved in. Such a service provides an excellent opportunity to invite the neighbors for the special occasion to get acquainted with them, and to establish one's family as a Christian witness in the neighborhood.

Careful differentiation should be made between a house blessing and a church dedication. A family's house may be set aside to be of spiritual service to its family and neighborhood, but only the church's house is set aside exclusively for the worship of God. It is proper that a house be blessed, but only a church is dedicated.

Typically, a house opening sets the building apart for:
1. Nurturing the love, unity, and spiritual growth of the family living there.
2. Witnessing to the neighborhood of the saving love of Jesus.

Who Officiates

No license or ordination is required for house blessing services. An elder may perform the service, but should do so with the knowledge and cooperation of the pastor.

Order of Service

Attendees often include non-Christian neighbors. People typically gather in the living room of the home and the room may be crowded. Some will likely be standing. Thus, the service should usually be no more than 30 minutes in length.

The following order is suggested:

Congregational Song	This ought to be considered optional, depending on the situation. Appropriate songs include "Happy the Home" and "Love at Home."
Prayer	Since there are three prayers in this short service, the first and last should be brief and not repeat the prayer of blessing. This first prayer is for the purpose of invoking God's presence in the service.
History of house/family	This could be given by a family member, perhaps the head of the household.
Message	The message might include: *Scripture* (see suggestions on page 233) *Poetry* (see suggestions on page 233) *Litany* (see suggestions on pages 233, 234)
Candle ceremony	Your message could close with the lighting of a candle to symbolize the light of Jesus present in this home and the use of this house to let that light shine throughout the neighborhood. The candle can remain burning throughout the remainder of the service.
Prayer of blessing	The family might kneel with joined hands in a circle surrounding the kneeling pastor. Others stand surrounding the family. Include in your prayer a blessing on the house, the family, and the neighborhood.
Special song	"Bless This House" is an ideal song for this setting.
Benediction	This prayer should be brief and not repetitious of the prayer of blessing. Perhaps a formal benediction is most appropriate: "And now may 'the Lord bless you and keep you; the Lord make His face shine upon you, and be gracious to you; the Lord lift up His countenance upon you, and give you peace,' now and evermore. Amen" (Num. 6:24-26).

HOUSE DEDICATION

House tour At this juncture the family may wish to invite guests to tour the house. Refreshments are optional.

Suggested Scriptures

Gen. 24:67	Home a place to find love and comfort.
2 Sam. 23:15	Home a precious place of refreshing.
Ps. 127	The Lord should build the house. He blesses it with children.
Isa. 65:21-24	"They shall build houses and inhabit them."
Micah 4:4	"Everyone shall sit under his vine."
Luke 10:38-42	The place of work and worship in the home.

Suggested Poetry

What Is a Home?

"What is a home? A roof to keep out the rain. Four walls to keep out the wind. Floors to keep out the cold. Yes, but home is more than that. It is the laugh of a baby, the song of a mother, the strength of a father. Warmth of loving hearts, light from happy eyes, kindness, loyalty, comradeship. Home is first school and first church for young ones, where they learn what is right, what is good, and what is kind. Where they go for comfort when they are hurt or sick. Where joy is shared and sorrow eased. Where fathers and mothers are respected and loved. Where children are wanted. Where the simplest food is good enough for kings because it is earned. Where money is not so important as loving-kindness. Where even the teakettle sings from happiness. That is home. God bless it."

—Ernestine Schuman-Heink.

The Four Corners

"Bless the four corners of this house.
Bless the rooms where each shall rest.
Bless the door that opens wide, to stranger, as to kin;
And bless each windowpane that lets the sunlight in.
And bless the roof overhead, and every sturdy wall.
But most of all bless those that will dwell herein.
May the peace of man, the peace of God,
 and the peace of love be on all."

Suggested Litany

Leader:	Eternal God, the heaven of heavens cannot contain You, much less the walls of temples or homes made with hands. Graciously receive our thanks for this place, and accept it as a home dedicated to Your service and offered to Your honor and glory.
People:	We thank You, Lord.
Leader:	For Your presence whenever two or three have gathered in Your name,
People:	We thank You, Lord.
Leader:	For making us Your children through Jesus Christ our Saviour,
People:	We thank You, Lord.
Leader:	For giving us families to love and to be loved,
People:	We thank You, Lord.
Leader:	For providing here shelter, and food, and friends,
People:	We thank You, Lord.
Leader:	For refreshing us day by day with the Bread of Life,
People:	We thank You, Lord.
Leader:	For this home where this family may be still and know that You are God,
People:	We thank You, Lord.
Leader:	For Your promise that You will soon come and take us to our heavenly home,
People:	We thank You, Lord.
All:	For everything in heaven and on earth is Yours, and we exalt Your name above all. Amen."

Alternate litany. — *Family questions.* You may want to ask questions of the family either informally or in a written litany and receive their answers as a family commitment. Questions such as:

1. Do you pledge to make this house a place of prayer, where the family altar and daily devotions are revered?
2. Do you pledge to make this house a place of family love and unity?
3. Do you pledge to make this house a light to the community?

CHAPTER 40

New Parish Induction

Seventh-day Adventists tend to take for granted the acceptance of a new pastor in the parish and community. As a result, new pastors are left alone to work their way into the affection of church members. Not enough emphasis is given on assisting the bonding process between new pastors and their congregation.

Difficulties of Transition

The transition of a pastoral family from one parish to another may engender anticipation and enthusiasm on the part of both family and parish. The change can also be delicate and difficult. It is invariably accompanied by some degree of grief.

Congregational grief. — In marriage a loss through divorce may be more devastating than a loss through death, for in divorce the loved one chooses to leave. As a result one feels rejected, and rejection leads to anger. Likewise, when a pastor chooses to move from one parish to another, the congregation feels some degree of grief, rejection, and anger: "What's wrong with us?" "Why would our pastor want to leave us?" "I got hurt loving the last pastor. I'm not going to love the new one and get hurt again."

If the previous pastor did not choose to leave, but was arbitrarily reassigned by the conference/mission, the congregation may be angry at the conference and resent the replacement. If the previous pastor was not appreciated, the congregation may feel distrust of and anger toward all ministers.

People tend to resent and resist change—especially conservative people, and these make up a large portion of most congregations. New pastors invariably represent change. Therefore, the temptation is to resent and resist the new pastor.

Pastoral family grief. — The pastoral family has much more to grieve over than the church family. They get uprooted—an experience

249

especially devastating to wives and children. They move into a new town and a strange house, with financial and social strains. The children have to start in a new school. The spouse may have to hunt for a new job.

Most serious of all, the pastoral family have had to leave their friends. Where the congregation may be grieving the loss of one family, the new family is grieving the loss of all their friends in their previous parish.

All of this adds up to potential problems during pastoral transitions.

Smoothing the Transition

Some suggestions for smoothing the transition to a new pastorate:

Bury the old. — The old must be set aside before the new can be accepted. The congregation can express its appreciation and verbalize its grief through a well-promoted and attended farewell for the outgoing pastor.

Adventist theology teaches that the dead do not return! Former pastors, having been lovingly buried, should seldom return. Pastoral families must sever ties in the old pastorate, no matter how painful.

Don't replace too soon. — Some may feel that the new pastor must assume responsibilities immediately after the former pastor leaves. Research, however, indicates that it typically takes about three months before a congregation is ready to welcome a new pastor. This interim period gives time for church members to separate themselves emotionally from the former pastoral family. It also provides a unique opportunity for the latent lay leadership of the parish to emerge. Meanwhile, the congregation rediscovers its need to be pastored.

Adapt church's program to pastor's gifts. — No pastor is good at everything. The expected skills are too many and too varied. For example, on one end of the spectrum the pastor is expected to be a scholarly theologian and biblical preacher. This requires a love for books, a preference for privacy of one's study. On the other end, the pastor is expected to be a counselor, visitor, and promoter. This takes the opposite personality—gregarious and outgoing. No pastor can fill both roles perfectly.

Unless a congregation allows the pastors to focus on areas of their strength, they will inevitably spend most of the time in the areas of their weakness, doing things they enjoy the least. This not only makes their work less fulfilling, but deprives the church of the best they have to offer.

Should a new pastor immediately set out to make radical changes in the parish organization? Congregational cooperation in effecting change in a new pastorate is often greater during the "honeymoon" period of the new pastor. However, without sufficient knowledge of the parish, the new pastor is hardly in a position to determine what changes are needed.

An effective middle ground is to begin with a self-examination of the church. Find out its background, current status, and future needs. Share with your members your background, strengths, and weaknesses. How can you blame a congregation for failing to support you in your ministry when you haven't told them what type of ministerial role you prefer, the things you do best, and the things you enjoy the least? Don't be too fearful of admitting your weaknesses. They'll find them out anyway. And they'll forgive you a lot sooner if they know you're aware of them too.

The Bible likens a church to a body. "For as we have many members in one body, but all the members do not have the same function, so we, being many, are one body in Christ, and individually members of one another" (Rom. 12:4, 5). Pastors must stop trying to represent the entire body. They are only one part of it. When there's a weakness in one part of the body, the rest of the body compensates. For example, when the eyes can't see, the senses of hearing and touch intensify to compensate for the weakness. Likewise, when a pastor is weak at some task, the natural thing to do is criticize; the Christian thing to do is compensate.

Like Aaron and Hur holding up Moses's hands (Ex. 17:12), the local church elders should support the pastor's hands. They should lead out in examining what the church wants done and what you as the new pastor do and don't do best. They ought to identify your strengths and let you major in those. They should assist you in delegating other duties among members in the congregation having gifts in other needed areas.

The theory is simple and beautiful, but implementation might be something else again. You may feel the biggest problem in a congregation is finding people to lead in those areas where that congregation previously expected the pastor to lead. Not necessarily so. One reason the best persons in a congregation will not accept responsibility is the unwillingness of the pastor to give up authority. Only weak or foolish leaders will accept responsibility without the authority that is necessary to carry out the job.

As pastor you are the principal leader of the church. But you must overcome the desire to retain control over every area of church ministry. Relinquishing an area of personal weakness means entrusting it to someone else—not an easy task for most ministers.

Celebrate the new. — Conferences/missions and congregations should make the service of installing a new pastor as significant an event as possible. Just as a wedding is an important symbolic act publicly establishing a new home, an installation service for a pastor is an important symbolic act publicly establishing a new pastorate. One difference, though, is that the bride can plan her own wedding. Pastors cannot plan their own installation. Elders and conference/mission officials must take the responsibility. Elders or other congregational leaders should not do it by themselves, as pastors are employed and assigned by the conference. Conference officials must not do it by themselves, as though they are authoritatively imposing the pastor on the congregation. The congregation is a community, a church family. The conference representative is normally not a member of that family and thus can hardly welcome the new pastor to it.

Too often the conference/mission official makes only a brief introduction of the new pastoral family on Sabbath morning. The church then plans only a secular, social event as a welcome. It is far better to have a formal, spiritual installation service. In some situations pastors and members of other churches in the area may be invited.

Pastoral Installation Service

Ideally the installation service should be part of the Sabbath worship service, when most members are present. The suggested service below emphasizes introduction of the entire pastoral family. Certain pastoral families might not prefer this much public exposure, but some agreeable emphasis should be placed on welcoming the whole family. The pastor's family, not the pastor, is most likely to feel least welcomed.

Introduction of conference/mission representative. — The head elder should introduce the conference representative as coming to present the new pastoral family.

Conference representative's remarks. — The conference representative should explain the purpose of the installation service: to help bond the church and pastoral family together and to dedicate the new pastor-church team to ministering in the community. The conference leader should also introduce each member of the pastor's family, presenting a brief biographical sketch of each. An additional option: the conference leader may present to the pastor a tray with a lighted candle for each church in the parish, and then a charge to keep the lights shining brightly and help them grow in number.

Welcome by local elder. — The elder speaks for the congregation in welcoming the pastor. The entire pastoral family may be invited to

NEW PARISH INDUCTION

the platform, in which case the elder's spouse may well give a special welcome to the pastor's spouse. A child, youth leader, or church school teacher from the congregation could welcome the pastor's children.

Litany

Elder:	We come on this day to open a new chapter in the history of our church—the beginning of a new pastorate.
Congregation:	We have received gifts from God, who has equipped us for ministry, and provided a new pastor to lead, train, and encourage us.
Pastoral family:	We come seeking to serve you in lifting up Jesus Christ, that together we might grow.
Congregation:	We invite you to lead us in our walk with God.
Pastoral family:	We seek your love as we become part of this church family.
Congregation:	We wish to have you as part of our family, and we open our hearts to you.
Conference Representative (to pastor):	God has given to you the challenge of leading these people in their preparation for the soon coming of our Lord Jesus Christ.
Pastor:	I accept this challenge. Under God, I pledge to do my best always to lift Him up.
Conference Representative:	As a church, you face the challenge of presenting the gospel to your community.
Congregation and pastor:	We accept this challenge to present the living Christ through our lives and our ministries.
All:	We covenant, before Christ and each other this day, to place Christ first, to seek the guidance of His Spirit, and to work together for the hastening of His coming.

Installation prayer. — The pastoral family might face the congregation with the conference representative on one side of them and the head elder on the other. Other elders or church leaders may be invited forward to form a human chain from the pastor and elder on the platform to the first pew. Everyone, including the congregation, is then invited to join hands and kneel together for the installation prayer. This act symbolizes a uniting of pastor and people.

The head elder prays, inviting the congregation's commitment in supporting the new pastor.

The conference/mission representative prays, officially installing the pastor as congregational leader.

The conference representative then leads the elders in welcoming the new pastoral family with a handshake.

Pastor's sermon

Church welcome
After the service closes, as the congregation leaves the sanctuary, members welcome the pastoral family. A fellowship meal provides an excellent closing to the installation.

CHAPTER 41

Prayer for Sick

When to Encourage Anointing

"Is anyone among you sick? Let him call for the elders of the church, and let them pray over him, anointing him with oil in the name of the Lord. And the prayer of faith will save the sick, and the Lord will raise him up. And if he has committed sins, he will be forgiven" (James 5:14, 15).

Prayer ought to be at the heart of every pastor's ministry, and prayer for the sick is a significant part of such a prayer ministry. A pastor should pray for healing: spiritual, emotional, and physical healing.

The formal anointing service, however, is typically reserved for the physically sick. The text asks, "Is anyone among you sick?" It does not ask, "Is anyone among you dying?" The anointing service ought not to be used for every frivolous physical complaint. It should be reserved for significant illness, but not just for fatal illness. In some places, anointing has become almost a lost rite because of the traditions of some non-Adventist denominations that have used anointing as though it were a last rite.

Anointing is not to bless the dying, but to heal the living. It is to recognize a serious physical problem and meet it by putting our trust in God even before we look to human sources. It is to turn to God first—not just at the last.

Early Seventh-day Adventist leaders frequently used the rite of anointing. Ellen White and her family were anointed a number of times for various types of ailments. Anointing was the practice rather than the exception.

Who Officiates

The sick should "call for the elders of the church." Local elders may officiate at an anointing service in the absence of a minister, but should do so with the pastor's approval. Ideally a minister leads out, assisted by the presence and prayers of available elders.

Preparing for the Service

Where held. — An anointing service may be held in church, home, nursing home, or hospital. If in a hospital, it should be conducted so as not to interfere with the physician and hospital staff. Length and formality of the service depend on the place it is held and the condition of the recipient.

Who attends. — In addition to the minister and the elders, others having a special gift of prayer may be present. The recipient may wish to invite friends. Non-Christian family or friends are usually not invited, but need not be asked to leave if present. Those who lead out should have a serious commitment to Christ, believe firmly in divine healing, and have prepared their hearts for the occasion.

Preparing the recipient. — "If I regard iniquity in my heart, the Lord will not hear" (Ps. 66:18). Encourage the sick person to examine his/her life before the anointing. An excellent way to prepare for the service is for the individual to study the chapter "Prayer for the Sick" in *The Ministry of Healing*.

Respect the privacy of persons not wanting to speak too specifically about their ailment. On the other hand, you should learn as much as the recipient is comfortable in sharing so your prayer can be specific.

Order of Service

Preliminary remarks. — As pastor, you should explain to the group the purpose of anointing and how it takes place. The recipient might be invited to testify to his/her faith and give the reason for requesting healing.

If the sick person is not too critical to warrant a brief service, take time to read from the Scriptures the prerequisites to divine healing. These principles include:

1. *Belief* that God can and does heal.
2. *Confession* of sin.
3. *Commitment to healthful living.* Much illness results from wrong habits of living. Assure the sick that God freely forgives our sins of the past, but it is presumptuous to ask God to heal our bodies if we intend to go on abusing them.
4. *Willingness to use human means.* "Every good gift and every perfect gift is from above" (James 1:17). God may already have engifted some physician to whom He will lead the sick person for healing. God works miracles, but He often chooses to work them through gifts He places in

human hands.

5. *Trust God's answer.* Sometimes God heals immediately, sometimes slowly, sometimes never. If the afflicted person is not healed immediately, it ought not to be interpreted as a sign either of the individual's spiritual weakness or of God's unwillingness to heal. The service should climax with the certainty that everything has been placed in God's hands and that God can be trusted.

Suggested Scriptures before anointing

James 5:14-16	"Let them pray over him, anointing him with oil."
Num. 21:8, 9	People were healed by following God's prescribed ritual.
Ps. 103:1-5	"Who heals all your diseases."
Ps. 107:19, 20	"Then they cried out to the Lord in their trouble."
Mark 16:15-20	"They will lay hands on the sick, and they will recover."

The anointing prayer. — You, or the person leading out, should have a small vial of olive oil. Everyone kneels. The recipient may wish to pray. If so, he/she should probably pray first. Other designated leaders pray in turn. You pray last. As you begin to pray, place a little oil on the fingertips of your hand. Near the close of your prayer, apply the oil to the forehead of the one you are anointing. This symbolizes the Holy Spirit's touching the afflicted one in a specific and special way.

Seventh-day Adventists do not follow or support the practice of some who apply oil to the part of the body in which the infirmity exists.

Concluding the service. — As soon as the prayer season ends, leave. A little time for getting acquainted and social fellowship might precede the anointing, but should not follow it. Leave while a spirit of reverence prevails and the presence of God permeates the room.

CHAPTER 42

Wedding

"The family tie is the closest, the most tender and sacred, of any on earth. It was designed to be a blessing to mankind. And it is a blessing whenever the marriage covenant is entered into intelligently, in the fear of God, and with due consideration for its responsibilities" (*The Adventist Home*, p. 18). Every wedding should therefore be a time of spiritual renewal, joyful celebration, and individualized service to the couple and their families.

Legal Requirements

As a minister, you are responsible to be informed on marriage laws of the state or country in which you function. Before performing a marriage ceremony, make sure that you comply with legal requirements, such as registration and licensing procedures. Laws for officiating are usually not complicated, but they are important. A brief visit or phone call to the county or district clerk's or registrar's office should give you the information you need.

In some countries an ordained minister may, so far as civil authorities are concerned, perform the ceremony in the church, but the marriage contract is legally signed by the district registrar, who usually sits in the vestry and listens to the approved form of marriage declaration.

In other countries the law requires that affidavits must be obtained from the contracting parties if they desire to have their wedding outside of the church building, as in the case of a home wedding.

In still other countries the minister cannot perform the ceremony at all, for it is recognized as a state responsibility and marriage is looked upon as a civil contract. In such cases our members usually retire to the church or a home after the civil ceremony, and there the ordained minister conducts a special service, asking the blessing of the Lord upon the couple.

You should examine the marriage license before performing the ceremony. Do not proceed if the date is not valid, the license was taken out in one place and the wedding is in another place where it is not valid, or if any other legal obstacle exists.

The statement "Therefore, if anyone can show just cause why these two may not lawfully be joined together, let him now speak, or else hereafter forever hold his peace" is often omitted now. It is no longer the responsibility of the minister or wedding ceremony to establish whether or not the two may "lawfully be joined together." That issue has supposedly been settled by civil authorities in the granting of the marriage license.

Denominational Guidelines

Who officiates. — In chapter 6, "Church Officers and Their Duties," the *Church Manual* stipulates, "In the marriage ceremony the charge, vows, and declaration of marriage are given only by an ordained minister except in those areas where division committees have taken action to approve that selected licensed or commissioned ministers who have been ordained as local elders may perform the marriage ceremony. Either an ordained minister, licensed or commissioned minister, or a local elder may officiate in delivering the sermonette, offering the prayer, or in giving the blessing."

When you should not officiate. — If the contracting parties are strangers to you, diligently question them until you are fully assured that there are no serious obstacles to the marriage. People presumably ask you, a minister, to perform their ceremony because they want God's blessing on their home. It's a great privilege, but an awesome responsibility. You dare not bless what you feel certain God cannot bless.

Inadvisable marriage. In counseling a couple contemplating marriage, the pastor must deal with some important areas, such as worship of God, Sabbathkeeping, training children, recreation, association, use of financial resources, disparity in age, poor health, and irreconcilable differences in ethnic and/or cultural backgrounds.

Scripture warns, "Do not be unequally yoked together with unbelievers. For what *fellowship* has righteousness with lawlessness? And what *communion* has light with darkness? And what *accord* has Christ with Belial? Or what *part* has a believer with an unbeliever?" (2 Cor. 6:14, 15).

Put all these cautions together, and we have a plain message: we should not "yoke" or join ourselves to those with whom we have too little in *common*. For Adventists, this includes even other Christian believers. The consistent Adventist young woman, for example, just doesn't have enough in common with even the most devout non-Adventist Christian man. This in no way disparages his genuineness as a Christian. The problem lies in lifestyle: the wholistic theology of Adventism leads to a lifestyle too different to encourage marital harmony. We tend to warn her that he won't make her happy. It is probably more Christian to warn her that she may not make him happy.

Likely, he won't prefer her vegetarian diet. She won't want to cook his bacon. She'll object to his beer in the refrigerator and his tobacco smoke in the living room. He won't want her to pay tithe. She won't approve of his TV on Sabbath. They miss the fellowship of attending church together or being part of the same church family. The most convenient time for him to shop may be Saturday, and she won't go along. She won't go dancing or to cocktail parties with him.

When children come, she objects to his having the babies christened. She doesn't want Father taking his son to games on Friday night or Saturday. She wants her children to have an Adventist education. He doesn't want to be burdened with the expense. He promotes one set of beliefs to the child, she promotes another, and the child, frustrated and confused, often ends up with none.

No wonder the Bible asks, "Can two walk together, unless they are agreed?" (Amos 3:3). "The happiness and prosperity of the marriage relation depends upon the unity of the parties; but between the believer and the unbeliever there is a radical difference of tastes, inclinations, and purposes. They are serving two masters, between whom there can be no concord. However pure and correct one's principles may be, the influence of an unbelieving companion will have a tendency to lead away from God" (*Patriarchs and Prophets*, p. 174).

Ellen White consistently argues against marriage between believer and unbeliever, and defines a believer as one who has "accepted the truth for this time." "Though the companion of your choice were in all other respects worthy (which he is not), yet he has not accepted the truth for this time; he is an unbeliever, and you are forbidden of heaven to unite yourself with him. You cannot, without peril to your soul, disregard this divine injunction" (*Testimonies*, vol. 5, p. 364).

Marriages are more likely to endure and family life to be happy and fulfilling if husband and wife share common spiritual values and lifestyles. For this reason the Seventh-day Adventist Church strongly discourages marriage between a Seventh-day Adventist and a non-Seventh-day Adventist, and strongly urges Seventh-day Adventist ministers not to perform such weddings.

The Church recognizes that it is the prerogative of the individual to make the final decision relative to the choice of the marriage partner. If a member chooses a partner who is not a member of the Church, the Church hopes that the couple will realize and appreciate that the Seventh-day Adventist pastor, who has covenanted to uphold the principles outlined above, should not be expected to perform such a marriage. If an individual does enter into such a marriage, the Church is to demonstrate love and concern with the purpose of encouraging the couple toward complete unity in Christ.

As a pastor it is important for you to show such a couple that you truly care about them. Try the following:

1. Offer to study Adventist beliefs with the nonmember or with both. Adventists usually don't court non-Adventists unless they are already struggling with their own Christian experience. Hasty baptisms are questionable, yet an open heart and mind can make much spiritual progress in very little time.

2. Offer premarital counseling. You can be their friend. In the counseling process, they may see for themselves possible problems with interfaith marriages.

3. You might offer to help them find another minister. If your congregation would not misunderstand, you may even feel justified in attending the ceremony. Having expressed your reservations about the marriage, you, of all people, have a right to show your interest in the couple involved.

4. *Once the wedding is over*, encourage the church to show its support and Christian love for the couple in every way possible to help their home be happy in spite of what we think to have been a mistaken beginning.

Inappropriate remarriage. No Seventh-day Adventist minister has the right to officiate at the remarriage of a person who has no scriptural right to remarry. Jesus declared, "And I say to you, whoever divorces his wife, except for sexual immorality, and marries another, commits adultery; and whoever marries her who is divorced commits adultery" (Matt. 19:9).

The *Church Manual*, in chapter 15, "Divorce and Remarriage," lists 10 statements and stipulations on the subject, then concludes, "No Seventh-day Adventist minister has the right to officiate at the remarriage of any person who, under the stipulation of the preceding paragraphs, has no scriptural right to remarry."

Do not perform the remarriage of a divorced member without first having accurate, objective information about the first marriage. Such information doesn't usually come from the person about to remarry. It is both professionally unethical and grossly unwise to perform such a marriage without first consulting a pastor or elder from the congregation where the breakup occurred.

Inappropriate ceremony. A church wedding involves both a legal contract and a spiritual commitment. Any wedding ceremony in which the secular overshadows the spiritual is inappropriate for a Christian minister to perform.

Congregational Guidelines

You should lead your church in preparing wedding guidelines. Do this at a time when no request for a wedding has been received and no feelings are likely to be hurt. Give these guidelines, along with a wedding application, to anyone requesting a wedding in the church.

The completed wedding application should list specific requests of the bride and reflect that the guidelines have been read and will be followed. Among other things, the guidelines should deal with the following.

Use of the church. — Study the *Church Manual* and *Minister's Handbook* with your church board, pointing out potential problems of interfaith marriages. If you, as their pastor, are not allowed to perform such a wedding, encourage the church not to allow it in a church facility. Otherwise, you are looked on as harsh and as following a standard separating you from your congregation.

Who may be married in the church? The congregation may adopt a guideline such as this: "Any couple who are *both* Seventh-day Adventists; any couple who are not Seventh-day Adventists. The couple must be willing to uphold Adventist standards in the church. No marriage shall be permitted in the church when one is a Seventh-day Adventist and the other is not."

Would your congregation allow a non-Adventist pastor to conduct a wedding in your church? A typical guideline from one congregation: "Who may perform weddings in the church? A pastor of another denomination or another Seventh-day Adventist pastor as long as the individual has been approved and is willing to cooperate with the church pastor."

Music. — A congregation's wedding guidelines often contain a long list of acceptable music. If no other music is allowed, it severely limits the bride's choice. A middle ground is to state that the listed music is preapproved and that other music must be approved by a designated church musician.

The guidelines may also state as to whether the church organ or other instrument may be used by persons other than the church's own musicians.

Other restrictions and services. —

1. *Wedding coordinator.* Does the church have one? Must this person be used?
2. *Decorations.* Which are permissible and which are not?
3. *Candles.* Brides love them. Custodians hate cleaning up after them, especially if the church is carpeted. Many congregations allow only dripless candles. In some cultures candles are not used in Adventist churches.
4. *Dress.* Are there standards for what is appropriate or inappropriate?
5. *Photographs.* Are there limitations? Many congregations allow no pictures during the sacred part of the service. Others allow them during

this time only if there is no flash and the audience is completely unaware of the photographer.
   6. *Rice or confetti.* Are they allowed inside the building?
   7. *Reception.* Are there rules about use of church facilities for the wedding reception?
   8. *Fees.* Is there a fee for a member's wedding? a Seventh-day Adventist from another congregation? a non-Adventist?
   9. *Equipment and services.* Does the church own stairs, candelabra, kneeling bench, aisle runner, etc.? Some congregations purchase these, and then rent them out for a small fee to pay for them eventually.

Exceptions to the guidelines should be few, and should be approved only by a designated committee. The pastor should not have to take full responsibility for dealing with the aggravation expressed by families whose plans have been contrary to the guidelines.

Premarital Counseling

Before marrying a couple, Adventist pastors should insist on intensive premarital counseling. Such counseling may require weekly meetings and homework assignments over several weeks prior to the wedding. Some may argue that premarital counseling does little good, because the couple is so romantically idealistic before the wedding. While this may be true, and while premarital counseling seldom helps a couple change their minds even when severe problems are pointed out, there is another benefit. Having established friendship with and faith in you, the couple will turn to you when problems come after the marriage.

The Family Life arm of the Church Ministries Department of the General Conference has prepared excellent material for premarital counseling, now available through Adventist Book Centers.

Planning the Wedding

Simplicity. — Adventist weddings should be simple and spiritual rather than fancy and frivolous. "Let every step toward a marriage alliance be characterized by modesty, simplicity, sincerity, and an earnest purpose to please and honor God" (*The Ministry of Healing*, p. 359).

In those parts of the world in which such items as veils, cords, and candles represent non-Christian rites, they should be eliminated from Adventist wedding ceremonies. Ministerial attire should be simple and appropriate.

Private planning. — You should have a private planning session with the bride and groom before conducting their wedding. Listen to the bride's specific plans. Encourage her to prepare a written order of service. Discuss their preference regarding the sermonette, vows, etc. Set the time for a rehearsal.

If formal pictures of the wedding party are to be taken, encourage the couple to plan on taking them just before the ceremony. This might not be acceptable if the bride does not want to be seen in her dress before the service begins. However, there are great advantages. Weddings often include a large number of participants, and they must dress specially for the occasion. If the wedding is their first appointment, it will invariably be held up by someone's not being ready.

If their first appointment is for pictures, the photography can begin before everyone is present. Later, since the entire wedding party was present and dressed for the pictures, the wedding itself is seldom held up. Also, if pictures are taken between the wedding and the reception, reception guests become restless from having to wait a long while before the bride and groom appear.

Rehearsal. — You, as minister, are likely the only wedding professional present at the wedding rehearsal. Women are usually presumed to be more knowledgeable than men in regard to weddings. You may have conducted 100 weddings, but even if a female wedding coordinator has coordinated only 10, do not be offended if she is perceived as the authority. Don't control too much unless called upon.

On the other hand, your counsel will at times be sought on matters such as the proper placement of families in the audience, correct position of the platform participants, and other details of a proper service. If you have little interest in such details, your spouse may be interested in reading up on appropriate procedures and team with you in giving counsel. You are responsible for seeing that church standards are upheld.

When wedding rehearsals are held too far ahead of the ceremony, participants may forget their part. If held too close to the ceremony, participants may be too excited over the imminence of the ceremony. Probably the ideal time for rehearsal is the night before the wedding.

If possible, do not use an organist or other instrumentalist who cannot attend the rehearsal. Musicians play a very central role in a wedding ceremony. No matter how accomplished the musician, no one can do one's best without knowing the details of the ceremony.

A wedding rehearsal tends to be disjointed and frustrating. A few helpful hints:

1. *Ask the bride to bring a written order of service.* This eliminates some of the chaos. Even then, many adjustments will likely be made during the rehearsal.

2. *Begin with a talk-through.* Seat the participants and go through the bride's written order of service together, clarifying and making changes as necessary. When finished, all should know their roles. This

talk-through can begin before latecomers arrive. Hopefully, a friend will fill them in when they come.

3. *Protect the bride.* An excellent little speech at the very beginning of the talk-through goes something like this: "We are here to create a memory for the bride and groom. It's our business to help make it a beautiful one. In settling the little details of the ceremony, the bride's wishes must always come first and the groom's next. Unless church regulations are involved, no decision by minister, wedding coordinator, family, or friends must be allowed to have preeminence over the wishes of the couple." Then quietly see that this principle prevails throughout the rehearsal.

4. *End with two walk-throughs.* If some are still absent, use stand-ins. The first time through will go slowly, and participants may groan if asked to do it again. However, the second time through usually takes only a few minutes and leaves participants feeling much more comfortable about knowing their roles.

5. *Relieve the couple of unnecessary responsibility.* As the rehearsal ends, remind the attendants that they are there to serve the bride and groom, to run errands, to take care of last-minute details, to relieve as much of the stress as possible. Have the bride and groom do as little as possible during the ceremony. They are there not to give a public performance, but to make a lifetime commitment to each other before God and enjoy family and friends.

Order of Service

Seventh-day Adventists have no prescribed nuptial liturgy. Being a world church, we must allow variations to fit local cultures. In cultures in which wedding services are different from the one outlined below, local divisions or unions might suggest adaptations that produce a more appropriate order of service.

Home weddings are typically much simpler and planned according to the taste and circumstances of the parties concerned. Attendance at home weddings is usually by invitation only. Attendance at church weddings is open to anyone.

Here is a suggested order of service. Probably no pastor will use every part of it. Adapt it to your own situation:

Musical prelude

Guestbook	The guestbook is usually signed in the foyer as guests enter. If attendance is large, have several pages being signed at the same time so people need not wait in line.

Guests ushered in	Ushers seat the bride's friends on the left side of the church, groom's on the right. Ushers offer their right arm to the lady entering, leading her down the aisle, followed by her escort. The bride's family is ushered to a reserved front section on the left, the groom's on the right. A special place may be reserved in the parents' pew for the grandparents.
Mothers enter	The groom's mother is the last to enter before the wedding begins. The bride's mother then enters, beginning the ceremony.
Candles lighted	
Special music	
Minister and groom's party enters	The minister enters, usually from a side room, goes to the center of the platform, and faces the audience. The groom follows and stands on the minister's left. Groomsmen follow.
Bride's party enters	The bridesmaids, maid of honor, Bible boy, and flower girl (if all these are used) enter down the center aisle.
Bride enters	Bride enters on the right arm of her father or guardian. If her mother stands, the audience stands. People see better if allowed to remain seated.
Groom meets bride	Groom meets bride as she and her father stand beside the family pew.
Bride given away	See details below.
Special music	
Bride and groom proceed to platform	Bride and groom proceed to platform as organ continues processional. Place them so they face each other. If they face you, their backs are to the audience and the audience is somewhat left out.
Sermonette	See details below.

Vows	See details below.
Prayer	The couple have just pledged themselves to each other. Now they kneel to ask God's help to keep that pledge. Invite God to come into their hearts that there may be love in their home, to help them make this home a little heaven to go to heaven in.

The prayer might end with: "And now may 'the Lord bless you and keep you; the Lord make His face shine upon you, and be gracious to you; the Lord lift up His countenance upon you, and give you peace' " (Num. 6:24-26). Or end by saying the Lord's Prayer in unison, giving the audience the opportunity of praying a blessing on the couple. |
| **Special Music** | Special music may follow while the couple are on their knees. "The Lord's Prayer" or "Wedding Prayer" are especially appropriate pieces. |
| **Embrace** | |
| **Introduction** | This may well be in three parts.

First, along with the bride and groom, step forward. Stand between them just before they leave, perhaps with a hand on the shoulder of each. Put your notes away. Nobody will likely have listened much to what you said before. They were busy watching the bride and groom and their attendants, and your part was quite formal. Now, be completely informal. Call the couple by their first names and share a few minutes of marital counsel designed especially to fit their personalities and individual situation.

Second, introduce the new family, using both the first and last name.

Third, invite guests to the reception if this is the bride's request. |
| **Recessional** | Recessional music begins. The bride and groom |

exit down the center aisle; other wedding party couples follow in reverse order to their coming in. The minister goes last. A thoughtful touch is for you to have asked your spouse to sit on the center aisle. Stop by your spouse's pew, offer your arm, and exit together.

It is ideal for the bride and groom to go directly to the reception to be ready in the receiving line for their guests to arrive. It is often superfluous for the entire party to stand in the reception line. Bride and groom and their parents are most needed.

Parents Parents of the bride and groom are ushered out, in reverse order of their coming in.

Audience dismissed Audience dismissed by row.

Bride Given Away

The traditional question "Who giveth this woman to be married to this man?" may be answered by the father saying "I do" or "Her mother and I do." The father may then withdraw his arm from the bride and insert her arm in the groom's as a symbol of his blessing on the union. The bride might wish to kiss her father.

Some brides may object to this traditional question, feeling it infers that women are possessions to be handed from one man to another. You may want to ask for a commitment from the parents of both bride and groom as follows: As bride and groom remain in the aisle, the bride's father goes to the bride's mother. Both sets of parents stand. The minister asks, "Who gives this couple to be joined in holy wedlock?" Both sets of parents answer, "We do." The minister continues, "Do you promise to release your child and accept this new family member to be loved as one of your own?" Parents answer, "We do." The bride and groom can then go to their parents and exchange appropriate greetings. The parents sit down as the couple proceed to the platform.

The wedding service provides an opportunity to underscore the blending and bonding of two families. If this emphasis is desired, the minister could obtain from the parents letters sharing their feelings about the new family member. The minister could then read portions of such letters during the service. This creates an environment of personal warmth and family acceptance.

A unique approach to the "giving away" begins after the bride has come to the family pew. The groom moves toward her as the minister says, "From an ancient love story we read that Isaac went out to meet Rebekah. It is recorded that they asked Rebekah if she was willing to go and be the wife of Abraham's son, Isaac. [Groom now stands facing bride.] So I ask you, [bride's name], will you go and become the wife of this man?" The bride answers, "I will go." The groom escorts her to the platform.

Sermonette

The sermonette should not be more than five or ten minutes in length under most circumstances. This is typically a rather formal part of the service. Everyone is watching the couple, waiting for the exchanging of the vows. Say little here and add a bit more, informally, just before the couple leaves. People will listen better then and benefit more.

Sample sermonette. — "We are gathered here in the sight of God, and in the presence of this company, to join together this man and this woman in the sacred estate of matrimony.

"But why in church? The bride and groom have chosen to begin their home in God's house as a symbol of their desire to have Him in theirs.

"God loves a wedding. The whole idea originated with Him when He performed the first wedding ceremony—in Eden. God said, 'It is not good that man should be alone; I will make him a helper comparable to him' [Gen. 2:18].

"God made both man and woman in such a way that neither is quite complete without the other. The Creator made Eve from Adam's rib to teach at least three lessons: (1) it was taken from his side, for woman was to be neither above nor beneath, but to stand by the side of man; (2) the rib was from under his arm, for she was to be protected by him; (3) it was taken from near his heart, for she was to be loved by him.

"Thus it was that Jesus quoted, 'For this reason a man shall leave his father and mother and be joined to his wife, and the two shall become one flesh' [Matt. 19:5].

"Into this holy estate these two persons here present come now to be joined."

Suggested sermonette texts

Gen. 1:26-28	"Male and female He created them."
Gen. 2:18-24	The first wedding.
S. of Sol. 2	Song of love.
S. of Sol. 8:6, 7	"Many waters cannot quench love."
Mark 10:6-9	"They are no longer two, but one flesh."

WEDDING

    John 2:1-10   Jesus can work a miracle at a wedding.
    John 15:9-12   "That your joy may be full."
    1 Cor. 13   "Love never fails."
    Eph. 5:22-28   "Wives submit." "Husbands love."
    Heb. 13:4   "Marriage is honorable."

Vows

The bride and groom join hands for the exchanging of vows. Traditionally they join right hands, but you could suggest that they hold both hands as a more intimate gesture. You might say, "Now, as the bride and groom join hands I invite husbands and wives in the audience to join hands and renew their vows as the bride and groom exchange theirs." Then follows the vow.

Traditional vow. — The minister asks the bridegroom: "And now, solemnly promising before God, and in the presence of these witnesses, will you, [groom's full name], have this woman, [bride's full name], to be your wedded wife, to live together after God's ordinance in the sacred estate of matrimony? Will you love her, comfort her, honor her, cherish her, in sickness and in health, in prosperity or adversity; and, forsaking all others, keep yourself only unto her so long as you both shall live? Do you so declare?"

The bridegroom answers: "I do."

Then the minister asks the bride: "Will you, [bride's full name], have this man, [groom's full name], to be your wedded husband, to live together after God's ordinance in the sacred estate of matrimony? Will you love, honor, and cherish him, in sickness and in health, in prosperity or adversity; and, forsaking all others, keep yourself only unto him, so long as you both shall live? Do you so declare?"

The bride answers: "I do."

Then the minister lays a hand on the joined hands of the bride and groom, saying: "Forasmuch as [groom's full name] and [bride's full name] have consented to be joined together in holy wedlock, and have witnessed the same before God and this company, and thereto have given and pledged their troth, each to the other, and have declared the same by joining hands, I, as a minister of the gospel and by the authority of the law of _____, do pronounce that they are husband and wife. What God hath joined together, let no one put asunder."

Alternate vow. — Minister asks the groom: "[Groom's full name], do you take this woman you clasp by the hand to be your lawfully wedded wife?"

Groom answers: "I do."

Minister asks the groom: "Do you solemnly promise before God and these witnesses to be to her a faithful loving husband in sunshine or in shadow, in gain or in loss, in trial or in triumph, and keep yourself only unto her so long as you both shall live, according to God's holy ordinance? Do you so declare?"

Groom answers: "I do."

Minister asks the bride: "[Bride's full name], do you take this man you clasp by the hand to be your lawfully wedded husband?"

Bride answers: "I do."

Minister asks the bride: "Do you solemnly promise before God and these witnesses to be to him a faithful loving wife in sunshine or in shadow, in gain or in loss, in trial or in triumph, and keep yourself only unto him so long as you both shall live, according to God's holy ordinance? Do you so declare?"

Bride answers: "I do."

Minister lays a hand on their joined hands: "Inasmuch as you, [groom's full name], and you, [bride's full name], have taken these pledges of affection and vows of fidelity, I, a minister of the gospel, being authorized by the Word of God and by the laws of this state, do hereby pronounce you husband and wife."

Vow spoken by couple. — Groom to bride: "In the name of God, I, [groom's full name], take you, [bride's full name], to be my wife, to have and to hold from this day forward, for better for worse, for richer for poorer, in sickness and in health, to love and to cherish, until we are parted by death. This is my solemn vow."

Bride to groom: "In the name of God, I, [bride's full name], take you, [groom's full name], to be my husband, to have and to hold from this day forward, for better for worse, for richer for poorer, in sickness and in health, to love and to cherish, until we are parted by death. This is my solemn vow."

The minister lays a hand on their joined hands and pronounces them husband and wife.

One problem with the couple's speaking their own vows is that they may be nervous about forgetting and may think of nothing else during the ceremony. They should be reminded of this in the process of making their decision. As a compromise the minister can hold a copy of the vows in an unobtrusive manner so that the couple can refer to it if necessary.

Vow prepared by couple. — Couples sometimes want to personalize their ceremony and exercise creativity by preparing their own vows. When such an option is desired, you must give guidance to the couple, for you have a legal and theological obligation to declare them man and wife only when certain commitments are made. The vows must say that the commitment is total and permanent. It should invoke God's help. Give them copies of traditional vows to be used as guidelines as they prepare their own.

Reception

At the reception, extend to the couple your congratulations, then lead out in the signing of the wedding license. (In some places this is done as part of the wedding ceremony.) Usually the bride and groom sign along with witnesses. Preferred witnesses are the maid of honor and the best man. Pictures are often taken of the signing.

You are legally responsible for registration of the marriage, so you must keep the designated copy of the signed document to send to the civil authorities. Some document should also be sent with the bride and groom as proof of their marriage.

If you wish to give a gift, present the couple with something to be used in the establishing of their family altar.

Adventist ministers do not charge a fee for weddings or any other of their services.

Additional Suggestions

Before the ceremony. — Keep copies of previous ceremonies and make them available to couples. This is particularly easy if you have a computer in which to store them.

Ask the bride and groom to write, separately, answers to such questions as "Why do you feel this is the right time for you to marry?" "Why do you feel this is the right person for you to marry?" "How do you want your wedding ceremony to be remembered by those attending?" Personalize the ceremony by including excerpts from what they have written.

Or ask the families of the couple to write a paragraph about some incident that demonstrated what made the bride and/or groom special to them. Sharing some of these during the ceremony affirms the couple and individualizes the service.

During the ceremony. — The trinity candle ceremony is very popular in some places. A candelabra holding three candles is placed just behind the minister. At the beginning of the service candlelighters light only the two on either end. During the ceremony, probably between the vows and the prayer, the bride and groom each remove one of the lighted candles. Together they light the center candle and blow out the candle they hold. Meanwhile, the minister repeats, "'Therefore a man shall leave his father and mother and be joined to his wife, and they shall become one flesh.' And they two shall become one."

A variation is to have none of the three candles lighted ahead of time. At the proper place in the service both sets of parents stand. The fathers light a candle held by each mother. The mothers go to the platform, light the two end candles, then return to their seats, and the couple continues as above. This can be a powerful symbol of uniting two lives, bonding two families, and creation of a new family apart from the parents.

Audience participation is limited at a wedding. One way to include the audience is to repeat the Lord's Prayer in unison so each person pronounces a blessing on the union. Another way is for the minister to turn to the audience just after the vows and just before the declaration of marriage and ask, "Will all of you witnessing these promises do all in your power to uphold these two persons in their marriage? If so, please answer 'We will.'"

A fitting climax to the ceremony, just before the bride and groom exit down the aisle, is for them to repeat, probably after the minister, "Whither thou goest, I will go; and where thou lodgest, I will lodge: thy people shall be my people, and thy God, my God: where thou diest, I will die, and there will I be buried; the Lord do so to me, and more also, if ought but death part thee and me" (Ruth 1:16, 17, KJV).

In the event that either the bride or the groom has children who will become part of the new home, include them in the wedding service. At some point call them to the platform, perhaps to hold the hands of bride and groom. The minister might say to the bride and groom: "We are here to affirm and to support the desire of these two people to provide a home for [names of children]; to provide a place where they might find security, warmth, love, and the challenges that will help them grow and mature. Do you take this newly created family as your own, and do you here pledge to love and care for them?" Bride and groom answer: "We do."

Mementos of the ceremony. — Signatures in a guestbook and gifts brought by friends become mementos of the wedding. An additional innovation is to write the vows on a parchment scroll. The bride and groom may actually read their vows from it. After the service they sign their names to the scroll, perhaps along with signatures of their families or members of the wedding party. The scroll is rolled up and tied with a special ribbon, and the couple keep it as a memento.

Or give each attendee a pretty piece of paper when he or she enters. If there is a printed program, a blank space on it may be used. Print the request "We invite you to share a word of encouragement, helpful advice, or a special Bible verse with the bride and groom as they begin their new home together. Please hand to the usher as you leave." Perhaps on every anniversary after, the couple will take out these notes, relive their wedding, and be encouraged by the thoughts of their friends.

CONCLUSION

"Those who sow in tears shall reap in joy. He who continually goes forth weeping, bearing seed for sowing, shall doubtless come again with rejoicing, bringing his sheaves with him" (Ps. 126:5, 6).

"Stir me, O, stir me, Lord! I care not how,
But stir my heart in passion for the world;
Stir me to give, to go, but most to pray;
Stir, till Thy blood-red banner be unfurled
O'er lands that still in heathen darkness lie,
O'er deserts where no cross is lifted high,

• • •

"Stir me, O, stir me, Lord; for I can see
Thy glorious triumph day begin to break;
The dawn already gilds the eastern sky.
O church of Christ, awake! awake!
O, stir us, Lord, as heralds of that day!
The night is past, our King is on His way!"
—Bessie Porter Head

Index

Anointing, 255
Authority, delegating, 115, 122, 125
Backsliding. *See* Inactive
Baptism, 199
  assistants, 201
  attire, 202
  children, 137
  church approval before, 137
  during, 203
  facilities, 201
  importance, 199
  obedience before, 135
Bible worker, 80
Board, church, 117
Budget, church, 187
Bulletin, church, 172
Burnout, 36, 37, 124
Business meeting, 117
Calling, 17
  divine appointment, 17
  from Christ, 17
  personal empowering, 19
  privilege, 17
  relationship with Christ, 18
  to sacrifice, 19
  to service, 18
Campaigns, church 189
Child dedication, 207
  additional suggestions, 213
  biblical, 207
  conducting, 209
  litanies, 211
  planning, 208
Children, ministers', 47
Choir, 149
Christian example. *See* example

Church building, 191
Church dedication, 215
  booklet, 220
  church opening, 221
  dedication weekend, 220
  litany, 218
  order of service, 215
  poems, 219
Church fellowship, 171
Church growth, 133
  establishing new members, 139
  finding new members, 133
  friendship system, 140
  obedience before baptism, 135
  preparing new members, 135
  put new members to work, 142
Church Manual, authority, 73
Church policies, 73
Churches, disbanding. *See* disbanding
Churches, organizing new. *See* organizing
Churches, uniting. *See* uniting
Code of ethics, 53
Communion, 223
  additional suggestions, 228
  foot washing, 226
  importance, 223
  Lord's supper, 227
  problems, 224
  recipes, 229
  sermon, 225
  who officiates, 223
  who participates, 223
Community relationships, 30
Conference, relationship with, 69
  conferences help pastors, 70

cooperation the key, 71
organization needed, 69
pastors help conferences, 70
Counseling, 167
   crisis, 168
   lay, 169
   limitations, 167
Credentials, 77
   Bible worker, 80
   commissioned ministers, 79
   expired, 78
   interns, 80
   ministerial, 79
   purpose, 77
   retirees, 78
Deaconess, 102, 227
Deacon, 101, 164, 227
Departments, conference, 70, 127
Devotional methods, 24
Diet, 35
Directory, church 173
Disbanding churches, 109
   for discipline or apostasy, 110
   for loss of members, 109
Disciplined members, 74, 180
Disciplined ministers, 54, 77
Dress, 39
Education, Christian, 195
   importance, 195
   practical suggestions, 195
Elder, local, 30, 48, 75, 100, 117, 118, 119, 125, 128, 129, 136, 137, 141, 147, 148, 150, 164, 179, 184, 200, 208, 233, 227, 251, 252, 255, 260
Ethics, pastoral, 53
   code, 53
   fellow ministers, 54
   job placement, 55
   race, 55
   sexual, 56
Evaluation, 61, 114
Evangelism, 133
Example, Christian, 65
   be aware your humanity, 65
   be what you teach, 65
   be willing to admit mistakes, 66
Exercise, 35
Expired credentials, 78
Facilities, church, 191
   designing, 192
   locating, 191
   maintaining, 194
   renting, 194
Family life, pastoral, 47, 249
   advantages of clergy families, 51
   ministry begins at home, 47
   prescription for happy family, 49
Fellowship, church, 171
   additional options, 178
   communicating members, 171
   discipline, 180
   small groups, 175
   social events, 177
   unity, 171
Finance, church, 185
   handling money, 187
   spiritual, 185
Freedom, organization limits, 71
Friendships, 28
Funeral, 231
   additional suggestions, 239
   before, 231
   committal, 238
   funeral service, 233
   graveside service, 237
   grieving, ministering to, 240
   viewing body, 232
   who officiates, 232
G.C. *Working Policy*, 73
Groundbreaking, 243
   order of service, 243
   planning, 243
   stonelaying, 244
Growth. *See* professional growth
Home, 47
Hospital visitation, 165

House opening 245
    order of service, 245
    purpose, 245
    who officiates, 245
Inactive members, 134
Induction, new parish, 249
    difficulties of transition, 249
    installation service, 252
    smoothing transition, 250
Induction service, 102
    commissioned ministers, 102
    deaconesses, 102
Installing church officers, 126
Intern, 54, 80, 90
Interpersonal relationships, 27
    community relationships, 30
    impact on ministry, 27
    intimate friendships, 28
    loving people, 27
Job description, pastor, 89
Job placement, 55
Law suits against church, 58
Leadership, church 113
    committees, 116
    committees, chairing, 118
    leadership style, 114
    leadership vs. lordship, 113
    management principles, 114
    servant leaders, 113
    setting objectives, 116
Letter, transferring, 74
Limitations, knowing your, 66
Litanies
    child dedication, 211, 212
    church dedication, 218
    communion, 229
    house opening, 248
    lay-leader installation, 126
    pastoral installation, 252
    voting members, 203
Loving people, 27
Marriage. *See* wedding
Members as ministers, 121
    choosing lay leaders, 124
    every member a minister, 121
    motivating volunteers, 123
    training members, 127
Membership transfer, 74
Ministerial calling. *See* calling
Ministerial credential. *See* credential
Ministerial ordination, 93
Ministers, disciplined, 54
Ministers, non-SDA, 30, 55
Money, personal finance, 43
Motivating volunteers, 123
Music, 149, 263
Newsletter, church, 172
Nominating committee, 126
Nurturing new members, 139
Objectives, 31, 116
Order of service
    anointing, 256
    child dedication, 209
    church dedication, 215
    communion, 227
    funeral, 234
    groundbreaking, 243
    house opening, 245
    organizing new church, 104
    ordination, 94
    pastoral installation, 252
    wedding, 266
    worship, 155
Ordination, 83
    authorizing, 86
    clergy converts, 89
    examination for, 89
    for particular service, 83
    ministry; a special call, 84
    not a reward, 87
    of nonpastors, 87
    qualifications for, 85
    responsibility, 86
    significance of, 84
Ordination service, elders and deacons, 100, 101
Ordination service, ministers, 93
    audience involvement, 93
    charge, 95

order of, 94
prayer, 95
spouse involvement, 93
welcome, 98
welcome to wife, 98
Organization needed, 69
Organizing new churches, 103
 how to start new churches, 103
 new churches needed, 103
 preparation for organizing, 104
 service organizing, 104
Pastoring large districts, 129
 quarterly district meetings, 131
 three secrets, 129
Pastor's Bible class, 136, 141
Pastor's job description, 89
Pastor's pastor, 22, 29, 37
Personal appearance, 39
 attract to Christ, 39
 importance, 39
 should go unnoticed, 40
Personal finance, 43
Personal health, 35
 physical health, 35
 psychological health, 36
Poems
 church dedication, 219
 funeral, 237
 house opening, 247
 ministerial ordination, 97
 spiritual formation, 25, 275
Policies, church, 73
 Church Manual, 73
 G.C. *Working Policy*, 73
 membership transfers, 74
Prayer, 24, 36
Prayer for sick, 255
 order of service, 256
 preparing, 256
 when to anoint, 255
 who officiates, 255
Prayer in worship, 150
Prayer meeting, 159

importance, 159
 increasing attendance, 159
Preaching, 22, 27, 34, 40, 123, 153
Pride, 65
Priorities, 23, 33
Professional growth, 61
 how, 61
 where, 61
 why, 61
Promotion, campaigns, 189
Race, 55, 171
Reading, 24
Relationships with conference, 69
Renting your church, 194
Rest, 36
Retirees, 78
Scripture reading, 152
Scripture texts
 anointing, 257
 child dedication, 210
 church dedication, 216
 communion, 225, 226
 funeral, 235, 236, 237
 groundbreaking, 244
 hospital visitation, 166
 house opening, 247
 wedding, 270, 271
Sex and ethics, 56
Small groups, 175
Socials, church, 177
Soul winning, 133
Spiritual formation, 21
 barriers to, 22
 devotional methods, 24
 essential to courage, 22
 essential to leadership, 21
 essential to preaching, 22
 essential to soul winning, 21
 primacy of, 21
Spiritual gifts, 121
Spouse, minister's 47
Stress, 36
Time management, 31
 timesaving tips, 31
 tyranny of time, 31

Training members, 130, 134
Transfer, membership, 74
Unity, 171
Uniting churches, 107
    after uniting, 108
    before uniting, 107
    service uniting, 108
Visitation, 161
    hospital, 165
    lay, 164
    pastoral, 161
Wedding, 259
    additional suggestions, 273
    bride given away, 269
    congregational guidelines, 262
    denominational guidelines, 260
    legal requirements, 259
    order of service, 266
    planning, 264
    premarital counseling, 264
    reception, 273
    sermonette, 270
    vows, 271
    who officiates, 260
Worship service, 145
    children, 147
    order of, 155
    parts of, 147
    purpose of, 145
    worship as encounter, 145